T0381169

Deep Learning Recommender Systems

Recommender systems are ubiquitous in modern life and are one of the main monetization channels for internet technology giants. This book helps graduate students, researchers, and practitioners to get to grips with this cutting-edge field and build the thorough understanding and practical skills needed to progress in the area.

It not only introduces the applications of deep learning and generative AI for recommendation models but also focuses on the industry architecture of the recommender systems. The authors include a detailed discussion of the implementation solutions used by companies such as YouTube, Alibaba, Airbnb, and Netflix, as well as the related machine learning framework including model serving, model training, feature storage, and data stream processing.

Zhe Wang is an engineering director at a Silicon Valley tech company, leading a machine learning team of over 40 members. Previously, he served as a Senior Manager at TikTok. He has more than 10 years of experience working in the field of recommender systems and computational advertising. He has published more than 10 academic papers and 3 technical books, with more than 100 000 readers.

Chao Pu is a machine learning engineer with extensive experience in scalable machine learning systems at large-scale IT companies. He has designed, developed, operated, and optimized multiple recommendation systems that serve millions of customers.

Felice Wang is a data scientist with a wealth of experience in creating analytics models, such as predicting customer retention and optimizing price. She has also implemented machine learning techniques to build data-driven resolutions for various business circumstances.

"Recommender systems hold immense commercial value, and deep learning is taking them to the next level. This book focuses on real-world applications, equipping engineers with the tools to build smarter, more effective recommendation systems. With a clear and practical approach, this book is an essential guide to mastering the latest advancements in the field."

Yue Zhuge, NGP Capital

"Reading this book allows you to witness the wealth of resources and engineering practices driving recommendation system development. The authors share unique insights into bridging academic research and industry applications, providing valuable technical perspectives for practitioners and students. The book emphasizes innovative thinking and inspires readers to develop new solutions in recommendation system technologies."

Zi Yang, Google DeepMind

Deep Learning Recommender Systems

ZHE WANG

CHAO PU

FELICE WANG

CAMBRIDGE
UNIVERSITY PRESS

Shaftesbury Road, Cambridge CB2 8EA, United Kingdom

One Liberty Plaza, 20th Floor, New York, NY 10006, USA

477 Williamstown Road, Port Melbourne, VIC 3207, Australia

314–321, 3rd Floor, Plot 3, Splendor Forum, Jasola District Centre, New Delhi – 110025, India

103 Penang Road, #05–06/07, Visioncrest Commercial, Singapore 238467

Cambridge University Press is part of Cambridge University Press & Assessment, a department of the University of Cambridge.

We share the University's mission to contribute to society through the pursuit of education, learning and research at the highest international levels of excellence.

www.cambridge.org
Information on this title: www.cambridge.org/9781009447508

DOI: 10.1017/9781009447515

First published 2025

A catalogue record for this publication is available from the British Library

A Cataloging-in-Publication data record for this book is available from the Library of Congress

ISBN 978-1-009-44750-8 Paperback

Cambridge University Press & Assessment has no responsibility for the persistence or accuracy of URLs for external or third-party internet websites referred to in this publication and does not guarantee that any content on such websites is, or will remain, accurate or appropriate.

Contents

Foreword

As the core applications of the internet, recommendation, search, and advertising have always been the main battlefields of development and innovation in the industry in this era of personalization. They are also the technical moats built by giant companies such as Google, Amazon, and Alibaba. These fields often deal with internet-scale problems, with high nonlinear complexity and large amounts of data, which makes them naturally suitable for data-driven methods. Around 2015, the wave of deep learning swept in, and immediately detonated a comprehensive technological revolution in the entire field.

For companies that pursue commercial value, the impact brought by deep learning goes far beyond the contribution of a new algorithm. Looking back at the entire history of internet technology development, machine learning, as a new production tool, was introduced very early and has been applied in search, advertising, and other fields. However, a large number of complex models researched and published by early academia can only stay in the laboratory stage and are difficult to apply on a large scale by the industry. There are two main reasons: One is that the assumptions of the models are too harsh and too far from the actual application, which makes it difficult to produce an effective result; the other reason is that the calculation scale in the industry is huge, and there are complex engineering challenges in training and solving the models. To successfully develop a new model, it often takes months or even years for a professional large-scale parallel computing team to work on it, from the initial design all the way to its application. At that time, there was very little intersection between industry and academia.

However, the emergence of deep learning has completely changed the game of technology R&D, driving exponential growth in productivity. Unlike traditional machine learning, deep learning breaks the closed loop of industrial-grade machine learning algorithm development that requires specialized modeling and optimization skills, as well as specialized programming skills for distributed computing. It provides a new paradigm of algorithm development that is modular and easily adaptable, like building blocks:

(1) With a large number of excellent and open-source deep learning training frameworks providing packaged basic modules, the work of designing new model algorithms has become tool assembly.

(2) The optimization of the deep learning model can be easily completed with a series of standard optimizers, without manual gradient derivation and algorithm design, and most optimizers have been embedded in the deep learning framework and don't need additional programming development.

(3) Machine learning engineers or scientists can focus on the understanding of domain problems and model design and build deep model architecture in a way similar to civil engineers' drawing. The next work is handed over to software engineers. Training of the model is done through optimization of the deep learning framework to achieve the best computing efficiency and performance. In other words, the design and implementation of the model are decoupled.

This innovative R&D approach has enabled the proliferation of new models and new algorithms in the era of deep learning, greatly raised up the technological level in industrial applications, and had a huge commercial influence on the information industry. In the previous decades, there were only a handful of machine learning models that could be applied in the industry. But today, a technical intern can easily complete several experimental attempts of deep model algorithms each day. This is a huge improvement in productivity. In a way, deep learning has lifted the fear and liberated the imagination of complex machine learning model applications in the industry.

The transformation of the R&D approach has further reshaped the internal driving force of technological innovation. Evidently, after the booming of deep learning, the innovation of core model algorithms has gradually been dominated by the industry and driven by industrial practices and domain applications in fields such as recommendation, search, and advertising. The most advanced algorithms often come from the top teams of leading companies and are no longer created by academic machine learning laboratories specializing in research based on hypothetical problems or theoretical developments.

These algorithms developed from the industry often have a strong domain dependency. They often put aside the beautiful theoretical appearance and pursue simplicity and pragmatism. This is exactly what young practitioners tend to overlook and also the most precious highlight of this book. The greatest value of this book is not to list a large number of typical model algorithms that are well known in the industry for detailed dissection, but to try to guide learning and mastery of the ideas behind industrial model design from the perspective of technology creation, using the specific scenarios that the technology was invented as blueprints. It presents the real "silver bullet" – what problem it is trying to solve.

Nowadays, there are generally two approaches in the industrial technology R&D:

(1) Finding nails with a hammer: Track the latest top conference papers or technical blogs of large companies, look for innovations, try them in one's own scenario, and rely on luck to get results.

(2) Problem-driven: Define the problem clearly, think about the technical requirements, and then find or conceive the corresponding technical tools.

Sadly, many technical teams or machine learning engineers in the industry are still accustomed to using the first approach, not due to lack of ability, but due to cognitive inertia and lack of technical confidence. As the leader of Alibaba's Targeted Advertising Model team, I will introduce the second approach taking the R&D path of our team as an example:

What we have been contemplating and looking for is a model algorithm that "can really make use of the large amount of personalized internet behavior data accumulated within the Alibaba's e-commerce system." With this goal in mind, in the past three to four years, we have creatively proposed, developed, and produced a series of personalized behavior prediction models such as DIN, DIEN, MIMN, and ESMM, which have brought tens of billions of revenue increment to Alibaba's advertising business. There are two main considerations behind these models:

(1) For a personalized internet behavior model in e-commerce, what kind of deep model structure should be used to recognize the inherent pattern? For this consideration, we chose to use the attention-style structure (reverse activation of user interest expression, see the DIN model), the GRU-style structure (the evolution of interest over time, see the DIEN model), and the memory-style structure (interest memory and induction, see the MIMN model) in the model design.

(2) The depiction of user interests is generally more accurate with more user behavior data, so what kind of technical architecture can be used to accommodate more data? For this consideration, we started with single-point behavioral modeling (DIN, DIEN, and MIMN) and further developed into joint modeling (ESMM) of multiple behavioral paths, and started with short-sequence behavioral data modeling (DIN and DIEN), built to ultra-long behavioral sequences modeling (MIMN).

In fact, the initial technical benefits of deep learning, which has become the industry standard for most companies since its inception, have been mostly depleted. As far as I know, most of the top teams in the industry with comprehensive deep learning adoption have entered the stage of stagflation. I refer to this phase of technological progress as the first stage (1.0) of industrial-grade deep learning. The signs that this 1.0 stage has reached its peak are:

(1) With the evolution of the modular model architecture, its marginal benefits are diminishing over time.

(2) Deep models have entered a data-starvation stage, where increasing the volume of data by 10× or 100× is expected to fill existing model capacity and improve accuracy.

(3) Most new large-scale algorithm optimizations and improvements require significant upgrades and modifications to the engineering systems architecture.

A bottleneck has emerged. Where can we find the next technological breakthrough? Since 2018, I have been advocating for and implementing a new systems architecture for recommendation, search, and advertising fields, in order to adapt to the explosive development of leading machine learning capabilities enabled by deep learning. I believe that the next evolution in technology will enter a new phase, which I refer to as the industrial-grade deep learning 2.0 stage. In this 2.0 stage, deep learning will no longer be a novel weapon, but rather new infrastructure and tools; computational power will no longer be the driving force of deep learning, but rather a new constraint due to the explosion of model complexity; technological advancements will move from relying on single-point breakthroughs in deep learning algorithms to more complex and systemic technology systems, further creating technological dividends. The key breakthrough point lies in the collaborative design of algorithms and systems architecture (algo-systems codesign).

To give a specific example, candidate generation has always been an important part of recommendation and advertising technology systems. Due to the computational scale far exceeding that of re-ranking, historically ranking models have gone through various iterations from the simplest statistical feedback models to lightweight LR or FM models under feature pruning, and currently mainstream two-tower deep learning models. However, the two-tower structure limits the ability to perform feature crossing between the users and the items, and the final target fitting can only be in the form of vector inner products and its related variations, greatly limiting the model's expressive ability. In 2019, our team made a bold and new attempt: We redefined the candidate generation architecture, using fully real-time computation, and introduced network quantization compression, distillation, and other technologies to balance computational cost and model accuracy. Under certain computational constraints, this architecture can support candidate retrieval models that adopt any complex deep network structure for online inference. This architecture allows our latest candidate generation models to almost approach the complexity of re-ranking models and support efficient online iteration, achieving more than double-digit percentage performance improvements in most scenarios after being put online (this is the biggest single-point model technology breakthrough we have made in 2018).

In the era of industrial deep learning 2.0, we can anticipate that the pattern of technological evolution will further upgrade: from algorithm-centric practice and problem-driven approaches to more holistic considerations of larger technical systems, including domain-specific problem characteristics, data, computing power, algorithms, architectures, and engineering systems, all of which will be integrated into a unified framework for technical innovation. For professionals working in the fields of recommendation, search, and advertising, machine learning engineers must take into account the thinking of system engineers, while system engineers must keep up with the algorithmic trend and try to lead the architecture of algorithms. This phase of technology appears "unfavorable": complex, high cost, difficult to replicate, and requiring high demands on individuals (both machine learning and engineering abilities), among other challenges. However, I believe that the profound rule of technological development is to evolve from simple to complex and further into a more simplified technical system and trend, which is also the thinking approach that this book hopes to convey to its readers.

This is the best of times and also the worst of times. I hope this foreword brings inspiration and motivates you to explore the fascinating world of deep learning!

Zhu Xiaoqiang
Alibaba Senior Staff Machine Learning Engineer

Preface

The Deep Learning Era of Recommender Systems

In 1992, David Goldberg and his colleagues from Xerox Palo Alto Research Center created a recommender system using a collaborative filtering algorithm [1], marking the beginning of this 31-year history of recommender system development. In these 31 years, especially in the past eight years, this technology has been completely revolutionized by deep learning. In 2012, with the deep learning network AlexNet winning the famous ImageNet competition [2], deep learning detonated the fields of image, speech, natural language processing, and so on. And even in the fields of recommendation, advertising, and search, where internet commercialization has been the most successful and machine learning models are widely used, the wave of deep learning has also been sweeping through them. In 2015, with companies such as Microsoft, Google, Baidu, and Alibaba successfully applying deep learning models to recommendation, advertising, and other business scenarios, the field of recommender systems officially entered the era of deep learning.

As recommender system machine learning engineers (hereinafter referred to as recommendation engineers) in the era of deep learning, we are fortunate to witness the most profound and rapid technological changes. Yet we are also unfortunate because in this age of rapidly evolving technology and models, we may be on the edge of being eliminated. However, this era ultimately leaves ample room for passionate engineers to develop. While enthusiastic recommendation engineers build their own technology blueprints and enrich their technical reserves, it is hoped that this book can serve as a mental map, helping them build the technical framework of deep learning recommender systems.

The Origin of This Book

The motivation behind writing this book stems from two reasons. First, I have always had the desire to structure my knowledge of recommender systems. Second, I was invited by an editor from the Electronic Industry Press. In December 2018, after reading my technical columns and some articles from my blog, Editor Zheng Liujie contacted me and invited me to write a technical book on recommendation or advertising algorithms. At that time, I had just finished coauthoring *The Quest for Machine Learning: 100+ Interview Questions for Algorithm Engineers* with my colleagues from Hulu. This book about machine learning interviews has received positive feed-back from the market and helped many readers. This writing experience made me realize that taking something seriously and writing technical content earnestly could really benefit many readers. On the other hand, I have been working in the fields of recommendation and advertising for eight years and have witnessed the wave of deep learning in the recommender system field. Therefore, I chose the topic of "Deep Learning Recommender Systems" in the hope of sharing my limited knowledge and experience with those peers who are interested in this field.

Following the publication of the Chinese edition in 2020, the book received very positive reviews and quickly rose to become the most popular technical work in its field. Consequently, I accepted an invitation from Liu Yongchen, an editor at Cambridge University Press, to translate the book into English. I've been fortunate to collaborate with two other translators, Felice Wang and Chao Pu, both recognized experts in the recommender system domain. Together, we have not only worked on the translation but also incorporated the most recent advancements from the past three years in this rapidly evolving field.

Features of This Book

This book hopes to discuss the "classic" or "cutting-edge" technical content related to recommender systems, with a particular focus on the application of deep learning in the industry. It should be noted that this book is not an introductory book on machine learning or deep learning. Although the book will intersperse the introduction of basic machine learning knowledge, most of the content assumes that readers have some machine learning background. Additionally, this book is not a purely theoretical book, but a technical book that introduces the application methods of deep learning in the field of recommender systems and industry cutting-edge technology related to recommender systems from the perspective of engineers' practical experience.

Readers of This Book

The target audience for this book can be divided into two categories.

The first group consists of professionals in the internet industry, especially those in the fields of recommendation, advertising, and search. By studying this book, these peers can become familiar with the development of deep learning recommender systems and the details of each key model and technology. This could enable them to apply or even improve these technologies in their work.

The second group consists of enthusiasts and students with some background in machine learning who wish to enter the field of recommender systems. This book aims to introduce the relevant principles and application methods of recommender system technology from a practical perspective, starting with the details and using plain language, helping readers to build a cutting-edge and practical knowledge framework of recommender systems from scratch.

Discussions Are Welcomed

The field of deep learning recommender systems is evolving rapidly, but my knowledge is limited, and it is inevitable that there will be some omissions and mistakes. I sincerely hope to work together with readers to iterate on and improve our knowledge of deep learning recommender systems. Please feel free to provide feedback during the reading process. Whether it is to point out errors, make improvement suggestions, or discuss technical issues with me, you can contact me through the following methods:

Email: wzhe06@gmail.com
I will respond to valuable feedback as soon as possible.

Appreciations

The process of writing this book has not been easy. Aside from devoting almost all of my free time to writing, it also required a significant amount of time to review research papers, organize technical frameworks, and even communicate with peers and authors in various companies to discuss technical details and stay up to date with the latest technological applications in the industry. I am deeply grateful to the industry colleagues who provided invaluable assistance for this book.

During the writing process, the editor, Liu Yongchen, offered numerous valuable and constructive suggestions for the book and made many professional edits to address detailed issues. I am deeply grateful to Liu Yongchen and the editors at Cambridge University Press who have contributed to this book.

I also wish to express my gratitude to my two coauthors, who diligently and meticulously completed the translation of this book to a high standard. Simultaneously, they enriched the book by including numerous cutting-edge developments. It has been an honor to work with them, and I have learned a great deal from our collaboration.

Last but not least, I would also like to thank my wife and daughter for their immense support and understanding during the writing process. Your care for our family and support for my work has been my greatest motivation in completing this book.

Thank you all!

Foster City, San Francisco Bay Area, USA
Wang Zhe

References

[1] David Goldberg, et al. Using collaborative filtering to weave an information tapestry. *Communications of the ACM*, 35(12), 1992: 61–71.
[2] Alex Krizhevsky, Ilya Sutskever, Geoffrey E. Hinton. Imagenet classification with deep convolutional neural networks. *Advances in Neural Information Processing Systems*. 2012. https://proceedings.neurips.cc/paper_files/paper/2012/file/c399862d3b9d6b76c8436e924a68c45b-Paper.pdf

1 Growth Engine of the Internet

Recommender Systems

This is an era where life is being influenced by recommender systems everywhere. For online shopping, the recommender system will pick thoughtful products; for searching for news, the recommender system will prepare interesting headlines; for learning something new, the recommender system will provide the most suitable courses; for looking for some relaxation, the recommender system will stream addicting short videos; or, if you simply want to close your eyes and rest, the recommender system will play the most appropriate music. In short, recommender systems have never impacted people's lives as much as they do now.

And the machine learning engineers behind the recommender systems have never been chasing the ever-changing recommendation technology like they are now. If recommender systems are the growth engine of internet development, then the machine learning engineer is the development engine of the recommender systems. In this chapter, we will start from the specific scenarios of recommender systems, introduce what recommender systems are, why recommender systems are called the "growth engine" of the internet, and how to view recommender systems from a technical point of view and build the overall architecture of recommender systems.

1.1 Why Are Recommender Systems the Growth Engine of the Internet?

For internet industry practitioners, the word "growth" is like a spear in the heart, constantly stimulating and motivating us. My understanding of the word "growth" comes from an experience in college. Sogou, Inc. has a long-term partnership with Tsinghua University's Department of Computer Science. As a result, my classmates from the same lab often talk about the cooperation projects with Sogou. There was one sentence that I remember to this day: "If we can recommend more suitable ads for Sogou users and increase their click-through rate by 1%, we can increase the company's profit by tens of millions." Since then, the word "growth" has been ingrained in my heart. This word has almost become the only criterion for the success of IT companies, and it has also become the eternal pursuit of all IT practitioners. The desire to "magically" achieve "growth" through algorithms and models has also guided me on my career path as a machine learning engineer.

1.1.1 The Role and Significance of Recommender Systems

The role and significance of recommender systems can be explained from the perspectives of users and companies.

User perspective: The recommender system solves the problem of how users can efficiently obtain interesting information in the case of "information overload." In theory, application scenarios for recommender systems are not limited to the internet. However, the massive information problem brought by the internet often causes users to get lost in the sea of information and unable to find the target content. This makes the internet the best scenario for recommender system applications. Like the fish that represents this book on the cover, it emerges from the shoal of fish, traverses the digital web and leaps onto the paper. I hope it can become the knowledge "koi" that was screened out for you. From the perspective of user needs, the recommender system works as a filter when the user's needs are not very clear. Therefore, compared with a search system (in which users input a clear "search keyword"), the recommender system makes more use of the historical information from the user to "guess" what they might like. This is the basic assumption that must be paid attention to when solving recommendation problems.

Company perspective: The recommender system solves the problem that products can attract users to the greatest extent, retain users, increase user stickiness, and improve user conversion rate, so as to achieve the purpose of continuous growth of the company's business goals. Companies with different business models define different optimization goals. For example, video companies pay more attention to users' viewing time; e-commerce companies pay more attention to users' conversion rate (CVR); and news companies pay more attention to users' click-through rate (CTR), and so on. It should be noted that the ultimate goal of designing a recommender system is to achieve the company's business goals and increase the company's revenue. It should be the starting point for engineers to consider problems from the company's perspective.

Because of this, the recommender system is not only an "engine" for users to efficiently obtain interesting content, but also an "engine" for internet companies to achieve business goals. These two aspects are two dimensions of the same problem and complement each other. Next, I will try to use two application scenarios to further explain how the recommender system plays the key role of "growth engine."

1.1.2 Recommender Systems and YouTube Watch Time Growth

As already mentioned, the "ultimate" optimization goal of a recommender system should include two dimensions: optimizing user experience and satisfying the company's business interests. For a healthy business model, these two dimensions should be in harmony. This is fully reflected in the YouTube recommender system.

YouTube is the world's largest UGC (User Generated Content) video-sharing platform (as shown in Figure 1.1). The most direct manifestation of its optimized user

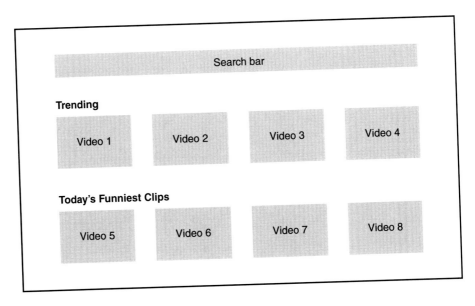

Figure 1.1 Homepage of YouTube.

experience is the increase in user viewing time. As an advertising-based company, YouTube's business interests are also based on the growth of user viewing time, because the user's viewing time is proportional to the total advertisement exposure. Only by continuously increasing the exposure of advertisements can the company's profits continue to grow. Therefore, YouTube's user experience and the company's interests are aligned on the "watch time".

Because of this, the main optimization goal of YouTube's recommender system is viewing time rather than the "click-through rate" that traditional recommender systems value. In fact, in a well-known engineering paper, *Deep Neural Networks for YouTube Recommendations* [1], YouTube engineers explicitly proposed a modeling method that uses watch time as an optimization objective. The general recommendation process is: first, build a deep learning model to predict the duration that the user watches a candidate video, and then sort the candidate videos according to the predicted duration to form the final recommendation list. The technical details of the YouTube recommender system are discussed in the following chapters.

1.1.3 Recommender Systems and Revenue Growth for E-Commerce Sites

While the recommender system plays a relatively indirect role in achieving YouTube's business goals, it directly drives the company's revenue growth on the e-commerce platform. This is because whether the products recommended by the recommender system for users are suitable directly affects the user's purchase CVR.

In 2019, the turnover of Tmall's "Double 11" was 268.4 billion yuan. What drives Tmall to achieve such an amazing turnover is Alibaba's famous "Thousands of People, Thousands of Faces" recommender system (as shown in Figure 1.2 on the homepage of Tmall's mobile terminal). Comparing the Tmall homepage seen by a man and

(a)

(b)

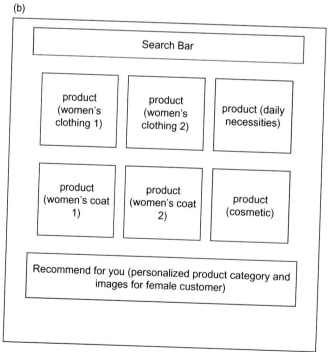

Figure 1.2 Homepage of Tmall's mobile terminal. (a) Tmall homepage seen by a male user. (b) Tmall homepage seen by a female user.

a woman, it can be seen that Tmall's recommender system not only recommends different categories of products for different users (for example, in the "Quick Snap" module, mobile phones and watches are recommended for men, while women's clothing and pajamas are recommended for women), but also different thumbnails of the same category are generated according to the user's characteristics (for example, in the "Recommended for you" module, the thumbnails of the same channel are personalized).

It can be said that Tmall's recommender system truly realizes the personalized recommendation of all elements of the homepage, and achieves a veritable "Thousands of People, Thousands of Faces." Everything behind this is driven by recommendation algorithms that focus on improving CVRs and click-through rates. Assuming that an improvement in the recommender system increases the overall conversion rate of the platform by 1%, then with a 268.4-billion-yuan turnover, the increase will reach 2.684 billion yuan (268.4 × 1%). In other words, machine learning engineers created a value of 2.684 billion yuan just by optimizing the recommendation technology. This is undoubtedly the greatest charm of recommender engineers.

The value of recommender systems goes far beyond that. In 2018, the global online advertising market reached 220 billion US dollars, and the driving force behind this is the advertising recommender systems of major companies. In the same year, the user viewing time of short video applications in China increased by 89.2%, for which video recommendation engines played an irreplaceable role. Since 2015, personalized information applications have overwhelmingly surpassed traditional portal websites and news applications, becoming the most important way for users to obtain information. It can be said that the recommender system has become the core technology system driving almost all fields of applications of the internet, and it deserves to be the strong engine that boosts the growth of the internet today.

1.2 Recommender Systems Architecture

Through the introduction of Section 1.1, the reader should already understand the following two points:

(1) The core demand of internet companies is "growth," and the recommender system is at the center of the "growth engine."
(2) The "user pain point" to be solved by the recommender system is how to efficiently obtain the information of interest for the user in the case of "information overload."

The first point tells us that the recommender system is important and indispensable. The second point clearly explains the basic problem to be solved in building it; that is, the recommender system needs to deal with the relationship between "people" and "information."

The "information" here refers to "product information" in product recommendation, "video information" in video recommendation, and "news information" in news recommendation. In short, it can be collectively referred to as "item information."

From the perspective of "user," in order to more reliably infer the interests of "user", the recommender system hopes to use a large amount of information related to "user," including past behavior, demographic attributes, relationship networks, and so on, which can be collectively referred to as "user information."

In addition, in a specific recommendation scenario, the user's final selection is generally affected by a series of environmental information such as time, location, and user status, which may be referred to as "scenario information" or "context information."

1.2.1   The Logical Framework for Recommender Systems

Based on the knowledge of "user information," "item information," and "context information," the problem to be handled by the recommender system can be formally defined as: for user U, under a specific context C, for massive information of "item," construct a function f(U, I, C), to predict the user's preference for a specific candidate "item" I, and then sort all candidate items according to the preference to generate a recommendation list.

According to the definition of the recommender system problem, the abstract logical framework can be obtained (as shown in Figure 1.3). Although this logical framework is highly generalized, it is on this basis that the entire technical architecture of the recommender system is produced by refining and expanding each module.

1.2.2   The Technical Architecture for Recommender Systems

To develop a functional recommender system, engineers must translate abstract concepts and modules into concrete implementations. Based on Figure 1.3, there are two types of problems that engineers need to focus on solving:

(1) Questions related to data and information, that is, what are "user information," "item information," and "context information"? How are they stored, updated, and processed?
(2) Issues related to the recommender system algorithms and models, that is, how to train the recommendation model, how to predict, and how to achieve a better recommendation?

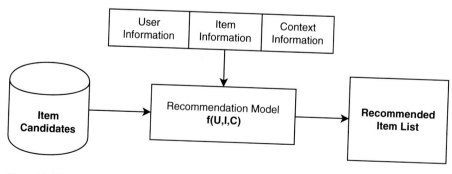

Figure 1.3 The logical framework for recommender systems.

These two types of problems can be divided into two parts: the "data and informa-tion" part has gradually developed into a data flow framework that integrates offline batch processing and real-time stream processing in the recommender system; the "algorithm and model" part is further refined as a model framework that combines training, evaluation, deployment, and online inference of the recommender system. Specifically, the schematic diagram of the technical architecture for recommender systems is shown in Figure 1.4.

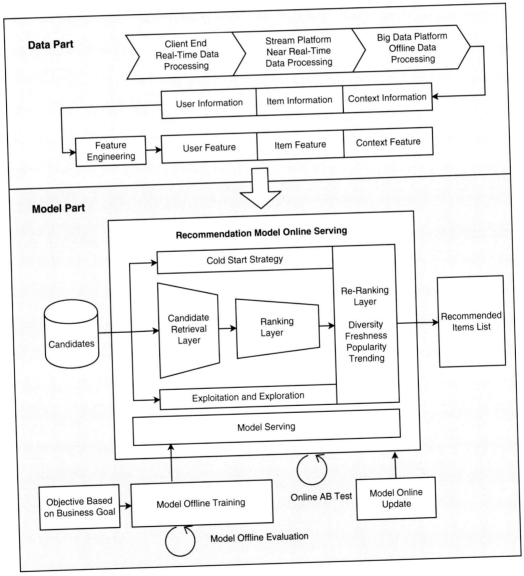

Figure 1.4 Schematic diagram of the technical architecture for recommender systems.

1.2.3   Data Part of the Recommender System

The data part of the recommender system (as shown in beige in Figure 1.4) is mainly responsible for the information collection and processing of "users," "items," and "context." Specifically, the three platforms responsible for data collection and processing are ranked according to the ability of real-time performance, namely "client-side and server-side real-time data processing," "quasi-real-time data processing on stream processing platform," and "offline data processing on big data platform." While the real-time performances decrease, the massive data processing capabilities of the platforms increase. Therefore, the data flow framework of a mature recommender system will use the three platforms to complement each other and utilize them together.

After obtaining the original data information, the data processing system will further process the original data. There are three main data exports after processing:

(1) Generate the sample dataset required by the recommendation model for training and evaluation.
(2) Generate the "features" required for the recommendation model serving for online inference of the recommender system.
(3) Generate statistical data required for system monitoring and business intelligence (BI) systems.

To some extent, the data part of the recommender system is the "water source" of the entire system. Only by ensuring the continuity and purity of the "water source" can the recommender system be continuously "nurtured" to operate efficiently and output accurately.

1.2.4   Model Part of the Recommender System

The "model part" is the main body of the recommender system (as shown in light blue in Figure 1.4). The structure of the model is generally composed of the "Retrieval Layer," "Ranking Layer" and "Re-ranking Layer."

- The "Retrieval Layer" generally uses efficient rules, algorithms or simple models to quickly retrieve items that users may be interested in from a massive candidate set.
- The "Ranking Layer" uses the sorting model to fine-sort the candidate sets that are initially screened.
- The "Re-ranking Layer" can combine some supplementary methods and algorithms to make certain adjustments to the recommendation list, so that additional factors such as "diversity," "popularity," and "freshness" of the results are taken into account, before finally forming a user-visible recommendation list.

This process, from the recommendation model receiving the set of all candidate items, to finally generating the recommendation list, is generally referred to as the model-serving process.

Before performing model services in an online environment, model training is required to determine the model structure, the parameter weights in the structure, and the parameters in related algorithms and strategies. According to the different training environments of the model, the training methods can be divided into two parts: "offline training" and "online updating." The advantage of offline training is that it can utilize the entire set of samples and features to make the model approach the global optimum; while online updating focuses on "digesting" new data samples in quasi-real-time and reflecting new data trends more quickly to meet the real-time requirements of the model.

In addition, to evaluate the recommendation model and facilitate iterative optimization, the model part of the recommender system provides various evaluation modules such as "offline evaluation" and "online A/B testing." These offline and online evaluation indicators are used to guide the next iterative model optimization.

All of these modules together constitute the technical framework of the model part of the recommender system. The model part, particularly the "Ranking Layer" model, is its focus, and it is also the focus of research in the industry and academia. Therefore, the following chapters focus on the model part, especially the mainstream technology of the "Ranking Layer" models and their evolution trends.

1.2.5 The Revolutionary Contribution of Deep Learning to Recommender Systems

The revolutionary contribution of deep learning to recommender systems lies in the improvement of the recommendation model part. Compared with traditional recommendation models, deep learning models are more capable of fitting data patterns and mining feature combinations. In addition, the flexibility of the deep learning model structure enables it to adjust the model according to different recommendation scenarios, making it a "perfect" fit with specific business data.

At the same time, the requirements of deep learning for massive training data and real-time data also pose new challenges to the recommender system's data flow. How to achieve real-time processing of massive data, real-time extraction of features, and real-time data acquisition in the online model service process are the difficult problems that need to be overcome in the data part of the deep learning recommender system.

1.2.6 See the Whole Picture, Supplement Details

The overall technical architecture of the recommender system and its corresponding technical details are extremely complex. It not only requires practitioners to have deep machine learning knowledge and theoretical understanding of recommendation models, but also demands the practitioners' engineering capabilities and the "business sense" to make the best choice by leveraging different technical solutions. Perhaps this is the charm of recommender systems.

By studying this chapter, you will gain an overall understanding of the framework of deep learning recommender systems. Don't worry if you are not clear about the technical terms and related concepts involved in this chapter. Just keeping the initial impression of the deep learning recommender system is good enough. I hope you can "see the whole picture" of the technical framework of recommender systems, and read specific chapters to "supplement details." I believe this book will help you answer the questions in your heart.

1.3   Structure of the Book

The contents of this book will follow the structure depicted in Figure 1.4, with an emphasis on introducing the applied knowledge and practical experience of deep learning in recommender systems. While introducing a specific technical topic, we will try to present a full picture of the development process and its cause and effect.

Since the ranking model is taking the absolute core position in the entire recommender system, the first few chapters of this book will focus on the technical evolution trend of the deep learning ranking model. In the following chapters, we will introduce some technical details and engineering implementations in the other modules of recommender systems, by presenting examples of industry-leading recommender systems. Specifically, the main content of this book is divided into nine chapters.

Chapter 1. The Growth Engine of the Internet: Recommender Systems

This chapter introduces the basic knowledge of recommender systems, their status and role in the IT industry. It introduces the main technical architecture of recommender systems so that readers can gain a high-level understanding and expand the content of this book from the whole to the details.

Chapter 2. Pre-Deep Learning Era: The Evolution of Recommender Systems

This chapter looks at the evolution history of the recommendation models in the pre-deep-learning era and introduces basic machine learning technology related to recommendation models, so as to lay a solid foundation for grasping the deep learning recommender system.

Chapter 3. Top of the Tide: Application of Deep Learning in Recommender Systems

This chapter examines the popular deep learning recommendation model structure in industry and the evolution maps among different models. It is hoped that readers can establish ideas and technical intuitions for improving recommendation models while mastering the main technical approaches of deep learning recommender systems.

Chapter 4. Application of Embedding Technology in Recommender Systems

This chapter focuses on the embedding technique, the core technique of deep learning, in recommender systems. This chapter includes the development process and technical details of the state-of-the-art embedding technique, as well as its applications.

Chapter 5. Recommender Systems from Multiple Perspectives

If the deep learning recommendation model is the core of the recommender system, then this chapter will re-examine it from perspectives beyond this core. It covers the different technical modules and optimization ideas of recommender systems. These include feature engineering, retrieval layer strategies, real-time recommender systems, optimization goals, business understanding, cold start, "exploration and exploitation," and many other important recommender systems topics.

Chapter 6. Engineering Implementations in Deep Learning Recommender Systems

This chapter introduces the engineering implementation approach and main technical platform of the deep learning recommender systems. It includes three parts: data processing platforms; offline training platforms; and online deployment and inference methods

Chapter 7. Evaluation in Recommender Systems

This chapter takes a closer look at the main indicators and methods of recommender system evaluation. It explains how to establish a multilayer recommender systems evaluation framework from traditional offline simulation and evaluation, to fast online evaluation test methods, and finally to online A/B testing.

Chapter 8. Frontier Practice of Deep Learning Recommender Systems

This chapter introduces the technical framework and model details of the industry-leading recommender systems. It mainly includes the cutting-edge practice of recommender systems from industry giants such as YouTube, Airbnb, Facebook, and Alibaba.

Chapter 9. Build Your Own Recommender Systems Knowledge Framework

The final chapter summarizes the knowledge of recommender systems related to this book, and introduces the main technical and analytical methodologies required for recommendation engineers.

Reference

[1] Paul Covington, Jay Adams, Emre Sargin. Deep neural networks for YouTube recommendations. Proceedings of the 10th ACM Conference on Recommender Systems, September 7, 2016 (pp. 191–198).

2 Pre-Deep Learning Era
The Evolution of Recommender Systems

Driven by the ever-increasing user growth demand for internet applications, recommender systems have seen tremendous progress in the technologies, from the one-size-fits-all Collaborative Filtering (CF) and Logistic Regression (LR) before 2010, to Factorization Machine (FM) and Gradient Boosting Decision Tree (GBDT). After 2015, deep learning models took off, and various model architectures emerged one after another. The mainstream recommender system models have developed from a single model to a combination of models, from classical frameworks to deep learning.

Frankly speaking, deep learning recommendation models have already become the mainstream in the fields of recommendation, advertising, and search. But before diving right in, it is still necessary to understand the recommendation models of the pre-deep learning era for the following reasons:

(1) Even with the unprecedented popularity of deep learning nowadays, traditional recommendation models, such as CF, LR, and FMs, still have irreplaceable advantages and extensively applicable scenarios. This is because they have high interpretability, low requirements of hardware environment, and are easy for rapid training and deployment. An excellent recommendation engineer should get familiar with the pros and cons of each model and be able to flexibly utilize and improve different algorithm models.

(2) Traditional recommendation models are the basis of deep learning models. The basic unit that constitutes the deep neural network (DNN) is a neuron, and a neuron can be represented by the widely used traditional LR models. Furthermore, the most influential deep learning recommendation models, such as Factorization machine-supported Neural Network (FNN), Deep Factorization Machine (DeepFM), and Neural Factorization Machine (NFM) have deep connections to the traditional FM models. In addition, training methods such as gradient descent, which are widely used in traditional model training, are still used in the deep learning era. Therefore, traditional recommendation models are the foundation of deep learning models, and it is also where we will start our journey in this book.

This chapter starts with the evolution diagram of the recommendation models in the pre-deep learning era and introduces the principles, advantages, and disadvantages of the main traditional models, as well as the evolutionary relationship between different models. Hopefully, this will serve as a comprehensive blueprint for readers to understand the development of traditional recommendation models.

2.1   Evolution Diagram of Traditional Recommendation Models

Figure 2.1 shows the evolution diagram of traditional recommendation models, which we will be using as an index for the entire chapter. Readers who already know some of these models can build a comprehensive model evolution relationship, and readers who have no prior knowledge of recommendation models can build the framework and general impression of traditional recommendation models based on this.

Briefly speaking, the development of the traditional recommendation model is mainly composed of the following four parts:

(1) Collaborative filtering algorithm family (the blue part in Figure 2.1). The classic CF algorithm used to be the preferred model for recommender systems. From the perspective of item similarity and user similarity, CF derived two algorithms: Item Collaborative Filtering (ItemCF) and User Collaborative Filtering (UserCF). In order to handle the sparse co-occurrence matrix and enhance the generalization ability, a Matrix Factorization model (MF) is derived from CF, and various branch models of matrix factorization are developed.

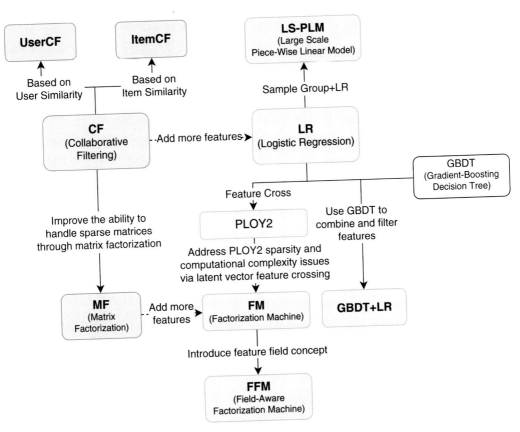

Figure 2.1 Evolution diagram of traditional recommendation models.

(2) Logistic regression model family. Compared with CF, which only utilizes explicit or implicit feedback information between users and items, LR can utilize and incorporate more user, item, and contextual features. Numerous models are derived from the LR model, including the Large-Scale Piece-wise Linear Model (LS-PLM) with enhanced nonlinear capabilities, the FM model developed from LR, and ensemble models integrating various types of models, and so on.

(3) Factorization machine model family. Based on traditional LR, the FM adds a second-order part, which enables the model to have the ability to combine features. Furthermore, the Field-Aware Factorization Machine (FFM) developed from the FM further strengthens the feature interaction capability of the model by adding the concept of feature field.

(4) Ensemble models. Combining different models into one is a common method for integrating the advantages of multiple models. The GBDT+LR ensemble model proposed by Facebook is the most influential ensemble method in the industry. In addition, the idea of feature engineering modeling embodied in ensemble models has also become one of the core ideas of deep learning recommendation models.

Next, we will go over each of the models in the evolution relationship diagram. After learning a new model, you may return to this diagram, find the position of the model, and embed the knowledge related to it into the model evolution knowledge graph.

2.2   Collaborative Filtering: A Classic Recommendation Algorithm

If recommender systems engineers are asked to select the most influential and widely used models in the industry, probably 90% of them would choose CF. Research on CF can even be traced back to 1992 [1]. Xerox's research center developed a CF-based mail screening system to filter out useless mail that users are not interested in. However, the rise in popularity of CF stemmed from the application of this method by the internet e-commerce giant Amazon.

In 2003, Amazon published the paper *Amazon.com Recommenders Item-to-Item Collaborative Filtering* [2], which not only made Amazon's recommender system widely known but also made CF a research hotspot and a mainstream model in the industry for a long time in the following years. Today, although the research on CF has been closely integrated with deep learning, the basic principles of the model are still not separated from the idea of classical CF. In this section, we will introduce what CF is and its technical details.

2.2.1   What Is Collaborative Filtering?

As the name suggests, "collaborative filtering" is a recommendation process used to filter massive amounts of information in conjunction with everyone's feedback,

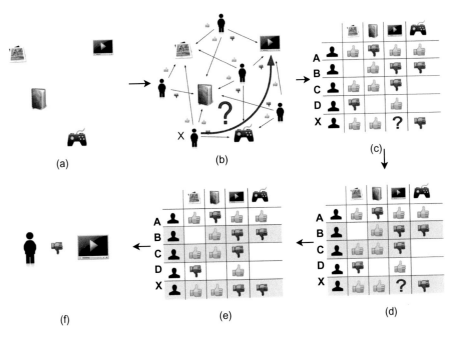

Figure 2.2 Recommendation process of collaborative filtering.

evaluations, and opinions, in order to select information that may be of interest to the target user. Here, an example of product recommendation is used to illustrate the recommendation process of CF (as shown in Figure 2.2).

Figure 2.2 describes the CF recommendation process for an e-commerce website. The recommendation process is divided into six steps in the order of Figure 2.2 (a) through (f):

(a) There are four products in the commodity library of the e-commerce website: game consoles, novels, magazines, and TVs.

(b) User X visits the e-commerce website, and the recommender system needs to decide whether to recommend a TV to user X. In other words, the recommender system needs to predict whether user X likes this TV. In order to make this prediction, the data that can be used are the historical evaluation from user X on other products and the historical evaluation data from other users on these products. In Figure 2.2 (b), the green "like" sign indicates the user's favorable evaluation of the product, and the red "dislike" sign indicates the negative evaluation. This way, users, products, and evaluation records constitute a directed graph with indicators.

(c) In order to facilitate the calculation, the directed graph is converted into a matrix (called the "co-occurrence matrix"), where users are the rows of the matrix, products are the columns, and the user evaluations of "like" and "dislike" are the elements of the matrix. Here, the value of "like" is set to 1, the value of "dislike" is set to -1, and the value of "no data" is set to 0 (if the user has a specific rating for the product, the element in the co-occurrence matrix can be taken as the specific score, the default value when there is no data can also take the average score).

(d) After the co-occurrence matrix is generated, the recommendation problem is transformed into a problem of predicting the value for the question mark in the matrix (shown in Figure 2.2 (d)). Since it is "collaborative" filtering, users are supposed to consider the opinions of other users with similar interests. Therefore, the first step is to find the top n users (where n is a hyperparameter) with the most similar interests to user X, and then combine the evaluations of these similar users on "TV" to get user X's opinion in "TV."

(e) From the co-occurrence matrix, user B and user C are selected as the top n (here, n is assumed to be 2) similar users because their row vectors are similar to user X. According to Figure 2.2 (e), the evaluations of "TV" from both users B and C are negative.

(f) Since similar users' evaluation of "TV" is negative, the prediction for user X's evaluation of "TV" is also negative. In the actual recommendation process, the system will not recommend "TV" to user X.

The algorithm flow of CF is described above, but the processes of "user similarity calculation" and "final result sorting" are not rigorously defined. The formal definitions of these two steps are described in the following sections.

2.2.2   User Similarity Calculation

In the process of CF, the calculation of user similarity is the most critical step. According to the introduction in Section 2.2.1, the rows in the co-occurrence matrix represent users. Then, the problem of calculating the similarity between user i and user j is to calculate the similarity between user vector i and user vector j. A few similarity calculation methods that are commonly used are as follows:

(1) Cosine similarity, as shown in Equation 2.1. Cosine similarity measures the vector angle between user vector i and user vector j. Obviously, the smaller the included angle is, the greater the cosine similarity is, and the more similar the two users are.

$$\text{sim}(i, j) = \cos(i, j) = \frac{i \cdot j}{\|i\| \cdot \|j\|} \tag{2.1}$$

(2) Pearson correlation coefficient, as shown in Equation 2.2. Compared with cosine similarity, the Pearson correlation coefficient reduces the impact of user rating bias by using the user average score to correct each independent rating.

$$\text{sim}(i, j) = \frac{\sum_{p \in P}\left(R_{i,p} - \bar{R}_i\right)\left(R_{j,p} - \bar{R}_j\right)}{\sqrt{\sum_{p \in P}\left(R_{i,p} - \bar{R}_i\right)^2}\sqrt{\sum_{p \in P}\left(R_{j,p} - \bar{R}_j\right)^2}} \tag{2.2}$$

where $R_{i,p}$ represents the rating of item p by user i. $\overline{R_i}$ represents the average rating of all items by user i, and P represents the set of all items.

(3) Based on the idea of the Pearson coefficient, the influence of item scoring bias on the results can also be reduced by introducing the average item score, as shown in Equation 2.3.

$$\text{sim}(i,j) = \frac{\sum_{p\in P}\left(R_{i,p} - \overline{R_p}\right)\left(R_{j,p} - \overline{R_p}\right)}{\sqrt{\sum_{p\in P}\left(R_{i,p} - \overline{R_p}\right)^2}\sqrt{\sum_{p\in P}\left(R_{j,p} - \overline{R_p}\right)^2}} \tag{2.3}$$

where $\overline{R_p}$ represents the average of all ratings for item p.

In the calculation of user similarity, in theory, any reasonable "vector similarity definition" can be used. While improving traditional CF, researchers also solve some of the shortcomings by improving the definition of similarity.

2.2.3 Sorting of the Final Results

After obtaining top n similar users, the process of using top n users to generate the final recommendation results is as follows. Assuming that "the preferences of the target user and its similar users are similar," the preference of the target user can be predicted according to the existing evaluations of similar users. The most commonly used method here is to obtain the preference prediction of the target user by using the user similarity and the weighted average of the evaluations of similar users, as shown in Equation 2.4.

$$R_{u,p} = \frac{\sum_{s\in S}\left(w_{u,s} \cdot R_{s,p}\right)}{\sum_{s\in S} w_{u,s}} \tag{2.4}$$

where the weight $w_{u,s}$ is the similarity between user u and user s, and $R_{s,p}$ is the rating of user s to item p.

After obtaining user u's preference predictions for different items, the final recommendation list can be obtained by sorting according to the prediction scores. So far, the entire recommendation process of CF is completed.

The algorithm introduced earlier makes recommendations based on user similarity; therefore, it is also called user-based collaborative filtering (UserCF). Intuitively, it makes sense because "items liked by friends with similar interests will be my preference as well." However, from a technical point of view, it also has some shortcomings, mainly including the following two points:

(1) In an internet application scenario, the number of users is often much larger than the number of items, and UserCF needs to maintain a user similarity matrix to quickly find top n similar users. The storage overhead of the user similarity matrix is very large, and with the development of the business, the increase of users will cause the requirement for storage to grow rapidly at the speed of n^2, which is an unbearable expansion of the online storage system.

(2) The user's historical data is often very sparse. For users with only a few purchases or click behaviors, the accuracy of finding similar users is very low, which
makes UserCF unsuitable for applications that are difficult to obtain positive
feedback for (such as hotel reservations, bulky commodity purchases, and other
low-frequency applications).

2.2.4   ItemCF

Due to the two disadvantages of the UserCF algorithm, neither Amazon nor
Netflix adopted UserCF, but instead used ItemCF algorithm to implement their original recommender system.

Specifically, ItemCF is a CF algorithm for a recommendation based on item similarity. The similarity matrix between items is obtained by calculating the similarity
between the item column vectors in the co-occurrence matrix, to find similar items
that received positive feedback from the user in the past, and then used for further
sorting and recommendation. The specific steps of ItemCF are as follows:

(1) Based on historical data, construct an $m \times n$-dimensional co-occurrence matrix
with users (assuming the total number of users is m) as the rows and items (the
total number of items is n) as the columns.
(2) Calculate the similarity between the two column vectors of the co-occurrence
matrix (the calculation method of similarity is the same as that of user similarity),
and construct an $n \times n$-dimensional item similarity matrix.
(3) Obtain a list of positive feedback items in the user's historical behavior data.
(4) Using the item similarity matrix for the list of positive feedback items in the
target user's historical behavior, find out the similar top k items to form a similar item set.
(5) Sort the items in the set using the similarity score to generate the final recommendation list.

In step 5, if an item is similar to multiple positive feedback items in the user's
behavior history, the final similarity score of the item should be the accumulation of
multiple scores, as shown in Equation 2.5.

$$R_{u,p} = \sum_{h \in H} \left(w_{p,h} \cdot R_{u,h} \right)$$

(2.5)

where H is the set of positive feedback items of the target user, $w_{p,h}$ is the item similarity between item p and item h, and $R_{u,h}$ is the rating of item h by user u.

2.2.5   Application Scenarios of UserCF and ItemCF

In addition to the difference in technical implementation, UserCF and ItemCF are
also different in specific application scenarios.

On the one hand, because UserCF recommends based on user similarity, it has
stronger social characteristics. Users can quickly know what people with similar

interests have recently liked. Even if a certain item was not within their scope of interest before, it is still possible to have a quickly updated recommendation list through the actions of "friends." Such characteristics make it very suitable for news recommendations. Because the interest of news itself is often scattered, the timeliness and hotness of news are often more important attributes than the user's preference. On that basis, UserCF is suitable for discovering and tracking the trend of hotspots.

On the other hand, ItemCF is more suitable for applications with relatively stable changes of interests. For example, in Amazon's e-commerce scenario, users are more inclined to look for one type of product in a period of time. At this time, it fits the user's motivation to use item similarity for recommendation. In Netflix's video recommendation scenario, users' interests in watching movies and TV series are often relatively stable, so it is a more reasonable choice to use ItemCF to recommend videos of similar styles and types.

2.2.6   The Next Step of Collaborative Filtering

Collaborative filtering is a very intuitive and interpretable model, but it does not generalize very well. In other words, the information of two items that are similar cannot be generalized into the similarity calculation of other items. This leads to a serious problem – popular items have a strong Matthew effect and are likely to be similar to a large number of items; while the tail items are rarely similar to other items due to sparse feature vectors, resulting in very rarely recommended.

For example, choose the vectors of four items A, B, C, and D from a co-occurrence matrix, and use the cosine similarity to calculate the item similarity matrix (as shown in Figure 2.3).

According to the item similarity matrix, the similarity between A, B, and C is 0, and the item most similar to A, B, and C is D. Therefore, in the recommender system based on ItemCF, the item D will be recommended to all users who have had positive feedback on A, B, and C.

But, in fact, the reason that item D is similar to A, B, and C is only because item D is a popular commodity. The main reason why the system cannot find similarity between A, B, and C is that their feature vectors are very sparse and lack the direct data for similarity calculation. This phenomenon reveals the natural defect of CF – the Matthew effect of the recommendation results is obvious, and it lacks the ability to deal with sparse vectors.

$$
\begin{array}{l}
A[0\ \ 0\ \ 0\ \ 1\ \ 1\ \ 0\ \ 1\ \ 0\ \ 1] \\
B[0\ \ 1\ \ 0\ \ 0\ \ 0\ \ 0\ \ 0\ \ 0\ \ 0] \\
C[0\ \ 0\ \ 1\ \ 0\ \ 0\ \ 0\ \ 0\ \ 0\ \ 0] \\
D[1\ \ 1\ \ 1\ \ 1\ \ 1\ \ 1\ \ 1\ \ 0\ \ 1]
\end{array}
\Rightarrow
\begin{array}{c}
\ \ \ \ \ A\ \ \ \ \ \ B\ \ \ \ \ \ C\ \ \ \ \ D \\
A\begin{bmatrix} - & 0.00 & 0.00 & 0.71 \\ 0.00 & - & 0.00 & 0.35 \\ 0.00 & 0.00 & - & 0.35 \\ 0.71 & 0.35 & 0.35 & - \end{bmatrix} \\
B \\
C \\
D
\end{array}
$$

Figure 2.3 From item vectors to similarity matrix.

In order to solve these problems and increase the model's generalization ability, the MF technique is proposed. Based on the CF co-occurrence matrix, this method uses denser latent vectors to represent users and items, and mines the implicit interests and features of users and items, which, to a certain extent, makes up for the problem of lacking the ability to deal with sparse matrices in CF models.

In addition, CF only uses the interaction information between users and items and cannot effectively include many other features from users, items, and contexts, such as user age, gender, product description, product classification, and current time, which undoubtedly results in the loss of important information. In order to include these features into the recommendation model, recommender systems have gradually developed into a machine learning model with LR as the core, so that different types of features can be integrated.

2.3   Matrix Factorization Algorithm: The Evolution of Collaborative Filtering

Section 2.2 introduced one of the most classic models in the field of recommender systems – CF. To address the CF algorithm's pronounced Matthew effect and weak generalization ability, a matrix factorization (MF) algorithm is proposed. Based on the "co-occurrence matrix" in the CF algorithm, MF incorporates the concept of a latent vector and strengthens the model's ability to deal with sparse matrices, which solves the main problems of CF.

In 2006, Netflix held its famous competition recommendation algorithms, the "Netflix Prize Challenge," in which algorithms based on MF demonstrated great potential and opened the prelude to the popularity of MF in the industry [3]. This section uses an example of the Netflix recommendation application to illustrate the principle of the MF algorithm.

2.3.1   Principle of Matrix Factorization Algorithm

Netflix is one of the largest streaming media companies. The main application of its recommender system is to use the user's past behavior to recommend movies, TV series, or documentaries in its streaming application. Figure 2.4 depicts the algorithm principle of CF and MF in the video recommendation.

As shown in Figure 2.4(a), it is very straightforward to find what videos the user may like using the CF algorithm. That is, based on the target user Joe's viewing history, it finds similar users who have watched the same video as Joe, and then finds out what other videos these similar users liked, which can be recommended to the target user Joe.

The MF algorithm, however, generates a latent vector for each user and video, and projects the users and videos on the coordinate space of latent vectors (as shown in Figure 2.4(b)). Users and videos that are close to each other indicate

(a)

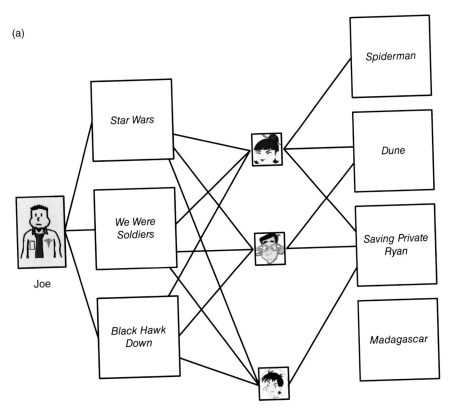

(b)

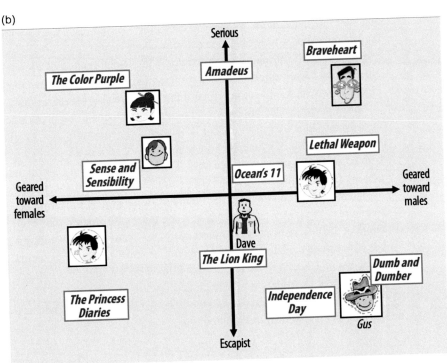

Figure 2.4 The algorithm principle of collaborative filtering and matrix factorization in the video recommendation: (a) schematic diagram of collaborative filtering and (b) schematic diagram of matrix factorization.

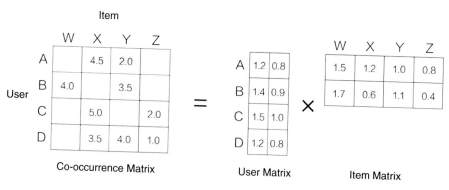

Figure 2.5 The matrix factorization process.

similar interest characteristics. In the recommendation process, videos within a small distance should be recommended to the target user. For example, if you want to recommend a video for user Dave in Figure 2.4(b), you can find that the two videos closest to Dave are *Ocean's Eleven* and *The Lion King*. Then the recommendation list for Dave can be generated by the distances of these videos, from near to far.

Use latent vectors to represent users and items, and also ensure that similar users and their interested items are close to each other – it sounds like a very good idea. But the key question is, how does one get such latent vectors?

In the context of "matrix factorization," the latent vectors of users and items are obtained by factorizing the co-occurrence matrix generated from CF (as shown in Figure 2.5), which is also the origin of the name "matrix factorization."

The algorithm decomposes the $m \times n$-dimensional co-occurrence matrix R into the product of a user matrix U ($m \times k$-dimensional) and an item matrix V ($k \times n$-dimensional), where m is the number of users, n is the number of items, and k is the dimension of the latent vectors. The size of k determines how much information is carried by the latent vectors. The smaller the value of k is, the less information the latent vectors contain, and the model's degree of generalization becomes higher. In contrast, the larger the value of k is, the more information the latent vectors contain, but the degree of generalization decreases accordingly. In addition, the value of k is also directly related to the complexity of solving MF. In the actual application, the value of k needs to be tested many times before finding a balance between the recommendation effect and the engineering cost.

Based on the user matrix U and the item matrix V, the estimated score of the item i by the user u is shown in Equation 2.6.

$$\hat{r}_{ui} = q_i^T p_u \tag{2.6}$$

where p_u is the corresponding row for user u in matrix U and q_i is the corresponding column for item i in matrix V.

2.3.2 Solving Matrix Factorization

There are three main methods to solve for MF: Eigenvalue Decomposition, Singular Value Decomposition (SVD), and Gradient Descent. Among them, Eigenvalue Decomposition can only be applied on square matrices, which makes it unsuitable for decomposing user–item matrices.

Here is a description of SVD:

Assuming an $m \times n$-dimensional matrix M. There must be a decomposition $M = U\Sigma V^T$, where U is an $m \times m$ orthogonal matrix, V is an $n \times n$ orthogonal matrix, and Σ is an $m \times n$ diagonal matrix.

Take the largest k elements in the diagonal matrix Σ as the latent factors, delete the other dimensions of Σ and the corresponding dimensions in U and V, and the matrix M is decomposed into $M \approx U_{m \times k}\Sigma_{k \times k}V_{k \times n}^T$. This is the MF with k-dimensional latent factors.

As it described earlier, SVD seems to solve the problem of MF perfectly. However, it has two defects, which make it yet unsuitable as the main method of MF in internet applications:

(1) SVD requires the original co-occurrence matrix to be dense. But in the internet application, most users have very little historical behavior data, which leads to a very sparse co-occurrence matrix. This is contrary to the application conditions of SVD. If SVD is applied, the missing elements must be filled in.
(2) The computational complexity of traditional SVD is as high as $O(mn^2)$ [4], which is almost unacceptable for internet applications with millions of products and tens of millions of users.

For the earlier two reasons, traditional SVD is also unsuitable for solving MF problems with large-scale sparse matrices. Therefore, the gradient descent method has become the main practice for MF, which is described in detail further.

Equation 2.7 is the objective function for solving MF with gradient descent. The purpose of this function is to minimize the difference between the original score r_{ui} and the product of the user vector and the item vector $q_i^T p_u$, so as to preserve maximum information of the original co-occurrence matrix.

$$\min_{q^*,p^*} \Sigma_{(u,i) \in K} \left(r_{ui} - q_i^T p_u \right)^2 \tag{2.7}$$

where K is the set of all user ratings. In order to reduce the overfitting problem, the objective function after adding the regularization term is shown in Equation 2.8.

$$\min_{q^*,p^*} \Sigma_{(u,i) \in K} \left(r_{ui} - q_i^T p_u \right)^2 + \lambda \left(\|q_i\|^2 + \|p_u\|^2 \right) \tag{2.8}$$

Basics: What Is Overfitting and Regularization?

The word "regularize" means to make something regular. As the name suggests, regularization is a technique used to make the trained model become more "regular" and more stable, so as to avoid producing some unstable "bizarre" results.

For example, the blue points in Figure 2.6 are the actual sample data, and the red curve is a function $f_{red}(x)$ fitted by a certain model. Although the red curve fits all sample points well, it fluctuates greatly. It is impossible to imagine that the real-world data pattern is like the red curve. This is an intuitive example of "overfitting."

In order to make the model more "stable," it is necessary to add some restrictions to the model. These restrictions are known as the regularization terms. After adding the regularization term and training again, the fitted function becomes the green curve, which minimizes the influence of individual "noisy points," and produces a more stable prediction output.

So what is the mathematical expression of the regularization term?

$$\frac{1}{2}\sum_{i=1}^{n}\left\{t_i - \boldsymbol{W}^{\mathrm{T}}\varnothing\left(\boldsymbol{X}_i\right)\right\}^2 + \frac{\lambda}{q}\sum_{j=1}^{M}|\boldsymbol{w}_j|^q \tag{2.9}$$

Equation 2.9 is the loss function of a model, where t_i is the actual output of the training set, $\boldsymbol{W}$ is the weight, and $\varnothing$ is the basis function. If the part after the plus sign is not included, Equation 2.9 is a standard L2 loss function.

The term after the plus sign is the regularization term, where λ is called the regularization coefficient, and the regularization restriction gets stronger with larger λ. The remainder is the sum of the model weights raised to the power of q. When q is 1, it is called L1 regularization, and when q is 2, it is called L2 regularization.

There is also another explanation for why adding a regularization term to the loss function will keep the model stable. For a loss function with regularization, increasing the model weights will cause the value of the loss function to increase. Gradient descent iterates in the direction of smaller loss, so the regularization term will actually minimize the weights of the model without affecting the loss between the model and the actual data as much as possible. The reduction of the weights will naturally decrease the fluctuation of the model, and thus achieve the purpose of making the model more stable.

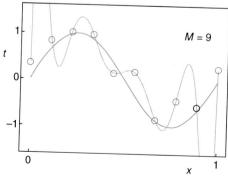

Figure 2.6 An example of overfitting.

To solve the objective function shown in Equation 2.8, standard gradient descent can be used.

(1) Determine the objective function, as shown in Equation 2.8.
(2) Calculate partial derivatives of the objective function and find the direction and magnitude of the gradient descent.

According to Equation 2.8, the partial derivative with respect to q_i is obtained as

$$-2\left(r_{ui} - q_i^T p_u\right)p_u + 2\lambda q_i$$

and the partial derivative with respect to p_u is

$$-2\left(r_{ui} - q_i^T p_u\right)q_i + 2\lambda p_u$$

(3) Use the results from step 2 to update the parameters in the opposite direction of the gradient:

$$q_i \leftarrow q_i + \gamma\left(\left(r_{ui} - q_i^T p_u\right)p_u - \lambda q_i\right)$$

$$p_u \leftarrow p_u + \gamma\left(\left(r_{ui} - q_i^T p_u\right)q_i - \lambda p_u\right)$$

where γ is the learning rate.

(4) Stop training when the number of iterations exceeds the upper limit n or the loss is lower than the threshold θ, otherwise repeat step 3.

After the matrix factorization process, the latent vectors of all users and items are obtained. When making recommendations for a user, take the inner product of the user's latent vector and all items' latent vectors one by one, to obtain the user's rating prediction for all items, and then sort them to obtain the final recommendation list.

With the understanding of the principle of matrix factorization, it can be more clearly explained why matrix factorization has a stronger generalization ability than CF. In the matrix factorization algorithm, due to the existence of the latent vectors, the predicted score can be obtained between any user and item. The generation of the latent vectors is actually a process of global fitting of the co-occurrence matrix. Therefore, the latent vectors are actually generated by using global information and have a stronger generalization ability. For CF, if two users do not have overlapping historical behavior, or two items are not purchased by the same person, then the similarity between the two users or the two items will be 0, because CF can only use the information of the specified user and the specified item to calculate the similarity, which makes it unable to generalize using global information.

2.3.3   Eliminating the Scoring Bias

Different users have different scoring systems (for example, on a scale of 1 through 5 with 5 being the best, some users think that a score of 3 is very low, while some users think that a score of only 1 is poor evaluation). The measurement standards for different items are also different (for example, the average score of electronic products and the average score of daily necessities may be quite different). In order to eliminate the scoring bias for users and items, a common practice is to add bias vectors to users and items in the matrix factorization, as shown in Equation 2.10:

$$r_{ui} = \mu + b_i + b_u + q_i^T p_u \qquad (2.10)$$

where μ is the global bias constant, b_i is the item bias coefficient, which can be the mean of all ratings received for item i, and b_u is the user bias coefficient, which can be the mean of all ratings given by user u.

In the meantime, the objective function for matrix factorization also needs to be changed from Equation 2.8 to 2.11.

$$\min_{q^*, p^*, b^*} \Sigma_{(u,i) \in K} \left(r_{ui} - \mu - b_u - b_i - p_u^T q_i \right)^2 + \lambda \left(\|p_u\|^2 + \|q_i\|^2 + b_u^2 + b_i^2 \right) \qquad (2.11)$$

Similarly, matrix factorization needs to be solved differently with the change of the objective function. The main difference is that a new gradient descent formula needs to be calculated by differentiating the new objective function. The details will not be repeated here.

After adding the scoring bias for users and items, the latent vectors obtained by matrix factorization can better reflect the "true" attitude distinctions of different users toward different items, and it is easier to capture valuable information in the evaluation data, thereby avoiding biased recommendation results.

2.3.4   Advantages and Limitations of Matrix Factorization

Compared with CF, matrix factorization obviously has a few advantages:

(1) Strong generalization ability. It partially solved the problem of sparse data.
(2) Low space complexity. Instead of storing the "huge" user similarity or item similarity matrix required in the CF model, just store the user and item latent vectors. The space complexity is reduced from n^2 to $(n + m) \cdot k$.
(3) Better scalability and flexibility. The final output of matrix factorization is the latent vectors for users and items, which is actually congruous with the idea of embedding in deep learning. Therefore, the result of matrix factorization can also be easily combined and spliced with other features, which enables it to combine with deep learning networks seamlessly.

Meanwhile, matrix factorization also has its limitations. Like CF, it is also inconvenient to add users, items, and context-related features, which makes it ineffective in utilizing additional information, and unable to make effective recommendations when lacking the user's historical behavior data. In order to solve this problem, the LR model and its subsequently developed models such as FMs have gradually become more widely used in the field of recommender systems because of their natural ability to integrate these features.

2.4   Logistic Regression: A Recommendation Model That Combines Multiple Features

While CF models make recommendations only based on user–item interactions, LR models can collectively utilize various features from users, items, and contexts to generate more "comprehensive" recommendation results. In addition, another form of LR, "perceptron," as the most basic single neuron in the neural network, is the basic structure of deep learning. Therefore, LR models capable of multifeature fusion have become another major direction of development for recommendation models other than CF.

Compared with CF and matrix factorization, which use the "similarity" of users and items for recommendation, LR treats the recommendation problem as a classification problem, and ranks items by the predicted probability of positive feedback. The positive feedback here can be the user "clicking" on a certain product, or the user "watching" a certain video. Therefore, LR transforms the recommendation problem into a Click Through Rate (CTR) estimation problem.

2.4.1   Recommendation Process Based on Logistic Regression Models

The recommendation process based on LR is as follows:

(1) Convert features such as user's age, gender, item attributes, item description, current time, and current location into numeric vectors.
(2) Determine the optimization goal of the LR model (taking optimization of the "click-through rate" as an example), use the existing sample data to train the model, and determine the parameters.
(3) In the model service stage, the features are input into the model, then through the inference of the LR, the probability of an item being "clicked" by a user (here, click is used as the positive feedback) is obtained.
(4) Use the probability of "clicking" to sort all candidate items to obtain the recommendation list.

The focus of this recommendation process is to use the features of the sample data for model training and online inference. The next sections will discuss the mathematical expression, inference process, and training methods of LR models.

2.4.2   Mathematical Expression of Logistic Regression Models

As shown in Figure 2.7, the inference process of LR models can be divided into the following steps:

(1) Take the feature vector $x = (x_1, x_2, \ldots, x_n)^{\mathrm{T}}$ as the input of the model.
(2) Assign weights $(w_1, w_2, \ldots, w_{n+1})$ to each feature to distinguish the feature's importance, then take the weighted sum of all features to obtain $x^{\mathrm{T}}w$.
(3) Input $x^{\mathrm{T}}w$ into the sigmoid function to map it to the interval between 0 and 1 and obtain the final "click-through rate."

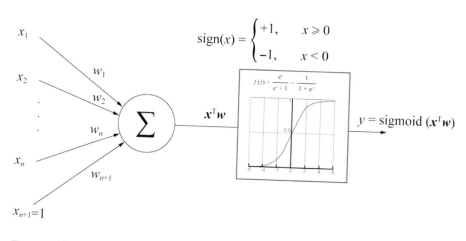

Figure 2.7 Mathematical inference of logistic regression models.

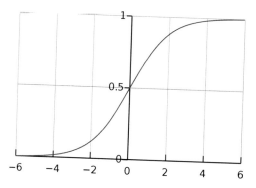

Figure 2.8 Sigmoid function.

Here, the sigmoid function is shown in Equation 2.12:

$$f(z) = \frac{1}{1+e^{-z}} \tag{2.12}$$

A graph of the function is shown in Figure 2.8. We can see that the value of sigmoid ranges between 0 and 1, which is in line with the definition of "click-through rate."

In summary, the mathematical expression of LR models is shown in Equation 2.13:

$$f(x) = \frac{1}{1+e^{-(w \cdot x + b)}} \tag{2.13}$$

For standard LR models, the parameter to be determined is w, that is, the weights corresponding to the features. The next section describes the training methods of the weights w for LR models.

2.4.3   Training Methods of Logistic Regression Models

The commonly used training methods for LR models include gradient descent, Newton's method, quasi-Newton method, and so on. Among them, gradient descent is the most widely used method, and it is also the basis for understanding various training methods in deep learning.

In fact, the steps of gradient descent were introduced in Section 2.3.

Basics: What Is Gradient Descent?

Gradient descent is a first-order optimization algorithm. Its goal is to find the local minimum of a function. To achieve this goal, an iterative search must be performed in the opposite direction of the gradient (or approximate gradient) corresponding to the current point on the function with a specified step distance. If the search is instead performed in the positive direction of the gradient, the local maximum of the function will be approached, and this process is called gradient ascent.

As shown in Figure 2.9, gradient descent is much like the process of finding the lowest point in a basin. In that sense, which direction has the fastest descent to find the lowest point?

This uses the nature of the "gradient": if a real-valued function $F(x)$ is differentiable and defined at x_0, then the steepest descent for $F(x)$ at x_0 is in the direction of the opposite of the gradient $-\nabla F(x)$.

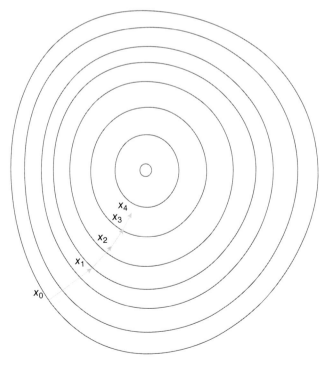

Figure 2.9 Illustration of gradient descent.

> Therefore, when optimizing a model's target function, you need to first take the derivative of the target function to obtain the direction of the gradient, then descend along the opposite direction of the gradient, and iterate this process until you find the local minimum.

The first step of solving an LR model using gradient descent is to determine the objective function. The mathematical expression of LR is shown in Equation 2.13, which can be denoted as $f_w(x)$. For sample x, the probability of the predicted result being positive (category 1) and negative (category 0) is shown in Equation 2.14.

$$\begin{cases} P(y=1 \mid x;w) = f_w(x) \\ P(y=0 \mid x;w) = 1 - f_w(x) \end{cases} \tag{2.14}$$

Combining the two equations in Equation 2.14, it can be re-written into Equation 2.15:

$$P(y \mid x;w) = \left(f_w(x)\right)^y \left(1 - f_w(x)\right)^{1-y} \tag{2.15}$$

The objective function can be obtained using the principle of maximum likelihood estimation, as shown in Equation 2.16.

$$L(w) = \prod_{i=1}^{m} P(y \mid x;w) \tag{2.16}$$

For the convenience of calculating derivatives, take the logarithm on both sides of Equation 2.16 and multiply by a coefficient $-(1/m)$. This way, the problem of finding the maximum value is converted into the problem of finding the minimum value. The final objective function is shown in Equation 2.17.

$$\begin{aligned} J(w) &= -\frac{1}{m} l(w) = -\frac{1}{m} \log L(w) \\ &= -\frac{1}{m} \left(\sum_{i=1}^{m} \left(y^i \log f_w(x^i) + (1 - y^i) \log\left(1 - f_w(x^i)\right) \right) \right) \end{aligned} \tag{2.17}$$

After obtaining the objective function, the gradient direction is calculated by taking partial derivatives with respect to each parameter. The partial derivative of $J(w)$ with respect to w_j is shown in Equation 2.18:

$$\frac{\partial}{\partial w_j} J(w) = \frac{1}{m} \sum_{i=1}^{m} \left(f_w(x^i) - y^i \right) x_j^i \tag{2.18}$$

With this gradient, the formula for updating the model parameters is shown in Equation 2.19:

$$w_j \leftarrow w_j - \gamma \frac{1}{m} \sum_{i=1}^{m} \left(f_w(x^i) - y^i \right) x_j^i \tag{2.19}$$

And that concludes the derivation of the updates of LR models.

We can see that both matrix factorization and LR can be solved with the basic steps of gradient descent. The crux of the problem is to use the mathematical expression of the model to find the objective function, and obtain the gradient descent formula by taking derivatives. In the following chapters, unless there are special circumstances, the parameter updating formulas are not derived in detail. Readers who are interested can try the derivation themselves or read papers related to it.

2.4.4 Advantages of Logistic Regression Models

Before deep learning models became popular, for a long time logistic regression (LR) models were one of the main choices in recommender systems and computational advertising. In addition to its flexibility for integrating different features and creating a more "comprehensive" recommendation result, there are three additional reasons for their popularity: mathematical support, strong interpretability, and engineering requirements.

2.4.4.1 Mathematical Support

As a type of generalized linear model, LR assumes that the dependent variable y follows the Bernoulli distribution. In fact, in CTR estimation problems, the model's dependent variable y is whether the "click" event occurs, and whether a user clicks on an advertisement is a classic eccentric coin tossing problem. Obviously, the dependent variable of the CTR model should follow the Bernoulli distribution. Therefore, using LR is in accord with the actual meaning of the "click" event.

In contrast, linear regression, as another special case of generalized linear models, assumes that the dependent variable y follows a Gaussian distribution, which is apparently not a mathematical assumption for binary classification problems such as clicks.

2.4.4.2 Strong Interpretability

Intuitively, the mathematical expression of an LR model is the weighted sum of features, transformed by a sigmoid function. Supported by its mathematical definition, the simple expression of LR is also very consistent with human intuition about the estimation process.

The weighted sum of each feature is used to synthesize the impact of different features on CTR. Because different features are not equally important, the weights are assigned to features to represent their importance. Finally, using the sigmoid function to map the values into a probability ranging between 0 and 1, which is exactly consistent with the meaning of CTR.

The immediate intuition of LR clearly has other benefits – making the model extremely interpretable. The importance of features can be easily explained by the value of the weights. It is also quite straightforward to locate which factors affect the final result when the prediction is off. This will make it easy to give explainable reasons when cooperating with colleagues in operations and products, effectively reducing communication costs.

2.4.4.3 Engineering Requirements

With terabytes of data processed every day in internet companies, model training overhead, and online inference efficiency are extremely important. Before 2012, when GPUs were not yet popular, LR models were the mainstream in the engineering field due to their easy parallelization, model simplicity, and low training overhead. Because of the limitations of the engineering team, even if the efficiencies of other complex models are improved, the company will not rashly increase the investment for computing resources to upgrade the recommendation model or the CTR model until LR is proven defeated. This is another important reason for its popularity.

2.4.5   Limitations of Logistic Regression Models

As a basic model, LR is apparently simple, intuitive, and easy to use. However, its limitations are also quite obvious: it lacks expressivity, and is not easy to perform a series of more "advanced" operations such as feature interaction and feature screening, thus inevitably causing information loss. In order to solve this problem, recommendation models continue to evolve into more complexity, and derive high-dimensional complex models such as FMs. After entering the era of deep learning, multilayer neural networks with powerful expressivity can completely replace LR models, and they are gradually being retired from companies. Companies will also jump into the applications of deep learning models instead.

2.5   From FM to FFM: A Solution for Automatic Feature Interaction

The lack of expressivity of LR models will inevitably lead to the loss of useful information. In the case of only using individual features instead of interacting features for prediction, sometimes it is not only a problem of information loss, but even a wrong conclusion. The "Simpson's Paradox" is a famous example that illustrates the importance of multidimensional feature interaction.

> ### Basics: What Is Simpson's Paradox?
> When conducting group research on a sample dataset, the group that has the advantage in comparison sometimes loses in the overall evaluation. This counter-intuitive phenomenon is called "Simpson's paradox." The following example of video recommendation will further illustrate what "Simpson's Paradox" is.
>
> Assume that Tables 2.1 and 2.2 show the data of videos clicked by male and female users:
>
> We can see that both male and female users have a higher click-through rate on video B than video A. Apparently, the recommender system should prioritize its recommendation of video B to users.
>
> **Table 2.1** Male users
>
> | Video | Click (count) | Impression (count) | CTR (%) |
> |---|---|---|---|
> | Video A | 8 | 530 | 1.51 |
> | Video B | 51 | 1520 | 3.36 |

Table 2.2 Female users

Video	Click (count)	Impression (count)	CTR (%)
Video A	201	2510	8.01
Video B	92	1010	9.11

Table 2.3 All users combined

Video	Click (count)	Impression (count)	CTR (%)
Video A	209	3040	6.88
Video B	143	2530	5.65

However, if we ignore gender, what conclusions can be drawn from the combined data (as shown in Table 2.3)?

Surprisingly, in the combined results, the click-through rate of video A is actually higher than that of video B. If a recommendation is made based on this, it will lead to the exact opposite conclusion from the previous results, which is the so-called Simpson's paradox.

In this example, the group experiment is equivalent to using the interacting feature of "gender" + "video id," while the combined experiment uses the individual feature of "video id" to calculate the click-through rate. The combined experiment reduces high-dimensional features and loses a lot of useful information, therefore unable to correctly characterize the data pattern.

Logistic regression only performs direct weighting on individual features, and does not have the ability to interact with features to generate high-dimensional combined features, so its expressivity is weak, and it may even draw erroneous conclusions like "Simpson's paradox." Therefore, it is necessary and urgent to improve the LR model to enable the capability of feature interactions.

2.5.1 POLY2 Model: The Beginning of Feature Interaction

For feature interaction, machine learning engineers often combine features manually and then filter the features through various analysis methods. But this method is undoubtedly inefficient. Unfortunately, human experience is often limited, and engineers usually do not have the time and energy to find the optimal combination of features. Therefore, a "brute force" combination of features using the POLY2 model becomes a viable option.

The mathematical expression of the POLY2 model is shown in Equation 2.20:

$$\varnothing \text{POLY2}(w, x) = \sum_{j_1=1}^{n-1} \sum_{j_2=j_1+1}^{n} w_{h(j_1,j_2)} x_{j_1} x_{j_2} \tag{2.20}$$

As you can see, the model interacts with all features pairwise (features x_{j_1} and x_{j_2}) and assigns weights $w_{h(j_1, j_2)}$ to all feature interactions. POLY2 solves the problem to a certain extent by interacting features with brute force. The POLY2 model is still a linear model in nature, and its training method is not different from LR, so it is convenient for engineering compatibility.

But the POLY2 model has two major flaws:

(1) While processing internet data, one-hot encoding is often used to process categorical data, resulting in extremely sparse feature vectors. And POLY2 performs nonselective feature interaction, which makes the feature vectors even more sparse. As a result, the learning of the weights for most of the interaction vectors cannot converge due to the lack of valid data.

(2) The number of parameters is increased from n to n^2, which greatly increases the training complexity.

Basics: What Is One-Hot Encoding?

One-hot encoding is an encoding method that converts categorical features into numerical vectors. Since categorical features do not have numerical significance, they cannot be directly used as one dimension in the feature space without one-hot encoding.

For example, a sample has three features, namely Weekday, Gender, and City, represented by [Weekday=Tuesday, Gender=Male, City=London]. Since the model's input feature vectors can only be numerical, the string "Tuesday" cannot be directly input into the model, and it needs to be numericalized. The most common method is one-hot encoding. The result of the encoding is shown in Figure 2.10.

Obviously, the feature space of Weekday has seven dimensions, and Tuesday corresponds to the second dimension, and thus set the corresponding dimension to one. Gender is divided into Male and Female, which corresponds to two dimensions with one-hot encoding. And the feature space for City is similarly generated.

Although the one-hot encoding method can convert categorical features into numerical vectors, it will inevitably result in a large number of features with zero value. This is especially evident in a massive user scenario such as the internet. Assuming that an application has 100 million users, after one-hot encoding of the user ID, only one dimension out of the 100 million features will be nonzero. This is the main reason for the sparsity of input features for internet-related models.

$$[0, 1, 0, 0, 0, 0, 0] \qquad [0, 1] \qquad [0, 0, 1, 0, \ldots, 0, 0]$$

Weekday = Tuesday   Gender = Male   City = London

Figure 2.10 One-hot encoded feature vectors.

2.5.2   FM Models: Interaction for Latent Features

To address the shortcomings of POLY2 models, in 2010, Rendle proposed the Factorization Machines (FM) model [5].

Equation 2.21 is the second-order part of FM. Compared with POLY2, the main difference is that the single weight coefficient $w_{h(j_1,j_2)}$ is substituted by an inner product of two vectors $(w_{j_1} \cdot w_{j_2})$. Specifically, FM learns a latent weight vector for each feature. When interacting features, the inner product of the two features' latent weight vectors is used as the weight of the interacted feature.

$$\varnothing \text{FM}(w, x) = \sum_{j_1=1}^{n-1} \sum_{j_2=j_1+1}^{n} (w_{j_1} \cdot w_{j_2}) x_{j_1} x_{j_2} \tag{2.21}$$

In essence, the practice of introducing latent vectors in FM is similar to the practice of matrix factorization using latent vectors to represent users and items. In other words, FM is a further expansion of the idea of using latent vectors in matrix factorization, from latent vectors of simple users and items to all features.

FM dramatically reduces the number of parameters from the order of n^2 for the POLY2 model to nk (k is the dimension of latent vectors, $n \gg k$ by introducing latent vectors for all features. While training FM models using gradient descent, the computational complexity can also be reduced to the order of nk, which greatly reduces the training overhead.

The introduction of latent vectors enables FM to better solve the problem of data sparsity. For example, in product recommendations, the sample has two features, namely channel and brand, and the feature combination of a training sample is (ESPN, Adidas). In POLY2, the model can only learn the weight corresponding to this combined feature when ESPN and Adidas appear in a training sample at the same time; in FM, however, ESPN's latent vector can also be updated by (ESPN, Gucci) samples, while Adidas' latent vectors can also be updated by (NBC, Adidas) samples, which greatly reduces the model's requirement for data sparsity. Even for a feature combination that has never appeared before, such as (NBC, Gucci), the model has the ability to calculate the weight of this feature combination based on its previously learned latent vectors for NBC and Gucci, respectively. This is something that POLY2 cannot achieve. Compared with POLY2, although FM loses the exact information of some feature combinations, the generalization ability is greatly improved.

In terms of engineering, FM can also be learned with gradient descent, making it real-time and flexible. Compared with the complex network structure of deep learning models, which makes it difficult to deploy and serve online, FM's easier-to-implement model structure makes the online inference process relatively simple, and it is easier to deploy and serve online. Therefore, FM became one of the mainstream recommendation models in the industry around 2012–2014.

2.5.3   FFM Model: Introducing the Concept of Feature Field

In 2015, the Field-aware Factorization Machines (FFM) model [6] developed from FM won the top prizes in several CTR prediction competitions. It was then adopted by many companies such as Criteo and Meituan in their recommender systems. Compared to FM models, the FFM model introduced the concept of field-awareness, which makes the model more expressive.

$$\oslash FFM(w,x) = \sum_{j_1=1}^{n-1} \sum_{j_2=j_1+1}^{n} \left(w_{j_1,f_2} \cdot w_{j_2,f_1} \right) x_{j_1} x_{j_2} \qquad (2.22)$$

Equation 2.22 shows the second-order part in the mathematical expression of FFM. The difference between FFM and FM is that the latent vector has changed from the original w_{j_1} to w_{j_1,f_2}, which means that each feature no longer corresponds to a single latent vector, but instead to a set of latent vectors. When feature x_{j_1} is interacted with feature x_{j_2}, x_{j_1} will interact with the latent vector w_{j_1,f_2} from x_{j_2}'s corresponding feature field f_2. Similarly, x_{j_2} will also interact with the latent vector from x_{j_1}'s corresponding feature field f_1.

What does the field mean here? Simply put, "field" represents the feature field, and the features in the field are generally a one-hot feature vector formed by one-hot encoding. For example, the gender of the user is usually divided into three categories: male, female, and unknown. For a female user, the feature vector from one-hot encoding is [0, 1, 0], and this three-dimensional feature vector is a "gender" feature field. Connecting all feature fields forms the overall feature space of the sample.

Next, an example from the Criteo FFM paper [6] is presented to illustrate the characteristics of FFM in details. Suppose the training samples received during the recommendation model training process are as shown in Figure 2.11. Here, Publisher, Advertiser, and Gender are the three feature fields, and ESPN, NIKE, and Male are the feature values of these three feature fields (one-hot encoding is still needed).

If it were in FM, the features ESPN, NIKE, and Male would have corresponding latent vectors $w_{ESPN}, w_{NIKE}, w_{Male}$. Then the weights for interacted feature pairs ESPN and NIKE, ESPN and Male would be $w_{ESPN} \cdot w_{NIKE}$ and $w_{ESPN} \cdot w_{Male}$. Among them, the latent vector w_{ESPN} is invariant in the two feature interactions.

On the other hand, in FFM, the weights of interacted feature pairs ESPN and NIKE, ESPN and Male are $w_{ESPN,A} \cdot w_{NIKE,P}$ and $w_{ESPN,G} \cdot w_{Male,P}$, respectively.

You may have noticed that ESPN uses different latent vectors $w_{ESPN,A}$ and $w_{ESPN,G}$, respectively, when interacting with NIKE and Male. This is because NIKE and Male are in different feature fields Advertiser (A) and Gender (G).

In the training process of FFM models, there are f feature fields with n features in each field, and each feature is represented by a k-dimensional latent vector. Hence, there are $n \cdot k \cdot f$ features that need to be learned with the model. In terms of training, the quadratic terms of FFM are not as simplified as in FM, and its complexity is kn^2.

Publisher(P)	Advertiser(A)	Gender(G)
ESPN	NIKE	Male

Figure 2.11 Example training sample.

Compared to FM, FFM's introduction of the concept of feature field includes more valuable information to the model and makes the model more expressive. But at the same time, the computational complexity of FFM increases to kn^2, which is much larger than the kn of FM. In the practical engineering applications, it is necessary to make a trade-off between model effect and engineering cost.

2.5.4   Model Evolution from POLY2 to FFM

In the last part of this section, we will present the model evolution from POLY2 to FM and then to FFM schematically. We still take the training samples shown in Figure 2.11 as an example.

The POLY2 model directly learns the weight of each interacted feature. If the number of features is n, the number of weights is of the order of n^2, specifically, $n(n-1)/2$. As shown in Figure 2.12, each colored dot represents one interacted feature.

The FM model learns the k-dimensional latent vector of each feature. The interacted feature is obtained by conducting the inner product of the corresponding feature latent vectors. The number of weights is nk. FM has a stronger generalization ability than POLY2, but its memorization is weakened. Its ability to deal with sparse feature vectors is much stronger than that of POLY2. As shown in Figure 2.13, each feature interaction is no longer a single dot, but an inner product of three colored dots, representing a three-dimensional latent vector for each feature.

The FFM model introduces the concept of the feature field, based on the FM model. When interacting features, each feature selects a latent vector corresponding to the field of the other feature, and performs an inner product to obtain the

$$\phi(\mathbf{w}, \mathbf{x}) = \bigcirc \quad + \quad \bigcirc \quad + \quad \bigcirc$$

$w_{ESPN,NIKE}$ $w_{ESPN,Male}$ $w_{NIKE,Male}$

Figure 2.12 Illustration of the POLY2 model.

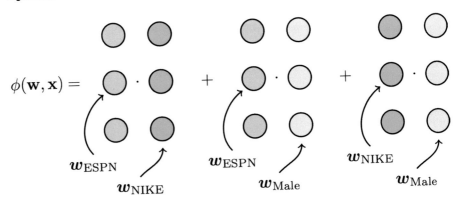

Figure 2.13 Illustration of the FM model.

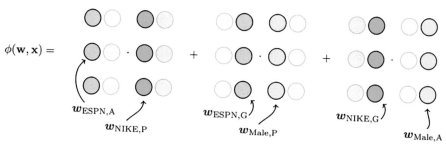

$$\phi(\mathbf{w}, \mathbf{x}) =$$

$w_{ESPN,A}$ $w_{NIKE,P}$ $w_{ESPN,G}$ $w_{Male,P}$ $w_{NIKE,G}$ $w_{Male,A}$

Figure 2.14 Illustration of the FFM model.

weight of the interacted feature. When there are n features, f feature fields and k dimensions in the latent vector, the number of parameters is $n \cdot k \cdot f$. As shown in Figure 2.14, each feature has two latent vectors, and the corresponding latent vector is selected when interacting with features from a different feature field.

In theory, the idea of using feature interaction in the FM model family can be extended to third-order or even higher orders. However, due to the combinatorial explosion problem, both the number of weights and the training complexity of the third-order FM are too high, making it difficult to implement in practice. Thus, how to break through the limitation of second-order feature interaction and further strengthen the ability of feature combination has become the direction of recommendation model development. The ensemble model introduced in Section 2.6 will to some extent address the problem of higher-order feature interaction.

2.6   GBDT+LR: The Beginning of Feature Engineering Modeling

FFM enhances the feature interaction capability of the model by introducing the concept of a feature field. But in any case, FFM can only perform second-order feature interaction. If the dimension of feature interaction continues to increase, it will inevitably result in combinatorial explosion and extremely high computational costs. So is there any method that can effectively deal with the problem of high-dimensional feature interaction and selection? In 2014, Facebook proposed a solution based on the GBDT+LR [7] ensemble model.

2.6.1   Structure of GBDT+LR Ensemble Model

In short, Facebook proposed a method to use gradient boosting decision tree (GBDT) to automatically perform feature interaction and selection, and then generate new discrete feature vectors. It uses the new feature vectors as the input of the LR model to predict CTR. The model structure is shown in Figure 2.15.

It should be noted that the GBDT and LR parts are trained separately, so there is no complex backpropagation of the gradient from LR to GBDT. The process of using LR to predict CTR has been introduced in detail in Section 2.4. In this section, we will focus on the process of using GBDT to construct new feature vectors.

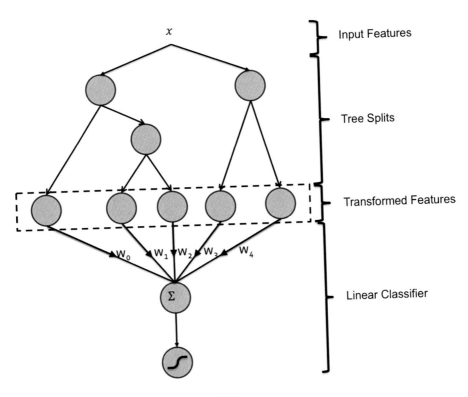

Figure 2.15 Structure of the GBDT+LR model.

Basics: What Is a GBDT Model?
The basic structure of GBDT is a forest of decision trees (as shown in Figure 2.16), and the learning method is gradient boosting.

Specifically, GBDT acts as an ensemble model, and its prediction method is to add up the results of all subtrees.

$$D(x) = d_{\text{tree1}}(x) + d_{\text{tree2}}(x) + \cdots$$

GBDT processed the subtree sequentially to generate the whole forest. The process of generating a new subtree is to use the residual between the sample label value and the predicted value from the current forest to construct a new subtree.

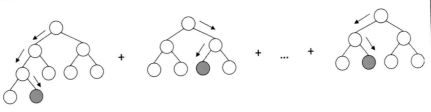

Figure 2.16 The structure of GBDT.

> Assuming three subtrees have been generated, the current predicted value is,
>
> $$D(x) = d_{tree1}(x) + d_{tree2}(x) + d_{tree3}(x)$$
>
> Next, GBDT will build the fourth subtree. The goal is to make the sum of the two prediction results, $D(x)$ from the current forest and $d_{tree4}(x)$ from the fourth subtree, further approximate the theoretical fitting function $f(x)$, that is
>
> $$D(x) + d_{tree4}(x) = f(x)$$
>
> Therefore, the process of generating the fourth subtree is based on the fitting function and the residual $R(x)$ from the current forest, where $R(x)$ is defined as
>
> $$R(x) = f(x) - D(x)$$
>
> In theory, if there are unlimited decision trees, then GBDT can infinitely approach the target fitting function based on all training samples, so as to reduce the prediction error.

GBDT is a forest composed of multiple decision trees, and the latter tree takes the residual between the predictions of the previous forest and the ground truth as the fitting target. The generation of each tree follows the standard decision tree generation process, so the splitting of each node is a natural feature selection process, and the multilayer node structure effectively combines the features automatically. It also solves the problem of feature selection and feature interaction in a very efficient way.

2.6.2 Feature Transformation with GBDT

After the GBDT model is trained using the training set, it can be used to transform the original feature vectors into new discrete feature vectors. Here are the specific processes:

After a training sample is fed into a subtree of GBDT, it will eventually fall into one of the leaf nodes according to the rules of each split. This leaf node is set to 1, and all the other leaf nodes are set to 0. The vector composed of all leaf nodes is the feature vector generated by this subtree. After concatenating the feature vectors from all subtrees of GBDT, we will get the final input feature vectors for the subsequent LR model.

For example, as shown in Figure 2.17, the GBDT model consists of three subtrees, each of which has four leaf nodes. After inputting a training sample, it falls into the third leaf node of the first subtree, so the feature vector is [0,0,1,0]. Then it falls into the first leaf node of the second subtree, giving a feature vector [1,0,0,0]. Finally, it falls into the fourth leaf node of the third subtree, resulting in a feature vector [0,0,0,1]. Lastly, all vector segments are concatenated to form the final feature vector [0,0,1,0,1,0,0,0,0,0,0,1].

In fact, the depth of the decision tree determines the order of feature interaction. If the depth of the decision tree is 4, after three node splits, the final leaf node is actually

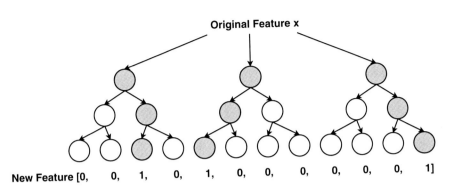

Figure 2.17 The generation of a feature vector with GBDT.

the result of a third-order feature interaction. Such a strong feature interaction capability is obviously not available in the FM model. However, GBDT is prone to overfitting, and the feature conversion method of GBDT actually loses a lot of numerical information in the original input features. Therefore, we cannot simply say that because GBDT has a strong feature interaction ability, it is better than FFM. While selecting and debugging models, there is always a trade-off between multiple factors.

2.6.3 New Trend of Feature Engineering after GBDT+LR Model

GBDT+LR ensemble models are an important approach to recommender systems, because it greatly advances the trend of feature engineering modeling. Before GBDT+LR models appeared, there were two main solutions for feature engineering – one was to perform manual or semi-manual feature interaction and feature selection; the other was to transform the objective function, improve the model structure, and increase the order of feature interaction. However, these two methods have their own drawbacks. The first method requires extensive experience and effort from algorithm engineers. The second method needs to fundamentally change the model structure, which requires the engineer's deeper understanding of model design.

The proposal of GBDT+LR models means that feature engineering can be completely done by modeling, and the input of the model can be the original feature vectors. Feature engineering will no longer require extensive manual selection and model design, which enables real end-to-end training.

Broadly speaking, automated feature engineering in deep learning models through various network structures and embedding layers is the continuation of the trend of feature engineering modeling started by GBDT+LR.

2.7 LS-PLM: Previous Mainstream Model by Alibaba

The last recommendation model in the pre-deep learning era introduced in this book is Alibaba's once mainstream recommendation model – Large Scale Piece-wise

Linear Model (LP-PLM) [8]. The LS-PLM is chosen as the final model of this chapter for two reasons. The first reason is its great impact. Although this model was only made public by Alibaba in 2017, it was actually Alibaba's mainstream recommendation model from as early as 2012, and was used in various advertising scenarios of Alibaba for a long time before deep learning models took over. The second reason is the significance of its structural characteristics. The structure of LS-PLM is very similar to a three-layer neural network, making it the perfect bridge connecting the two eras of recommender systems.

2.7.1   Main Structure of LS-PLM

LS-PLM is also known as a mixed logistic regression (MLR) model. Essentially, LS-PLM is a natural extension of LR. It adopts the idea of divide and conquer based on LR. It first partitions the sample set by clustering, and then applies LR to predict CTR in the sample cluster.

In LS-PLM, the idea of adding clustering to LR is inspired by the observation of sample characteristics in the field of advertising recommendation. For example, if the model is to estimate the CTR of female users clicking on ads for women's clothing, then obviously, we do not want to take into account the data of male users clicking on digital products, because such data are not only irrelevant to the target group's interests, but also perturbing the weights of relevant features during model training. In order to make CTR models more targeted for specific user groups and use cases, it first partitions the full sample, and then applies LR models to each cluster to predict the CTR. The idea of LS-PLM is generated from this inspiration.

The mathematical expression of LS-PLM is shown in Equation 2.23. Firstly, it uses the clustering function π to partition the samples (here π uses the softmax function to classify the samples), and then uses the LR model to calculate the CTR of the samples in each partition. Lastly, it multiplies the two terms and adds them up,

$$f(x) = \sum_{i=1}^{m} \pi_i(x) \cdot \eta_i(x) = \sum_{i=1}^{m} \frac{e^{\mu_i \cdot x}}{\sum_{j=1}^{m} e^{\mu_j \cdot x}} \cdot \frac{1}{1 + e^{-w_i \cdot x}} \tag{2.23}$$

where m is the number of partitions. The hyperparameter m can balance the fitting and generalization ability of the model. When $m = 1$, LS-PLM turns into ordinary LR. When m gets larger, the fitting ability of the model is also stronger. At the same time, the size of model parameters also increases linearly with the increase of m, and the training sample required for model convergence also increases. In practice, the empirical value of m given by Alibaba is 12.

In Figure 2.18, the two clusters of training data are shown in red and blue, respectively. The traditional LR model has insufficient fitting ability and cannot find a nonlinear classification boundary, while the MLR model can perfectly outline the rhombus classification boundary with four partitions.

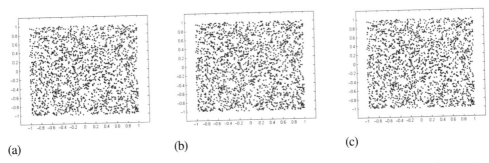

(a)   (b)   (c)

Figure 2.18 Fitting the MLR model to the training data. (a) Training dataset. (b) LR model. (c) LS-PLM model.

2.7.2 Advantages of the LS-PLM Model

The LS-PLM model is suitable for industrial-level recommendation, advertising, and other large-scale sparse data scenarios, mainly because of the following two advantages:

(1) **End-to-end nonlinear learning ability:** LS-PLM has the ability to partition the training sample. Thus, it can mine the nonlinear patterns contained in the data and save a lot of manual data processing and feature engineering. As a result, the LS-PLM algorithm can make the training end-to-end, which facilitates the unified modeling of different applications and business scenarios with a global model.

(2) **Strong model sparsity:** LS-PLM incorporates L1 and L2 norm regularization during modeling, which gives the final fitted model higher sparsity and lightweight deployment. In model online service, it only needs to use features with nonzero weights, so the sparse model also makes it more efficient for online inference.

Basics: Why L1 Norm Is More Likely to Produce Sparse Solutions Than L2 Norm

The model loss function with a regularization term is defined in the "Basics" of Section 2.3, as shown in Equation 2.9.

When $q = 1$, the regularization term is the L1 norm; when $q = 2$, the regularization term is the L2 norm.

It is very important to understand the characteristics of the L1 norm and the L2 norm. Why can adding the L1 norm to the LS-PLM model increase the sparsity of the model?

Here is a two-dimensional example to explain why the L1 norm is more prone to sparsity. The curve of L2 norm $|w_1|^2 + |w_2|^2$ is shown as the red circle in Figure 2.19(a), and the curve of L1 norm $|w_1| + |w_2|$ is shown as the red diamond in Figure 2.19(b). The loss function of the model without regularization is represented by the blue curve.

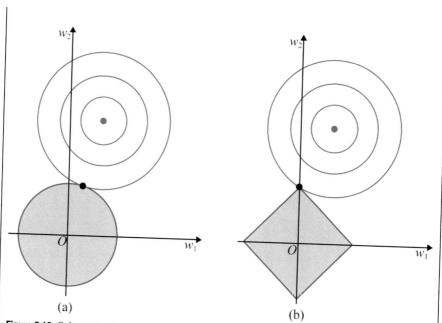

(a)   (b)

Figure 2.19 Schematic diagram of (a) L2 norm and (b) L1 norm and loss function contour.

Finding the minimum value of the loss function with a regularization term is to find the minimum value of the sum of some point on the red circle and some point on the blue circle. This value is usually at the tangent of the red curve and the blue curve (if not at the tangent, then at least two points have the same value, contradicting the definition of extremum). The L1 norm curve is more likely to tangent to the blue curve at the vertex. This results in the weights of other dimensions being 0 except for the dimension at the tangent point, which makes it easy to generate a sparse solution of the model.

2.7.3   Viewing LS-PLM from the Perspective of Deep Learning

In 2012, when LS-PLM models were just put into production, deep learning was still far from being a successful application in the field of recommender systems. But if we look at it today and revisit LS-PLM models from the perspective of deep learning, it would seem that LS-PLM models already had a strong sense of deep learning.

The next section explains the LS-PLM model with concepts of deep learning. It can be read as a warm-up for the deep learning sections that follow.

LS-PLM can be viewed as a three-layer neural network model with some attention mechanism. The input layer is the feature vector of the sample, and the middle layer is a hidden layer composed of m neurons, where m is the number of partitions. For a CTR estimation problem, the last layer of LS-PLM is naturally an output layer composed of a single neuron.

So where is the attention mechanism applied? In fact, between the hidden layer and the output layer, the weights between neurons are determined by the attention score obtained by the partitioning function. That is, the probability of a sample belonging to a partition is equivalent to its attention score.

Of course, this revisit of LS-PLM models from the perspective of deep learning is more about the model structure. In terms of implementation details, it is still different from a typical deep learning model nowadays. But undeniably, LS-PLM has approached the door of deep learning in its own way as early as 2012.

2.8 Summary: The Eve of Deep Learning Recommender Systems

In Section 2.1, we mention the importance of revisiting the model evolution relationship diagram in Section 2.1 after completing the study of this chapter, and re-embed the detailed knowledge of the model into the entire knowledge graph of recommendation models. This section summarizes the characteristics of all models that have been introduced in this chapter (as shown in Table 2.4), hoping to give readers a full picture of the key knowledge points.

When summarizing traditional recommendation models, readers should also be aware that there are inextricable connections between traditional recommendation models and deep learning models. It is the continuous accumulation of traditional model research that has laid a solid theoretical and practical foundation for deep learning models.

In 2006, the technology of matrix factorization was successfully applied to recommender systems. The idea of latent vectors is aligned with the idea of embedding technology in the deep learning world. In 2010, FM was proposed, and the concept of feature interaction was introduced into recommendation models. Its core idea of feature interaction was carried forward in deep learning models. In 2012, LS-PLM was applied on a large-scale application in Alibaba, and its structure was very close to a three-layer neural network. In 2014, Facebook used GBDT to automatically process features and unveiled a new chapter on feature engineering modeling. These concepts will continue to be applied in deep learning recommendation models and continue to shine.

In addition, standing on the shoulders of masters such as Geoffrey Hinton, Yann LeCun, Yoshua Bengio, and so on, Alex Krizhevsky proposed AlexNet [9] in 2012, which detonated the whole wave of deep learning. This model officially raised the curtain of deep learning, and its application quickly spread from images to speech and then to natural language processing. And naturally, recommender systems followed and joined the tide of deep learning.

Since 2016, with the introduction of a large number of excellent recommendation model architectures, such as FNN, Wide&Deep, Deep Crossing, and so on, deep learning models have gradually dominated the world of recommendation and advertising. They become the well-deserved mainstream of the new generation of recommendation models. Chapter 3 continues to discuss the relevant knowledge of recommendation models. We will follow the evolution history and unveil the technical details of state-of-the-art deep learning recommendation models.

Table 2.4 Summary of traditional recommendation models

Model Name	Mechanisms	Characteristics	Limitations
Collaborative Filtering	Generate a user–item co-occurrence matrix based on the user's behavior history, and use user similarity and item similarity for recommendation	The concept is simple, straightforward, and widely used	Poor generalization ability, lack of ability to deal with sparse matrices, and obvious popularity bias in the recommended results
Matrix Factorization	Decompose the co-occurrence matrix in the collaborative filtering algorithm into a user matrix and an item matrix; the inner product of the user latent vector and the item latent vector is used to compute the ranking score for recommendation	Compared with collaborative filtering, the generalization ability has been strengthened, and the processing ability of sparse matrices has been improved.	It is difficult to use contextual information and additional user/item features other than users' historical behavior data
Logistic Regression	Convert the recommendation problem into a binary classification problem such as CTR estimation; Convert different features like users, items, and contexts into feature vectors, and input into the logistic regression model to get the CTR prediction; Then sort by the predicted CTR score	Ability to integrate multiple types of features	The model does not have the ability to combine features, and shows poor expressivity
FM	Based on logistic regression, the second-order interacted features are added to the model; the corresponding feature latent vectors are obtained for each dimension through training; the interacted feature weights are obtained by the inner product between the latent vectors.	Compared with logistic regression, it includes second-order feature interactions, and the expressivity of the model is enhanced.	Due to the limitation of combinatorial explosion problem, the model is not easily extended to third-order feature interactions
FFM	Based on FM models, the concept of "feature field" is added, so that each feature adopts different latent vectors when it interacts with features from different fields	Compared with FM, it further strengthens the ability of feature interaction	
GBDT+LR	Use GBDT for automatic feature interaction; convert the original feature vectors into new discrete feature vectors, and input it into the logistic regression model for final CTR prediction	Feature engineering modeling, so that the model has the ability for higher-order feature interactions	The training complexity of the model has reached $O(n^2)$ and the training overhead is relatively large GBDT cannot perform fully paralleled training, so the training time is relatively long for model updates
LS-PLM	First partition the whole training sample; then build a logistic regression model inside each partition, and perform a weighted average of the partition probability of each sample and the logistic regression score to obtain the final prediction	The model structure is similar to a three-layer neural network, with strong expressivity	Compared with the deep learning model, the model structure is still relatively simple, and there is room for further improvement

References

[1] David Goldberg, et al. Using collaborative filtering to weave an information tapestry. *Communications of the ACM*, 35(12), 1992: 61–71.

[2] Greg Linden, Brent Smith, Jeremy York. Amazon.com Recommenders: Item-to-item collaborative filtering. *IEEE Internet Computing*, 1, 2003: 76–80.

[3] Yehuda Koren, Robert Bell, Chris Volinsky. Matrix factorization techniques for recommender systems. *Computer*, 8, 2009: 30–37.

[4] Alan Kaylor Cline, Inderjit S. Dhillon. Computation of the singular value decomposition. In: Leslie Hogben (ed.), *Handbook of linear algebra* (pp. 45-1–45-13). New York: Chapman and Hall, 2006.

[5] Steffen Rendle. Factorization machines. In 2010 IEEE International Conference on Data Mining, December 13, 2010 (pp. 995–1000).

[6] Yuchin Juan, et al. Field-aware factorization machines for CTR prediction. Proceedings of the 10th ACM Conference on Recommender Systems, September 7, 2016 (pp. 43–50).

[7] Xinran He, et al. Practical lessons from predicting clicks on ads at Facebook. Proceedings of the Eighth International Workshop on Data Mining for Online Advertising, August 24, 2014 (pp. 1–9).

[8] Kun Gai, et al. Learning piece-wise linear models from large scale data for ad click prediction: arXiv preprint arXiv: 1704.05194, 2017.

[9] Alex Krizhevsky, Ilya Sutskever, Geoffrey E. Hinton. ImageNet classification with deep convolutional neural networks. *Communications of the ACM*, 60(6), 2017: 84–90.

3 Top of the Tide

Application of Deep Learning in Recommender Systems

With the introduction of Microsoft's Deep Crossing, Google's Wide&Deep, and a large number of excellent deep learning recommendation models such as Factorization-machine-supported Neural Network (FNN) and Product-based Neural Network (PNN) in 2016, the field of recommender systems and computational advertising has fully entered the era of deep learning. Today, deep learning models have become a well-deserved mainstream in the field of recommender systems and computational advertising. In Chapter 2, we discuss the structural characteristics and evolution of traditional recommendation models. After entering the era of deep learning, the recommendation model has made significant progress mainly in the following two aspects:

(1) Compared with traditional machine learning models, deep learning models have stronger expressivity and can mine more hidden patterns in data.
(2) The model structure of deep learning is very flexible. The model structure can be adjusted according to business use cases and data characteristics, so that the model fits perfectly with the application scenario.

From a technical point of view, the deep learning recommendation model learns from many deep learning techniques in computer vision, and in speech and natural language processing, and has undergone rapid evolution in its model structure.

This chapter summarizes the deep learning recommendation models with great influence in the recommendation field, constructs the evolution map between them, and introduces the technical characteristics of each model. The criteria for selecting a model should follow the following three principles:

(1) Models have great influence in industry and academia.
(2) The model has been successfully applied by well-known IT companies such as Google, Alibaba, and Microsoft.
(3) It plays an important role in the development of deep learning recommender systems.

Now, we will enter the "top of the tide" of recommender systems technology and explore how deep learning is transforming its application.

3.1 Evolution Graph of Deep Learning Recommendation Models

Figure 3.1 shows the evolution graph of the state-of-art deep learning recommendation models. Taking the Multi-Layer Perceptron (MLP) as the core, by changing

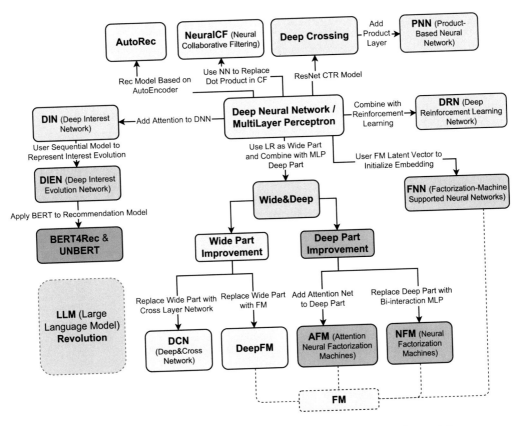

Figure 3.1 Evolution graph of mainstream deep learning recommendation models.

the structure of the neural network, a deep learning recommendation model with different characteristics is constructed. The main evolution directions are as follows:

(1) Changing the complexity of the neural network. From the simplest single-layer neural network model AutoRec (autoencoder recommendation) to the classic deep neural network structure Deep Crossing (deep feature crossing), the main evolutionary method is increasing the depth, that is, the number of layers and the structural complexity of the neural network.

(2) Changing the way features are crossed. The main change in this type of model is to enrich the way features are crossed in deep learning networks. For example, the NeuralCF (Neural Collaborative Filtering) changes the manner of user vector and item vector interoperability, and the PNN (Product-based Neural Network) model defines multiple types of feature vector cross operations.

(3) Ensemble models. This type of model mainly refers to the Wide&Deep model and its subsequent variants, for example, Deep and Cross, DeepFM, and so on. The idea is to improve the model's comprehensive ability by combining

two deep learning networks with different characteristics and complementary advantages.

(4) Evolving the FM models based on deep learning framework. The traditional recommendation model FM has many upgraded versions in the deep learning era, including NFM (Neural Factorization Machine), FNN (Factorization-machine-supported Neural Network), AFM (Attention neural Factorization Machine), and so on. These upgraded models improve FM in different directions. For example, NFM mainly uses neural networks to improve the capability of feature interaction on the second-order term. AFM is an FM model that introduces an attention mechanism, and FNN uses the results of FM to initialize the network.

(5) Combining attention mechanism and recommendation models. This type of model mainly applies the "attention mechanism" to the deep learning recommendation model, mainly including AFM, which combines FM and attention mechanism, and DIN (Deep Interest Network), which introduces the attention mechanism for CTR prediction.

(6) Combining sequence models and recommendation models. This type of model is characterized by using a sequence model to simulate the evolving trend of user behavior or user interest. The representative model is DIEN (Deep Interest Evolution Network).

These summaries clearly show the rapid development and broad thinking of deep learning models in recommendation applications. But each model is not a tree without roots, and its appearance is traceable. As with the structure of Chapter 2, we will explore together to learn the details of each model on the evolution graph as shown in Figure 3.1.

3.2   AutoRec: A Single Hidden-Layer Neural Network Recommendation Model

The AutoRec [1] model was proposed by the Australian National University in 2015. It combines the idea of AutoEncoder with collaborative filtering, and proposes a single hidden-layer neural network recommendation model. Because of its concise network structure and easy-to-understand theory, AutoRec is very suitable for learning as an entry model for deep learning recommender systems.

3.2.1   Theories of AutoRec

The AutoRec model is a standard autoencoder, and its basic theory is to use the co-occurrence matrix in collaborative filtering to complete the autoencoding of item vectors or user vectors. Then it uses the result of self-encoding to get the user's estimated rating of the item, and lastly performs recommendation ranking.

Basics: Autoencoder

As the name suggests, an autoencoder is a model that is capable of "self-encoding" data. Whether it is image, audio, or text data, it can be converted into a vector for expression. Assuming the featured data vector is r, the function of the autoencoder is to take the vector r through a reconstruction function. It will keep the obtained output vector as close to itself as possible after it is applied.

Assuming that the reconstruction function of the autoencoder is $h(r; \theta)$, then the objective function of the autoencoder is

$$\min_{\theta} \sum_{r \in S} \left\| r - h(r; \theta) \right\|_2^2 \qquad (3.1)$$

where S is the entire training dataset.

After completing the training of the autoencoder, it is equivalent to storing the "essence" of all data vectors in the reconstruction function $h(r; \theta)$. In general, the number of parameters in the reconstruction function is much smaller than the number of dimensions of the input vector, so the autoencoder is functionally equivalent to data compression and dimensionality reduction.

Due to the "generalization" process, the output vector generated by the autoencoder will not be completely equivalent to the input vector, so it has a certain prediction ability for the missing dimensions. This is also the reason why the autoencoder can be used for recommender systems.

Assuming that there are m users and n items, the user will rate one or several of the n items, and the unrated items can be represented by the default value or the average score. Then the ratings of all m users can form a scoring matrix with the dimension of $m \times n$, which is also known as a co-occurrence matrix in collaborative filtering.

For an item i, the ratings of all the m users can form an m-dimensional vector $r^{(i)} = \left(R_{1i}, \ldots, R_{mi} \right)^T$. As mentioned in *Basics: Autoencoder*, the problem that AutoRec solves is to construct a reconstruction function $h(r; \theta)$, so that the sum of the squared residuals between all the score vectors generated by the reconstruction function and the original score vector is minimized (Eq. 3.1).

After obtaining the reconstruction function of the AutoRec model, the final recommendation list can be obtained through the process of score estimation and ranking. The following section will introduce two key points of the AutoRec model: the model architecture of the reconstruction function, and the process of using the reconstruction function to obtain the final recommendation list.

3.2.2 Network Structure of the AutoRec Model

AutoRec uses a single hidden-layer neural network to build a reconstruction function. As shown in Figure 3.2, the input layer of the network is the item's rating vector r, and the output is a multiclassification layer. The blue neurons in Figure 3.2 represent a k-dimensional hidden layer of the model, where $k \ll m$.

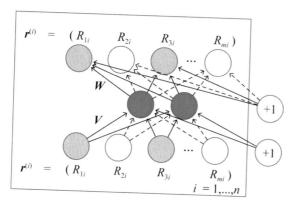

Figure 3.2 Architecture of the AutoRec model.

V and W in Figure 3.2 represent a parameter matrix from the input layer to the hidden layer and the hidden layer to the output layer, respectively. The reconstruction function is defined as follows,

$$h(r;\theta) = f\left(W \cdot g(Vr + \mu) + b\right)$$

(3.2)

where $f(\cdot)$ and $g(\cdot)$ are the activation functions of the output layer and the hidden layer, respectively.

In order to prevent overfitting of the reconstruction function, the L2 regularization term is added. Then, the AutoRec objective function becomes,

$$\min_{\theta} \sum_{i=1}^{n} \left\| r^{(i)} - h\left(r^{(i)};\theta\right) \right\|_{\mathcal{O}}^{2} + \frac{\lambda}{2} \cdot \left(\|W\|_{F}^{2} + \|V\|_{F}^{2} \right)$$

(3.3)

Since the AutoRec model is a standard three-layer neural network, the model can be trained using a gradient backpropagation approach.

Basics: Neuron, Neural Network, and Backpropagation

In this section, the basic concepts related to deep learning are mentioned many times, such as neurons, neural networks, and gradient backpropagation – the main training method of neural networks. We will briefly walk through these concepts.

Neuron, also known as Perceptron, is the same as a logistic regression unit from the model structure perspective. Here, we will use an example of a two-dimensional input vector to elaborate it. Assuming that the input vector of the model is a two-dimensional feature vector (x_1, x_2), the model structure of a single neuron is depicted in Figure 3.3.

In Figure 3.3, the elements in the blue circle can be viewed as a linear weighted summation, plus a constant bias b, and the final input can be expressed as follows

$$(x_1 \cdot w_1) + (x_2 \cdot w_2) + b$$

The entire blue circle in Figure 3.3 is a representation of the activation function. Its main role is to map an unbounded input variable to a normalized, bounded range of values. In addition to the sigmoid function introduced in Section 2.4, the other common activation functions are tanh, ReLU, and so on. Due to the limitation of the simple structure, the single neuron has poor fitting ability. Therefore, when solving complex problems, multiple neurons are often linked as a network, so that it can have the ability to fit any complex function. Such a network is what we often call a *Neural Network*. Figure 3.4 illustrates a simple neural network consisting of an input layer, a two-neuron hidden layer, and a single-neuron output layer.

In Figure 3.4, the neurons (blue circles) have the same structure as that of the perceptron described here. The inputs to neurons h_1 and h_2 are the feature vector (x_1, x_2) and the inputs to neuron o_1 are h_1 and h_2. Here, we show the simplest form of neural network. As the development of deep learning continues, researchers' exploration of different connection methods of neurons leads to different generations of deep learning networks with different characteristics.

After introducing the structure of a basic neural network, the next important question is how to train a neural network. We will start with two important concepts in the neural network training – *Forward Propagation* and Backpropagation.

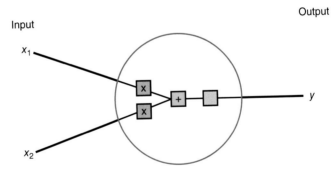

Figure 3.3 The model structure of a single neuron.

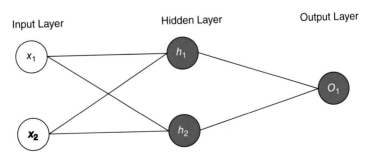

Figure 3.4 A simple neural network.

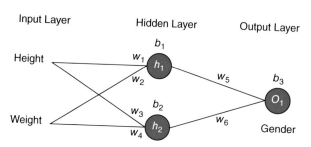

Figure 3.5 A schematic diagram of neural network structure and its weights.

The purpose of forward propagation is to obtain the predicted value of the model's input based on the current network parameters. This process is also often referred to as the model inference. After getting the predicted value, you can use the definition of the *loss function* to calculate the loss of the model. For the output layer neurons (o_1 in Figure 3.4), the gradient descent method can be used directly to calculate the gradient of the associated weights (that is, the weights w_5 and w_6 in Figure 3.5), so as to update the weights. But for the hidden layer, how could we use the gradient descent to update the parameters for the neurons in the hidden layer (for example, w_1 in Figure 3.5) based on the loss from the output layer?

It can be solved through the gradient backpropagation. The gradient backpropagation is used to derive model weights based on model loss utilizing the *chain rule*. As shown in the following equation, the gradient of the final loss function to the weight w_1 is obtained by multiplying the partial derivative of the loss function to the output of the neuron h_1 and the partial derivative of the output of the neuron h_1 to the weight w_1. That is, the final gradient is propagated back layer by layer, leading to the update of the weight w_1.

$$\frac{\partial L_{o_1}}{\partial w_1} = \frac{\partial L_{o_1}}{\partial h_1} \cdot \frac{\partial h_1}{\partial w_1}$$

In the specific calculation, it is necessary to clarify the form of the final loss function and the form of the activation function of each layer of neurons, and then calculate the partial derivative according to the specific function.

To summarize, a neuron is the basic structure in neural networks. The specific implementation, mathematical expression, and training methods are consistent with logistic regression models. A neural network is a network formed by connecting multiple neurons in a certain way. The training method of a neural network is gradient backpropagation based on the chain rule.

3.2.3   Recommendation Process Based on the AutoRec Model

The recommendation process based on the AutoRec model is not complicated. Given the rating vector of the input item i is $r^{(i)}$, the output vector of the model $h(r^{(i)}; \theta)$ is the prediction of ratings for the item i by all users. Then, $\hat{R}_{ui}$ represents the rating prediction of user u for item i, as shown in Eq. 3.4.

$$\hat{R}_{ui} = \left(h\left(r^{(i)}; \hat{\theta} \right) \right)_u \tag{3.4}$$

By traversing the input item vector, the rating predictions of all items from user u can be obtained. Then the recommendation list can be generated based on the rating predictions.

Like the collaborative filtering algorithm introduced in Section 2.2, AutoRec is also divided into item-based AutoRec and user-based AutoRec. The input vector in the formula introduced here is the rating vector of the item, so it can be called I-AutoRec (Item-based AutoRec). If the user's rating vector is used as the input vector, then we will get U-AutoRec (User-based AutoRec). In the process of recommendation list generation, the advantage of U-AutoRec over I-AutoRec is that it only needs to input the user vector of the target user once, and then the user's rating vector for all items can be constructed. That is to say, only one model inference process is needed to obtain the user's recommendation list; the disadvantage is that the sparsity of the user vector may affect the model's effectiveness.

3.2.4 Strengths and Limitations of the AutoRec Model

The AutoRec model uses a single hidden layer autoencoder to generalize user or item ratings, so that the model has a certain level of generalization and expressivity. Because the structure of the AutoRec model is relatively simple, it has a certain problem of insufficient expressivity.

In terms of model structure, the AutoRec model is exactly the same as the later word-to-vector model (Word2vec), but with different optimization targets and training methods. After learning Word2vec, interested readers can compare the similarities and differences between these two models.

From the perspective of deep learning, the proposal of the AutoRec model opened the prelude to the use of deep learning to solve the recommendation problem, and provided ideas for the construction of complex deep learning networks.

3.3 Deep Crossing Model: A Classic Deep Learning Architecture

If the AutoRec model is an initial attempt to apply deep learning to the recommender system, then the Deep Crossing model [2] proposed by Microsoft in 2016 is a complete application of the deep learning architecture in the recommender system. Although companies have claimed that they have applied deep learning models in their recommender systems since 2014, it was not until the year when the Deep Crossing model was released that there were official papers sharing the technical details of the complete deep learning recommender system. Compared with some problems of poor expressivity caused by the simple network structure of the AutoRec model, the Deep Crossing model completely solves a series of deep learning implementation issues from feature engineering, sparse vector densification, and multilayer neural network optimization target fitting. The solutions provided in this model have laid a good foundation for much subsequent research.

3.3.1 Application Scenarios of the Deep Crossing Model

The application scenario of the Deep Crossing model is the search advertisement recommendations in the Microsoft search engine Bing. After a user enters a search term in the search box, the search engine will not only return relevant results but also return advertisements related to the search term, which is also the main profit source of most search engines. Based on the business model, the most important module of an ads system is to build a CTR model to accurately predict click-through rate and further lift performance of ads recommendation. Therefore, CTR naturally become the optimization objective of the Deep Crossing model.

The features used by Microsoft under this use case are shown in Table 3.1. These features can be divided into three categories – the categorical features that can be processed into one-hot or multi-hot vectors, including user search terms (that is, query), ad keyword, ad title, landing page, match type; the numeric features, which Microsoft calls counting features, including CTR and click prediction; the other one is the features that need further processing, including advertising campaign, impression, click, and so on. Strictly speaking, these are not independent features but rather a group of features that need further processing. For example, the budget in the advertising campaign can be used as a numerical feature, and the ID of the advertising plan can be used as a categorical feature.

Categorical features can be processed into feature vectors through one-hot or multi-hot encoding, and numerical features can be directly concatenated into

Table 3.1 Features in the Deep Crossing model

Feature	Feature meaning
Search term	The search term entered by the user in the search box
Ad keyword	Keywords that the advertiser adds to the ad to describe their product
Ad title	The titles of the ads
Landing page	The first page after ad is clicked
Match type	Advertiser-selected ad-search term match type (including exact match, phrase match, semantic match, and so on)
CTR	Ad's historical CTR
Click prediction	CTR prediction from another CTR model
Ad campaign	The ad delivery plan created by the advertiser, including budget, targeting conditions, and so on
Impression Sample	An example of an ad "impression" that records the contextual information about the ad in the actual impression scene
Click Sample	An example of an ad "click" that records the contextual information about the ad in the actual click scenario

feature vectors. After generating the vector representation of all input features, the Deep Crossing model uses the feature vectors to predict CTR. The characteristic of a deep learning network is that the network structure can be flexibly adjusted according to the business and engineering needs, so as to achieve the end-to-end training from the original input features to the final optimization target. Next, by analyzing the network structure of the Deep Crossing model, we can explore how deep learning can accurately predict the CTR through the layer-by-layer processing of features.

3.3.2 Network Structure of Deep Crossing Model

In order to achieve end-to-end training, the Deep Crossing model needs to solve the following problems in its network:

(1) How to solve the problem of densification of sparse feature vectors since one-hot encoding feature is too sparse, which is not in favor of direct training;
(2) How to solve the problem of automatic feature crossovers;
(3) How to achieve the optimization target set by the problem in the output layer.

The Deep Crossing model sets up different neural network layers to solve these problems. As shown in Figure 3.6, the network structure mainly includes four layers: the embedding layer, the stacking layer, the multiple residual units layer, and the scoring

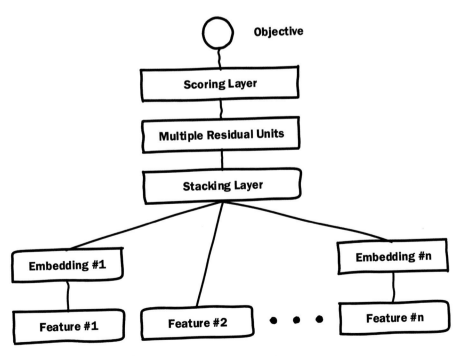

Figure 3.6 Structure diagram of the Deep Crossing model.

layer. Next, the functions and implementations of each layer will be introduced from bottom to top.

- *Embedding layer*: The role of the embedding layer is to convert sparse categorical features into dense embedding vectors. As can be seen from Figure 3.6, each feature (such as Feature#1, here refers to the one-hot encoded sparse feature vector) will be converted into the corresponding embedding vector (such as Embedding#1) after passing through the embedding layer.

  The structure of the embedding layer is mainly based on the classic fully connected layer structure, but the embedding technology itself, as a very widely studied topic in the deep learning domain, has derived many other different embedding methodologies such as Word2vec, Graph Embedding, and so on. Chapter 4 will give a more detailed introduction to the state-of-the-art embedding models.

  Generally speaking, the dimension of the embedding vectors should be much smaller than the original sparse feature vector, and tens to over one hundred dimensions can generally meet the requirements. It should be noted here that Feature#2 in Figure 3.6 actually represents a numerical feature. The numerical feature does not need to go through the embedding layer, but directly enters the stacking layer.

- *Stacking layer*: The function of the stacking layer is relatively simple. It is to concatenate different embedding features and numerical features to form a new feature vector containing all features. This layer is also usually referred as the concatenate layer.
- *Multiple Residual Units layer*: The main structure of this layer is a MLP. Compared with the standard neural network with a perceptron as the basic unit, the Deep Crossing model uses a multilayer residual network as the MLP implementation. The most famous residual network is the 152-layer residual network proposed by Microsoft researcher Yuming He in the ImageNet competition [3]. The application of residual networks in the Deep Crossing model is also the first successful extension of residual networks outside the field of computer vision.

  Through the multilayer residual network, the various dimensions of the feature vector are fully crossed, so the model can capture more information about non-linear features and combined features. As a result, the deep learning model is more expressive than traditional machine learning models.

Basics: Residual Neural Networks and Its Characteristics

Residual neural network is a neural network composed of residual units. The specific structure of the residual unit is depicted in Figure 3.7.

Different from the traditional perceptron, the residual unit has two main characteristics:

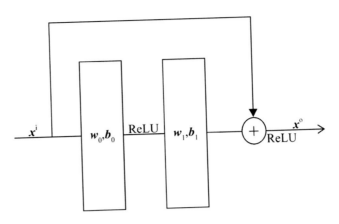

Figure 3.7 The specific structure of a residual unit.

(1) The residual unit contains a fully connected layer with ReLU as the activation function.
(2) The input is directly connected with ReLU output through a shortcut path.

Under such a structure, what the residual unit is actually fitting is the "residual difference" $(x^0 - x^1)$ between the output and the input, which is the origin of the name of the residual neural network.

The birth of the residual neural network is mainly to solve two problems:

(1) For traditional perceptron-based neural networks, when the network is deepened, there is often an overfitting problem; that is, the deeper the network, the worse the performance on the test set. In the residual neural network, due to the existence of short-circuit of the input vector, the two-layer ReLU network can be skipped in many cases to reduce the occurrence of overfitting.
(2) When the neural network is deep enough, there is often a serious gradient vanishing phenomenon. The vanishing gradient phenomenon means that in the process of gradient backpropagation, the closer to the input end, the smaller the magnitude of the gradient, and then the slower the parameter convergence speed. To solve this problem, the residual unit uses the ReLU activation function to replace the original sigmoid activation function. In addition, short-circuiting the input vector is equivalent to directly passing the gradient to the next layer without modification, which also makes the residual network converge faster.

- *Scoring layer*: The scoring layer, as the output layer, is to fit the optimization objective. For binary classification problems such as CTR prediction, the scoring layer often uses a logistic regression model, while for multiclassification problems such as image classification, the scoring layer often uses a softmax model.

This is the model structure of Deep Crossing. On this basis, the gradient backpropagation method is used for training, and finally the CTR prediction model based on Deep Crossing is obtained.

3.3.3   The Revolution to Feature Crossing Method by Deep Crossing Model

From the view of the current deep learning world, the Deep Crossing model is unremarkable, because it does not introduce any special model structure such as attention mechanism, sequence model, and so on. It just uses the typical deep learning architecture with embeddings and a multilayer neural network. But from a historical perspective, the emergence of the Deep Crossing model is revolutionary. There is no manual feature engineering involved in the Deep Crossing model. The original features are fed into the neural network layer after the embedding layer, and the task of feature crossing is all handed over to the model. Compared with the previously introduced FM and FFM models, which only have the ability to cross second-order features, the Deep Crossing model can perform "deep crossover" among features by adjusting the depth of the neural network, which is the origin of the name Deep Crossing.

3.4   NeuralCF Model: Combination of CF and Deep Learning

In Section 2.2, we introduce the classic algorithm of a recommender system – collaborative filtering. The Matrix Decomposition technique is then developed along the idea of collaborative filtering (Section 2.3), which decomposes the co-occurrence matrix in collaborative filtering into the user vector matrix and item vector matrix. In this model, the inner product of the hidden vector of user u and the hidden vector of item i is the prediction of the rating of item i by user u. Following the development path of Matrix Decomposition and combining with deep learning knowledge, researchers from the National University of Singapore proposed a deep-learning-based collaborative filtering model NeuralCF [4] in 2017.

3.4.1   Revisiting Matrix Factorization Models from the Perspective of Deep Learning

As mentioned in the introduction to the Deep Crossing model in Section 3.3, the main function of the embedding layer is to convert sparse vectors into dense vectors. In fact, if we view the Matrix Decomposition model from the perspective of deep learning, the user-hidden vector and item-hidden vector of the matrix decomposition layer can be treated as one kind of embedding method. The final "scoring layer" is to obtain the "similarity" after the inner product of the user's latent vector and the item's latent vector. The "similarity" here is the prediction of the rating. In summary, the architecture of the matrix factorization model can be described by a deep learning network like structure, as shown in Figure 3.8.

In the process of training and evaluating models using Matrix Decomposition, it is often found that the model is prone to underfitting. The reason is that the model structure of matrix decomposition is relatively simple, especially the output layer (that is, the scoring layer), which cannot effectively fit the optimization objective.

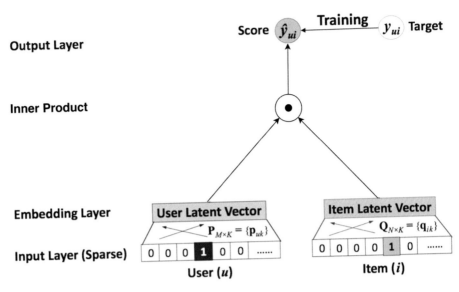

Figure 3.8 Representation of matrix factorization in a deep learning network-like structure.

This requires the model to have stronger expressivity. Inspired by this motivation, researchers from the National University of Singapore proposed the NeuralCF model.

3.4.2   Network Structure of the NeuralCF Model

As shown in Figure 3.9, NeuralCF replaces the simple inner product operation in the matrix factorization model with the structure of the multilayer neural network and output layer. The benefits of doing so are intuitive. First, the user vector and the item vector can be more effectively crossed to obtain more valuable feature combination information; the second is to introduce more nonlinear features to make the model more expressive.

In fact, the interaction layer of user and item vectors can be replaced by any other form of manipulations. Such type of model is the so-called Generalized Matrix Factorization model.

The original matrix decomposition uses the "inner product" method to allow the user to interact with the item vector. In order to further allow the vectors to fully cross in each dimension, the element-wise product (that is, multiplying the corresponding elements from two vectors with the same dimension) is used for interoperability. Then the final prediction target is fitted through the output layer, such as logistic regression. The use of neural networks to fit interaction functions in NeuralCF is a generalized form of feature crossing. In the chapters that introduce the PNN model and the Deep and Cross model, more feasible forms of interaction functions will be introduced.

Further, the feature vectors obtained through different interaction networks can be concatenated and passed to the output layer for fitting. An example of integrating two

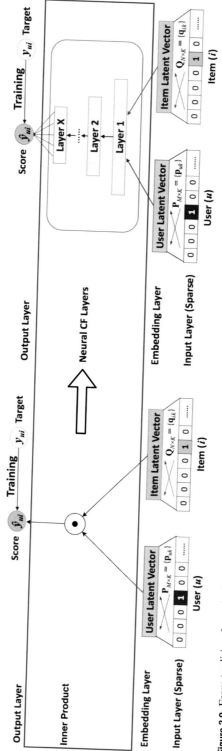

Figure 3.9 From traditional matrix factorization to NeuralCF.

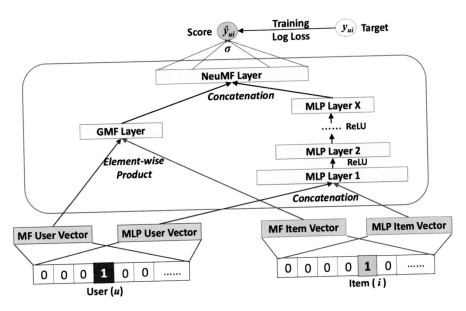

Figure 3.10 The hybrid NeuralCF model.

networks is given in the NeuralCF paper [4] (shown in Figure 3.10). Such a model is called the hybrid NeuralCF. It can be seen that the hybrid NeuralCF model integrates with the original NeuralCF model mentioned earlier and the generalized matrix factorization model with element-wise results, such as interoperability. This allows the model to have stronger feature crossing and nonlinearity.

Basics: What Is the Softmax Function?

While introducing the Deep Crossing and NeuralCF models, it has been mentioned many times that the softmax function is used as the final output layer of the model to solve the fitting of multiclassification problems. So what is the softmax function and why is the softmax function able to solve multiclassification problems?

Mathematical Definition of Softmax Function

Given an n-dimensional vector, the softmax function maps it to a probability distribution. The standard softmax function $\sigma : \mathbb{R}^n \to \mathbb{R}^n$ is defined by the following formula,

$$\sigma(X)_i = \frac{\exp(x_i)}{\sum_{j=1}^{n} \exp(x_j)} \quad \text{where } i = 1, \cdots, n \text{ and } X = [x_1, \cdots, x_n]^T \in \mathbb{R}^n$$

It can be seen that the softmax function solves the problem of mapping from an original n-dimensional vector to an n-dimensional probability distribution. Then in the multiclass classification problem, assuming that the number of classes is n, what the model wants to predict is the probability distribution of a sample on n classes. If a

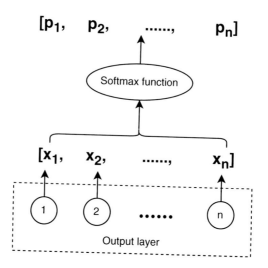

Figure 3.11 The structure of the softmax output layer.

deep learning model is used for prediction, then the final output layer is composed of n neurons. The output of the n neurons then become the input (a n-dimensional vector) to the final softmax function. Eventually, the final multiclass probability distribution can be obtained from the output of the softmax function. In a neural network, the structure of the softmax output layer can be presented as shown in Figure 3.11.

In multiclass classification problems, the softmax function is often used together with the cross-entropy loss function,

$$\text{Loss}_{\text{Cross Entropy}} = -\sum_i y_i \ln\left(\sigma(x)_i\right)$$

where y_i is the ground truth label value of the ith category, and $\sigma(x)_i$ represents the predicted value of the ith category by the softmax function. Because the softmax function normalizes the classification output into the probability distribution of multiple classifications, and the cross entropy describes the similarity between the predicted classification and the actual result, the softmax function is often used in conjunction with the cross entropy. When using cross-entropy as the loss function, the gradient descent form of the entire output layer becomes extremely simple. The derivative of the softmax function turns,

$$\frac{\partial \sigma(x)_i}{\partial x_j} = \begin{cases} \sigma(x)_i \left(1 - \sigma(x)_j\right), & i = j \\ -\sigma(x)_i \cdot \sigma(x)_j, & i \neq j \end{cases}$$

Based on the chain rule, the derivative of the cross-entropy function to the jth-dimensional input x_j of the softmax function can be expressed as,

$$\frac{\partial \text{Loss}}{\partial x_j} = \frac{\partial \text{Loss}}{\partial \sigma(x)} \cdot \frac{\partial \sigma(x)}{\partial x_j}$$

In a multiclass classification problem, only one dimension of 1 is in the ground truth label, and the rest of the dimensions are all 0. Assuming that the kth dimension is 1, that is, $y_k = 1$, then the cross-entropy loss function can be simplified into the following form,

$$\text{Loss}_{\text{Cross Entropy}} = -\sum_i y_i \ln\left(\sigma\left(\mathbf{x}\right)_i\right) = -y_k \cdot \ln\left(\sigma\left(\mathbf{x}\right)_k\right) = -\ln\left(\sigma\left(\mathbf{x}\right)_k\right)$$

Then,

$$\frac{\partial \text{Loss}}{\partial x_j} = \frac{\partial\left(-\ln\left(\sigma\left(\mathbf{x}\right)_k\right)\right)}{\partial \sigma\left(\mathbf{x}\right)_k} \cdot \frac{\partial \sigma\left(\mathbf{x}\right)_k}{\partial x_j} = -\frac{1}{\sigma\left(\mathbf{x}\right)_k} \cdot \frac{\partial \sigma\left(\mathbf{x}\right)_k}{\partial x_j} = \begin{cases} \sigma\left(\mathbf{x}\right)_j - 1, j = k \\ \sigma\left(\mathbf{x}\right)_j, j \neq k \end{cases}$$

From this, it can be seen that the combination of softmax function and cross entropy is not only perfectly aligned in mathematical meaning, but also makes the gradient formula concise. Based on this gradient equation, the update of the weight of the entire neural network can be completed by the method of gradient backpropagation.

3.4.3   Strengths and Limitations of NeuralCF Models

The NeuralCF model actually proposes a model framework – it is based on the two embedding layers of the user vector and the item vector, uses different interaction layers to cross the features, and can flexibly concatenate different interaction layers. From this, we can see the advantages of deep learning in building a recommendation model – using the ability of neural networks to fit arbitrary functions in theory, flexibly combining different features, and increasing/decreasing the complexity of the model as needed.

In practice, it should be noted that it is not always true that the more complex the model structure and the more features, the better. We need to understand the consequence induced by adding more complexities to the model: (1) risk of overfitting; (2) demand of a larger amount of training data; and (3) longer training time. These aforementioned aspects are what algorithm engineers need to consider while making trade-off decisions between model practicability, real-time performance, and effectiveness.

The NeuralCF model also has its own limitations. Since it is developed on the basis of collaborative filtering, the NeuralCF model does not introduce other types of features, which undoubtedly wastes other valuable information in practical applications. In addition, there is no further exploration and categorization of feature interaction types in the model. It requires deeper dives in the follow-up research.

3.5   PNN Model: A Way of Enhancing Feature Cross Capabilities

The main idea of the NeuralCF model introduced in Section 3.4 is to use a multilayer neural network to replace the dot product operation of classical collaborative filtering to enhance the expressiveness of the model. In a broader sense, any manipulation method between vectors can be used to replace the inner product operation of collaborative filtering, and the corresponding model can be called a generalized matrix factorization model. However, the NeuralCF model only mentions two fields of feature vectors, the user vector and the item vector. How to design the feature crossing method if multiple sets of feature vectors are added? In 2016, the PNN (Product-based Neural Networks) model proposed by researchers from Shanghai Jiao Tong University [5] gave several design ideas for feature interaction.

3.5.1　Network Structure of the PNN Model

The purpose of the PNN model proposal is also to solve the problem of CTR prediction in the recommender system, so the application scenarios of the model will be omitted here. Figure 3.12 shows the model structure diagram. Compared with the Deep Crossing model (as shown in Figure 3.6), the PNN model is similar in most parts of the overall structure, including the input layer, embedding layer, MLP layer, and final output layer. The only difference is that the PNN model replaces the stacking layer in the Deep Crossing model with a product layer. In other words, the embedding vectors of different features are no longer simply concatenated; instead, a product operation is applied to each pair of embedding vectors to capture cross-feature information in a more structured manner.

In addition, compared with NeuralCF, the input of the PNN model not only includes user and item information but can also have more features in different forms

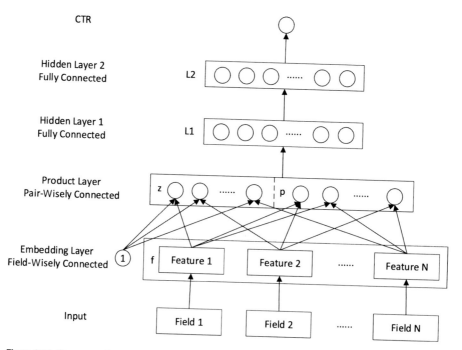

Figure 3.12 Structure diagram of the PNN model.

and sources, followed by generating the dense embedding feature vectors of the same length through the encoding of the embedding layer. To model feature crossing, the PNN model also provides more specific interaction methods.

3.5.2   Multiple Feature Intersection Forms in the Product Layer

The main innovation of the PNN model for the deep learning structure is the introduction of the product layer. Specifically, the product layer of the PNN model consists of a linear operation part (block z of the product layer in Figure 3.12) and a product operation part (block p of the product layer in Figure 3.12). Among them, the product feature interaction part can be divided into inner product type and outer product type. The PNN model using inner product operation is called Inner Product-based Neural Network (IPNN), and the PNN model using outer product operation is called Outer Product-based Neural Network (OPNN).

Whether it is an inner product type or an outer product type, it is a form of pairwise combination of different feature embedding vectors. In order to ensure the smooth operation of the product, the dimensions of each embedding vector must be the same.

The inner product is a classic vector manipulation method. Assuming that the input feature vectors are f_i and f_j respectively, the inner product equation $g_{inner}(f_i, f_j)$ can be defined as,

$$g_{inner}(f_i, f_j) = \langle f_i, f_j \rangle \tag{3.5}$$

The outer product operation is to cross each dimension of the input feature vectors f_i and f_j for each pair of elements to generate a feature cross matrix. The outer product equation $g_{outer}(f_i, f_j)$ can be defined as,

$$g_{outer}(f_i, f_j) = f_i f_j^T \tag{3.6}$$

The outer product operation generates a square matrix with the dimension of $M \times M$, where M is the dimension of the input vector. It is clear that such an operation will directly increase the complexity of the algorithm from the order of M originally to M^2. In order to reduce the burden of model training, a dimensionality reduction method was introduced in the PNN model paper. The results of the outer product of the feature embedding vectors are super-positioned to form a combined outer product matrix p, as shown,

$$p = \sum_{i=1}^{N}\sum_{j=1}^{N} g_{outer}(f_i, f_j) = \sum_{i=1}^{N}\sum_{j=1}^{N} f_i f_j^T = f_\Sigma f_\Sigma^T, f_\Sigma = \sum_{i=1}^{N} f_i \tag{3.7}$$

From the final form of Equation 3.7, the final superposition matrix p is similar to applying an average pooling on all the feature embeddings and then performing the outer product operation.

In practical applications, the operation of average pooling should also be treated with caution. Because the corresponding dimensions of different features are averaged, it is actually assumed that the corresponding dimensions of different features have similar physical meanings. But obviously, if one feature is "age" and the other is "region," then after these two features have passed through their respective embedding layers, the embedding vectors of the two are not in the same vector space, which is obviously not comparable. At this time, averaging the two will obscure a lot of valuable information. The average pooling often occurs in the embeddings in the same domain; for example, the embedding of multiple items browsed by the user is averaged. Therefore, the outer pooling operation of the PNN model needs to be cautious, and carefully balanced between training efficiency and model performance.

In fact, after the linear and product operations of the features, the PNN model does not directly send the results to the upper L_1 fully connected layer (as shown in Figure 3.12), but performs a local fully connected layer conversion inside the product layer. It maps the linear portion z, the product portion p into D_1-dimensional input vectors l_z and l_p respectively. D_1 is the number of hidden units in the L_1 hidden layer. The mapped vectors l_z and l_p are superimposed and passed into the hidden layer. This part of the operation is commonly seen and can be replaced by other types of transformation operations, so it will not be described in detail here.

3.5.3   Strengths and Limitations of the PNN Model

The highlight of the PNN model is that it emphasizes the versatility of interaction methods between feature embedding vectors. Compared with the simple, undifferentiated processing in the fully connected layer, the inner product and outer product operations adopted by the PNN model obviously focus more on the interaction between different features, which makes it easier for the model to capture the interacting relationship of the features.

However, the PNN model also has some limitations. For example, in the practical application of the outer product operation, a lot of simplification operations have to be performed to optimize the training efficiency. Furthermore, performing an indiscriminate crossover of all features, to some extent, ignores the valuable information contained in the original feature vector. It then comes down to questions such as how to integrate original features and crossed features to make feature crossing more efficient. The Wide&Deep model and various deep learning models based on FM introduced in the later sections will give their solutions.

3.6   Wide&Deep Model: Combining Memorization and Generalization

This section introduces a model that has had great influence in the industry since it was proposed: the Wide&Deep model, presented by Google in 2016 [6]. The main idea of the Wide&Deep model, as its name suggests, is a hybrid model consisting of a single-layer "wide" substructure and a multilayered "deep" substructure. Among them, the main function of the wide part is to make the model have strong memorization ability, while the main responsibility of the deep part is to make the model have more generalization ability. It has the advantages of logistic regression as well as deep neural network. That is, it can quickly process and memorize a large number of historical behavioral characteristics, and also has strong expressivity. It not only quickly became the state-of-art model in the industry at that time, but also derived a large number of hybrid models based on the foundations of the Wide&Deep model. Its influence still continues today.

3.6.1 Memorization and Generalization of the Wide&Deep Model

The original intention of the Wide&Deep model and its greatest value are from strong memorization ability and generalization ability at the same time. This is the first time we have mentioned the Memorization concept in this book. Although generalization has been mentioned many times in previous chapters, it has never given a detailed explanation. In this section, we will give a detailed explanation of both these two concepts.

Memorization can be understood as the ability of the model to directly learn and utilize the "co-occurrence frequency" of items or features in the historical data. Generally speaking, simple models such as collaborative filtering and logistic regression have strong "memorization capabilities." Due to the simple structure of this type of model, the original data can often directly affect the recommendation results, resulting in inductive recommendations like "if you have clicked on A, recommend B." This is equivalent to the model directly remembering the distribution of historical data characteristics, and use these memories to make recommendations.

Since the Wide&Deep model was originally proposed by the Google Play recommendation team, here we take the scenario of app recommendation as an example to explain the model's memorization capability.

Suppose that the following combined features are adopted during the training process of the Google Play recommendation model, $\text{AND}\left(\text{user}_{\text{installed\_app}} = \text{netflix}; \text{impression}_{\text{app}} = \text{pandora}\right)$, or (netflix & pandora). This feature means that the user has installed the Netflix app and sees the Pandora app recommended in the Google Play App store. If we use a successful Pandora installation as a positive label, it is easy to count the co-occurrence frequency between the feature of (Netflix and Pandora) and the positive labels of Pandora installation. Assuming that the co-occurrence frequency of the two is as high as 10% (the global average application installation rate is 1%), this feature is so strong that when designing a model, we expect that the model will recommend Pandora as soon as it finds this feature. It is like a memorable point imprinted in people's minds. This is the so-called memorization of the model. For simple models such as logistic regression, if such a "strong feature" is found, its corresponding weight will be greatly adjusted during the model training process, thus reflecting the direct memory of this feature. On the other hand, for a multilayer neural network, the feature will be processed through multiple layers and continuously crossed with other features, so the model's memory of any strong feature is not as prominent as that of a simple model.

The generalization ability can be understood as the relevancy in the feature transfer, and the ability to discover the latent correlation between the features and ground truth label, especially when the features are sparse or never appeared. Matrix decomposition has a stronger generalization ability than collaborative filtering, since matrix decomposition introduces a structure such as a hidden vector, which lets users or items with sparse data generate hidden vectors to obtain data-driven recommendation scores. This is a typical example of passing global data to the sparse items to improve generalization. For another example, deep neural networks can deeply explore latent patterns in data through multiple automatic crossings of the features. Even with very sparse input feature vectors, we can still obtain a relatively stable and smooth recommendation probability through a deep neural network structure. This is the generalization ability that simple models lack.

3.6.2   Network Structure of the Wide&Deep Model

Given the strong memorization ability of the simple model and the strong generalization ability of the deep neural network, the direct motivation for designing the Wide&Deep model is to combine these two structures. The specific model structure is shown in Figure 3.13.

The Wide&Deep model combines a wide part with a single input layer, and a deep part, which consists of the embedding layer and multiple hidden layers. Then both parts are fed to the final output layer to generate the prediction. The single-layer side (wide side) is good at dealing with a large number of sparse ID features while the deep side uses the strong expressive ability of the neural network to perform deep feature crossing and mine the data patterns hidden behind the features. Finally, using the logistic regression model, the output layer combines the outputs from the wide part and the deep part to generate the final prediction.

The specific feature engineering and input layer design present a deep understanding of the business use cases from the Google Play Recommendation team. From Figure 3.14, we can learn in detail which features the Wide&Deep model uses as the input of the deep part and which features are used as the input of the wide part.

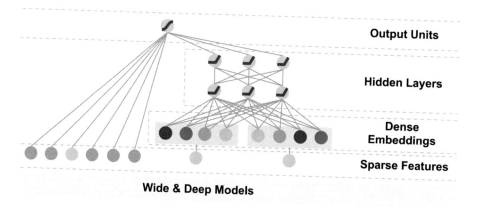

Figure 3.13 The structure of the Wide&Deep model.

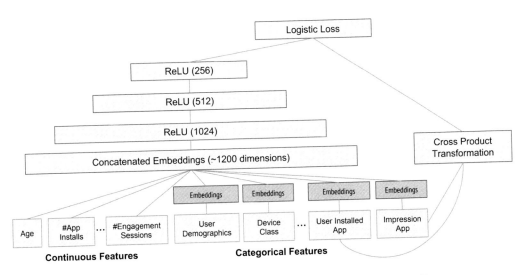

Figure 3.14 The structure of the Wide&Deep model with more feature details.

The input of the deep part is the full set of feature vectors, including user age, number of installed applications, device type, installed applications, impression applications, and so on. The category features, such as installed applications and impression applications, need to go through the embedding layer before entering the connection layer, where embeddings are concatenated into a 1200-dimensional vector. Then this vector is passed through three layers of ReLU fully connected layers, and finally fed to the output layer with the log-loss function.

The input of the wide part only includes two types of features – installed applications and impressed applications, where the installed applications represent the user's historical behavior, and the impressed applications represent the current application candidate to be recommended. The reason for choosing these two types of features is to take full advantage of the memorization ability of the wide part. As mentioned in the memorization example in Section 3.6.1, simple models are good at memorizing information in user behavior characteristics, and can directly influence recommendation results.

The function of combining the feature installed application and impressed application in the wide part is called the *Cross Product Transformation* function, and its definition is shown as follows,

$$\varnothing_\kappa(X) = \prod_{i=1}^{d} x_i^{c_{ki}} \quad c_{ki} \in \{0,1\} \tag{3.8}$$

where c_{ki} is a Boolean variable and x_i is the ith feature. When the ith feature belongs to the kth crossed feature, the value of c_{ki} is 1, otherwise it is 0. For example, for the crossed feature AND($\text{user}_{\text{installed\_app}}$ = netflix; $\text{impression}_{\text{app}}$ = pandora), the corresponding cross-product transform function output is 1 only when both two individual features $\text{user}_{\text{installed\_app}}$ = netflix and $\text{impression}_{\text{app}}$ = pandora are positive, otherwise it is 0.

After the features are crossed through the cross-product transformation layer operation, the wide part feeds the combined features into the final log-loss output layer, and participates in the final objective fitting together with the output from the deep part.

3.6.3   Evolution of the Wide&Deep Model: The Deep and Cross Model

The development of the Wide&Deep model not only integrates memorization and generalization, but also opens up a new idea for the integration of different network structures. After the Wide&Deep model, more and more works focus on improving the Wide&Deep parts, respectively. A representative model is the Deep and Cross model (DCN) proposed by researchers from Stanford University and Google in 2017 [7].

The structure diagram of the Deep and Cross model is shown in Figure 3.15. The main idea is to use the cross network to replace the original wide part. Since the design idea of the deep part has not changed substantially, this section focuses on the design idea and specific implementation of the cross part.

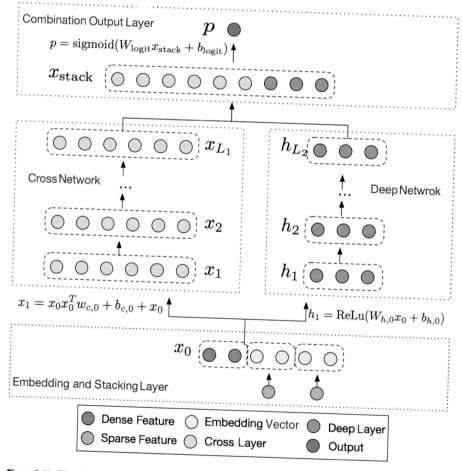

Figure 3.15 The structure of the Deep and Cross model.

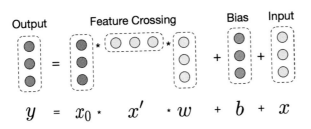

Figure 3.16 The operation of the cross-layer.

The purpose of designing the cross network is to increase the interaction strength between the features, and use a multilayer cross layer to perform feature crossover on the input vector. Assuming that the output vector of the lth cross layer is x_l, then the output vector of the $(l+1)$th layer can be expressed as,

$$x_{l+1} = x_0 x_l^T W_l + b_l + x_l \tag{3.9}$$

It can be seen that the second-order term of the cross-layer operation is very similar to the outer product operation mentioned in the PNN model in Section 3.5. On this basis, the weight vector w_l of the outer product operation, as well as the original input vector x_l and bias vector b_l are added. The operation of the cross layer is shown in Figure 3.16.

It can be seen that the cross layer is relatively "conservative" in increasing parameters. Each layer only adds an n dimensional weight vector w_l, where n is the input vector dimension, and the input vector is retained in each layer. So the change between output and input will not be particularly noticeable. The cross network composed of multiple interaction layers performs automatic feature crossover, which is more advanced than the wide part in the Wide&Deep model. This can help reduce the efforts on feature crossing based on human business understanding. Similar to that in the Wide&Deep model, the deep part of the Deep and Cross model is more expressive than the cross part, which gives the model a stronger learning ability on nonlinear relationships.

3.6.4 Influence of the Wide&Deep Model

The influence of the Wide&Deep model is undoubtedly significant. Not only has it been successfully applied to many first-tier IT companies, but its subsequent improvement and innovation work has continued to this day. In fact, DeepFM, NFM, and other models can be viewed as extensions of the Wide&Deep model. The key to the success of the Wide&Deep model is that:

(1) It grasps the essential characteristics of business problems, and can integrate the advantages of memorization ability from the traditional models and generalization ability from the deep learning models;

(2) The structure of the model is not complicated, and it is relatively easy to implement, train and productionize, which accelerates its popularization and application in the industry.

It is also from the Wide&Deep model that more and more model structures are added to the recommendation model, and the structure of the deep learning model begins to develop in a diversified and complex direction.

3.7   Integration of FM and Deep Learning Models

The evolution of the FM model family has been presented in detail in Section 2.5. After entering the era of deep learning, the evolution of FM has never stopped. The FNN, DeepFM, and NFM models introduced in this section use different methods to apply or improve the FM model, and integrate them into the deep learning model, continuing the advantages in an easy feature combination.

3.7.1   FNN: Embedding Layer Initialization with the Hidden Vector of FM

The FNN model was proposed by researchers at University College London in 2016 [8]. The structure of this model (as shown in Figure 3.17) is a classic deep neural network similar to the Deep and Cross model. It also includes a typical embedding layer to map the sparse input vector to dense vector. So how exactly is the FNN model combined with the FM model?

The key to the problem is the improvement of the embedding layer. In the parameter initialization process of the neural network, random initialization is often used,

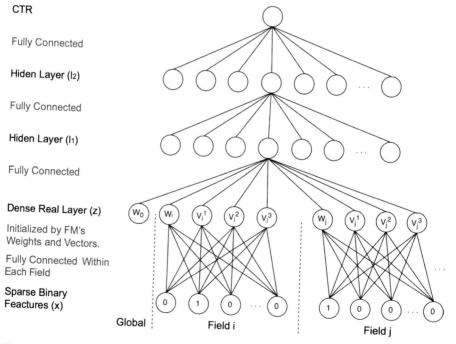

Figure 3.17 Structure of the FNN model.

which does not contain any prior information. Because the input of the embedding layer is extremely sparse, the convergence rate of the embedding layer is very slow. In addition, the number of parameters of the embedding layer often accounts for more than half of the parameters of the entire neural network, so the convergence speed of the entire model is often limited by the embedding layer.

Basics: Why the Convergence Rate of the Embedding Layer Tends to Be Slow

In a deep learning network, the role of the embedding layer is to convert the sparse input vector into a dense vector, but the existence of the embedding layer often slows down the convergence speed of the entire neural network for the following two reasons:

(1) The number of parameters in the embedding layer is huge. A simple calculation can be done here. Assuming that the dimension of the input layer is 100 000, the output dimension of the embedding layer is 32. There are five layers of 32-dimensional fully connected layers added above the embedding layer, and the final output layer dimension is 10. Then, the number of parameters from the input layer to the embedding layer is $32 \times 100\,000 = 3\,200\,000$. The total number of parameters for all remaining layers is $(32 \times 32) \times 4 + 32 \times 10 = 4416$. As a result, the total weight of the embedding layer is $3\,200\,000 / (3\,200\,000 + 4416) = 99.86\%$. That is to say, the weight of the embedding layer accounts for the vast majority of the weight of the entire network. It is not hard to understand that most of the training time and computational overhead are attributed to the embedding layer.

(2) Since the input vector is too sparse, in the process of stochastic gradient descent, only the weight of the embedding layer connected to the nonzero feature will be updated (please refer to the parameter update formula in the stochastic gradient descent for understanding), which further reduces the embedding layer convergence speed.

Aiming at the problem of the convergence speed of the embedding layer, the solution of the FNN model is to initialize the parameters of the Embedding layer with each feature latent vector trained by the FM model, which is equivalent to introducing valuable prior information when initializing the neural network parameters. That is to say, the starting point of neural network training is closer to the target optimal point, which naturally accelerates the convergence process of the entire neural network.

Let's review the mathematical form of FM again, as shown in (Eq. 3.10).

$$y_{\text{FM}}(x) := \text{sigmoid}\left(w_0 + \sum_{i=1}^{N} w_i x_i + \sum_{i=1}^{N} \sum_{j=i+1}^{N} \langle v_i, v_j \rangle x_i x_j\right) \tag{3.10}$$

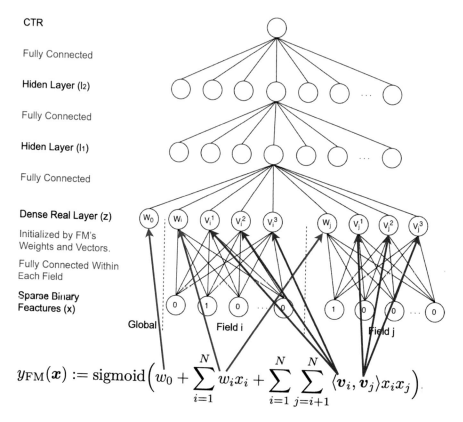

CTR

Fully Connected

Hiden Layer (l2)

Fully Connected

Hiden Layer (l1)

Fully Connected

Dense Real Layer (z)

Initialized by FM's
Weights and Vectors.

Fully Connected Within
Each Field

Sparse Binary
Feactures (x)

$$y_{\mathrm{FM}}(\boldsymbol{x}) := \mathrm{sigmoid}\left(w_0 + \sum_{i=1}^{N} w_i x_i + \sum_{i=1}^{N}\sum_{j=i+1}^{N} \langle \boldsymbol{v}_i, \boldsymbol{v}_j \rangle x_i x_j\right).$$

Figure 3.18 The process of using FM to initialize the embedding layer.

The parameters mainly include constant bias w_0, the first-order term parameter w_i and second-order hidden vector v_i. The corresponding relationship between the parameters of FM and the parameters of the embedding layer in FNN is depicted in Figure 3.18.

It should be noted that although the parameters in FM are pointed to each neuron in the embedding layer in Figure 3.18, its specific meaning is to the connection weight between the embedding neuron and the input neuron. Assuming that the dimension of the FM hidden vector is m, the hidden vector of the k-th dimension feature of the i-th feature field is $v_{i,k} = (v_{i,k}^1, v_{i,k}^2, \ldots, v_{i,k}^l, \ldots, v_{i,k}^m)$, then the l-th dimension $v_{i,k}^l$ of the hidden vector will become the initial value of the connection weight between the input neuron k and embedding neuron l.

In the process of the FM model training, the feature fields are not distinguished. However, in the FNN model, the features are divided into different feature fields. Each feature field has a corresponding embedding layer, and the dimension of embedding in each feature field should be consistent with the dimension of the FM hidden vector.

In addition to using FM parameters to initialize the weights of the embedding layer, the FNN model also introduces another processing method for the embedding layer in the real application – pre-training. More details are introduced in Chapter 4.

3.7.2   DeepFM: Replacing the Wide Part with FM

FNN uses the training result of FM as the initialization weight, and does not adjust the structure of the neural network, while DeepFM [9] jointly proposed by Harbin Institute of Technology and Huawei in 2017 integrates the model structure of FM with the Wide&Deep model. Its model structure diagram is shown in Figure 3.19.

As mentioned in Section 3.6, after the Wide&Deep model, many other models follow the structure of the dual-model combination, and DeepFM is one of them. The improvement of DeepFM on top of the Wide&Deep model is that it replaces the original wide part with FM, which strengthens the ability of partial feature combination of the shallow network. As shown in Figure 3.19, the FM part on the left shares the same embedding layer with the deep neural network part on the right. The FM part on the left crosses the embeddings of different feature fields in pairs, that is, the embedding vector is treated as the feature hidden vector in the original FM. Finally, the output of the FM and the output of the deep part are input into the final output layer to participate in the final prediction.

Compared with the Wide&Deep model, the improvement of the DeepFM model is mainly aimed at mitigating the shortage that the wide part of the Wide&Deep model does not have the ability to automatically cross features. The motivation for improvement here is exactly the same as that of the Deep and Cross model. The only difference is that the Deep and Cross model uses a multilayer cross network for feature

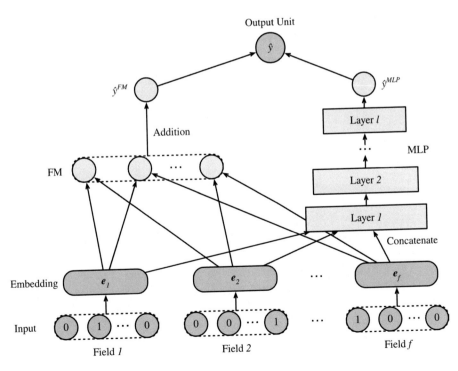

Figure 3.19 The structure diagram of the DeepFM model.

combination, while the DeepFM model uses FM structure for feature combination. Of course, the specific application effects still need to be compared through experiments.

3.7.3   NFM: FM Model's Neural Network Attempt

When we introduced the limitations of FM in Section 2.5, it mentions that whether it is FM or its improved model FFM, it is still basically a simple model with the second-order feature intersection. Affected by the "Curse of Dimensionality" issue, it is almost impossible for FM to extend the feature crossing beyond the third order, which inevitably limits the expressivity of the FM model. So is it feasible to use the stronger expressive power of deep neural networks to improve the FM model? In 2017, researchers from the National University of Singapore made an attempt to explore this and proposed the NFM [10] model.

The mathematical form of the classical FM is presented in Eq. 3.10. The main idea of the NFM model is to replace the part of the inner product of the second-order latent vector in the original FM with a function with stronger expressivity, as shown in Figure 3.20.

If the traditional machine learning idea is used to design the function $f(x)$ in the NFM model, it usually leads to a more expressive function through a series of mathematical derivations. But after entering the era of deep learning, since theoretically the deep learning network has the ability to fit any complex function, the construction of $f(x)$ can be completed by a deep learning network and learned through gradient backpropagation. In the NFM model, the neural network structure used to replace the second-order part of the FM is shown in Figure 3.21.

The characteristic is to add a feature cross-pooling layer (Bi-Interaction Pooling Layer) between the embedding layer and the multilayer neural network. Assuming that V_x is the embedding set of all feature domains, the specific operation of the feature cross-pooling layer is shown in Eq. 3.11,

$$f_{\mathrm{BI}}\left(V_x\right) = \sum_{i=1}^{n} \sum_{j=i+1}^{n} \left(x_i v_i\right) \odot \left(x_j v_j\right) \tag{3.11}$$

where $\odot$ represents the element-wise product operation of two vectors, that is, the corresponding dimension of two vectors with the same length is multiplied to obtain an element-wise product vector. The element-wise product operation on the kth dimension is as follows,

$$\left(v_i \odot v_j\right)_k = v_{ik} v_{jk} \tag{3.12}$$

After performing the element-wise product operation of the two embedding vectors, the crossed feature vectors are summed to obtain the output vector of the pooling layer. The vector is then input into the upper multilayer fully connected neural network for further interaction.

The first-order structure has been omitted in the NFM architecture diagram shown in Figure 3.21. If the first-order part of NFM is viewed as a linear model, then the architecture of NFM is equivalent to the evolution of the Wide&Deep model.

$$\hat{y}_{FM}(x) = w_0 + \sum_{i=1}^{N} w_i x_i + \boxed{\sum_{i=1}^{N} \sum_{j=i+1}^{N} v_i^T v_j \cdot x_i x_j}$$

$$\hat{y}_{NFM}(x) = w_0 + \sum_{i=1}^{N} w_i x_i + \boxed{f(x)}$$

Figure 3.20 Improvement of NFM to the second-order term of FM.

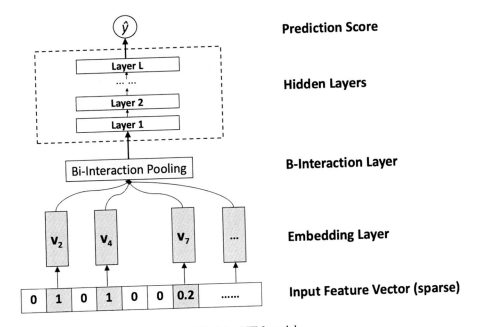

Figure 3.21 The model structure (partial) of the NFM model.

Compared with the original Wide&Deep model, the NFM model adds a cross-pooling layer to its deep part, which strengthens the feature interaction. This is another aspect to understand with the NFM model.

3.7.4   Strengths and Limitations of FM-Based Deep Learning Models

This section introduces three deep learning models (FNN, DeepFM, NFM) that were developed on top of FM approach. They are all characterized by adding targeted feature crossover operations to classic multilayer neural networks, so that the model has stronger nonlinear expressivities.

Following the idea of feature engineering automation, the deep learning model has come all the way from PNN, through Wide&Deep, Deep and Cross, FNN, DeepFM,

NFM and other models, and has made a lot of attempts based on different feature interaction ideas. However, the idea of feature engineering has almost exhausted all possible attempts, and the room for further improvement of the model is quite small, which is also one limitation of such type of model.

Since then, more and more deep learning recommendation models have started to explore some "structural" modifications. For example, attention mechanism, sequence model, reinforcement learning, and other model structures that shine in other fields have gradually entered the field of recommendation world. These attempts have achieved remarkable results in the improvement of the recommendation model.

3.8   Application of Attention Mechanism in the Recommendation Model

The "attention mechanism" comes from the natural human habit of attention. The most typical example is that when users browse the web, they will selectively pay attention to specific areas of the page and ignore other areas. Figure 3.22 is the heat map of page attention from research by the Google Search team by conducting eye-tracking experiments on a large number of users. It can be seen that the distribution of users' attention to the areas of the page is very different. Based on this observation, it indicates that considering the attention mechanism on the prediction in the modeling process may result in some good benefits.

In recent years, the attention mechanisms have been widely used in various fields of deep learning studies, and attention models have achieved great success in the fields of natural language processing, speech recognition, or computer vision. Since 2017, the recommendation field has also begun to try to introduce the attention mechanism into the model, among which the most influential works are AFM [11], proposed by Zhejiang University, and DIN [12], proposed by Alibaba.

3.8.1   AFM: FM Model with Attention Mechanism

The AFM model can be considered as a continuation of the NFM model introduced in Section 3.7. In the NFM model, the feature embedding vectors of different domains are crossed by the feature cross-pooling layer, and the crossed feature vectors are "summed" and input to the output layer through a multilayer neural network. The crux of the problem lies in the operation of sum pooling, which is equivalent to treating all intersecting features "equally," regardless of the degree of influence of different features on the result. In fact, this sum operation eliminates a lot of valuable information.

Here, the "attention mechanism" comes in handy. It is based on the assumption that different crossed features have different effects on the results. Take a more intuitive business scenario as an example to illustrate how users may pay different attention to different cross-features. If the application scenario is to predict the likelihood of a male user buying a keyboard, the cross-feature of "gender=male & purchase history

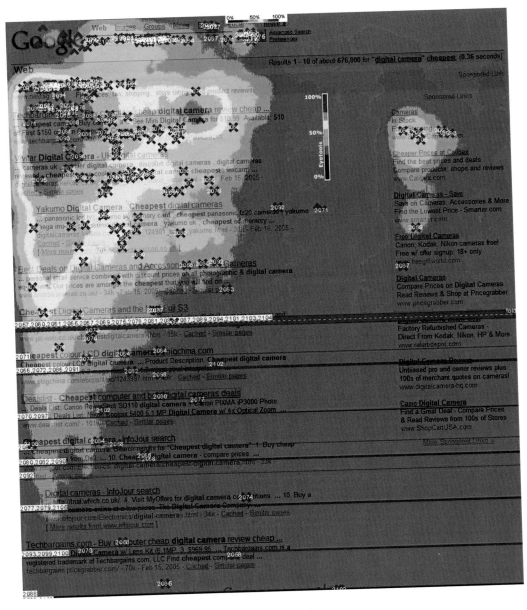

Figure 3.22 Google search engine page attention heatmap.

includes a mouse" is likely more important than the feature "gender=male & user age=30." Thus, the model pays more "attention" to the preceding features. Because of this, it makes sense to combine the attention mechanism with the NFM model.

Specifically, the AFM model introduces an attention mechanism by adding an attention net between the feature intersection layer and the final output layer. The model structure of AFM is shown in Figure 3.23. The role of the attention network is to provide weights for each cross feature, that is, the attention score.

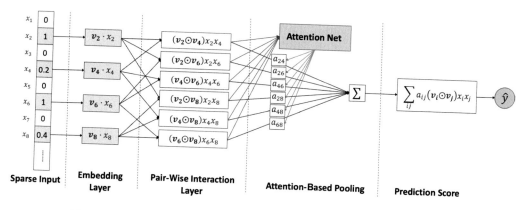

Figure 3.23 The structure diagram of the AFM model.

Like NFM, the feature intersection process of AFM also uses the element-wise product operation, as shown next,

$$f_{PI}(\varepsilon) = \left\{ \left(v_i \odot v_j \right) x_i x_j \right\}_{(i,j) \in \mathcal{R}_x} \tag{3.13}$$

The pooling process after AFM is added to the attention score is expressed as,

$$f_{Att}\left(f_{PI}(\varepsilon)\right) = \sum_{(i,j) \in \mathcal{R}_x} a_{ij} \left(v_i \odot v_j \right) x_i x_j \tag{3.14}$$

For the attention score a_{ij}, the easiest presentation method is to use a weight parameter. But in order to prevent the weight parameter from convergence issues due to the sparse problem of crossed feature, the AFM model uses a pairwise feature interaction and the attention network between the pooling layer to generate the attention score.

The structure of the attention network is a simple structure of a single fully connected layer plus a softmax output layer, and its mathematical form can be expressed as,

$$a'_{ij} = h^T \text{ReLU}\left(W \left(v_i \odot v_j \right) x_i x_j + b \right)$$

$$a_{ij} = \frac{\exp\left(a'_{ij}\right)}{\sum_{(i,j) \in \mathcal{R}_x} \exp\left(a'_{ij}\right)} \tag{3.15}$$

The model parameters to be learned are the weight matrix W from the feature intersection layer to the fully connected layer of the attention network, the bias vector b, and the weight vector h from the fully connected layer to the softmax output layer. Together with the other components in the model, the attention network is also trained through backpropagation to obtain the final weight parameters.

AFM is a positive attempt by researchers to improve the model structure. It has nothing to do with specific application scenarios. However, Alibaba's introduction of the attention mechanism into its deep learning recommendation model is a model improvement based on business observation. Next we will introduce Alibaba's well-known recommendation model in the industry: the DIN model.

3.8.2   DIN: Deep Learning Network with Attention Mechanism

Compared with many previous deep learning models with academic style, the DIN model proposed by Alibaba is obviously more business-centric. Its application scenario is Alibaba's e-commerce advertisement recommendation. When predicting the probability of a user u clicking on an advertisement a, the input features of the model are naturally divided into two parts. One part is the feature group of user u, as shown in Figure 3.24, and the other part is the feature group of candidate advertisement a, as shown in the advertisement feature group in Figure 3.24. Both users and advertisements contain two very important features – product ID (good_id) and shop ID (shop_id). The product ID in the user feature is a sequence, representing the set of products that the user has clicked on, and the same is true for the store ID. The product ID and store ID in the advertisement feature set are the IDs corresponding to the advertisement (the advertisement on the Alibaba platform). Most of them are products that participate in some promotional program).

In the original basic model (the base model in Figure 3.24), the product sequence and store sequence in the user feature group enter the upper neural network for further training after a simple average pooling operation. The product and store sequences have not distinguished the level of importance, and have no explicit relationship with the product ID in the advertisement features.

However, in fact, the degree of correlation between advertising features and user features is very strong, and the use case introduced in Section 3.7 can illustrate the strong correlations. Assuming that the product in the advertisement is a keyboard, there are several different product IDs in the user's click history, for example, mouse, T-shirt, and facial cleanser. Based on common sense, the historical commodity ID of "mouse" should be more important for predicting the click-through rate of "keyboard" ads than the latter two. From the model's point of view, the "attention" given to different features in the modeling process should be different, and the calculation of the "attention score" should be related to the advertising features.

It is also intuitive to reflect the aforementioned idea of "attention" into the model. A weight is calculated by using the correlation between candidate products and historically interacted products. This weight represents the strength of "attention." The DIN model adds the attention weight in the network structure, in which the attention part is formularized as,

$$V_{\mathrm{u}} = f\left(V_{\mathrm{a}}\right) = \sum_{i=1}^{N} w_i \cdot V_i = \sum_{i=1}^{N} g\left(V_i, V_{\mathrm{a}}\right) \cdot V_i \qquad (3.16)$$

where V_{u} is the embedding vector of the user u, V_{a} is the embedding vector of the candidate advertisement product, and V_i is the embedding vector of the ith action of the user u. Here, the user's action is to browse the product or store, so the embedding vector of the action is the embedding vector of the browsed product or store.

Because the attention mechanism is added, V_{u} has changed from the simple sum of V_i in the past to the weighted sum of V_i and the weight w_i of V_i is determined by the relationship between V_i and V_a, which is $g(V_i, V_{\mathrm{a}})$ in Eq. 3.16. This term is also known as the Attention Score.

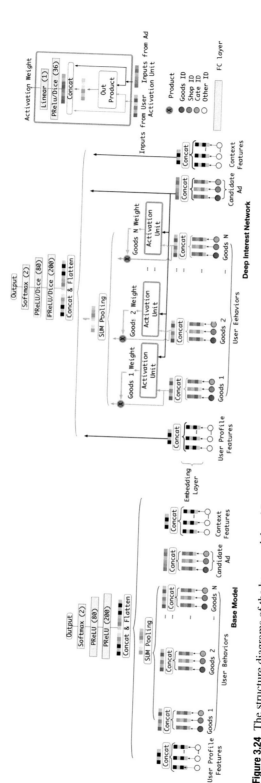

Figure 3.24 The structure diagrams of the base model and DIN model.

Then, what is the good representation for the $g(V_i, V_a)$ function? The answer is to use an attention activation unit to generate the attention score. This attention activation unit is essentially a small neural network, and its specific structure is shown in the activation unit at the upper right corner of Figure 3.24.

It can be seen that the input layer of the activation unit is two embedding vectors. After the element-wise minus operation, they are connected with the original embedding vector to form the input of the fully connected layer. Finally, the attention score is generated through the single neuron output layer.

If you pay attention to the red line in Figure 3.24, you can find that the store ID from the advertisement feature only interacts with the store ID sequence in the user's historical behavior, and the product ID of advertisement only works with the user's product ID sequence, as the weight of attention should be determined more by the correlation of same category of information.

Compared with the FM-based AFM model, the DIN model is a more typical attempt to improve the deep learning network structure. Since the introduction of the DIN model starts from an actual business scenario, it also gives recommendation engineers more substantial inspiration.

3.8.3 Inspiration of Attention Mechanism to Recommender Systems

From the perspective of the mathematical formula, the attention mechanism just replaces the past average or sum operation with a weighted sum or weighted average operation. However, the inspiration of this mechanism for deep learning recommender systems is significant, because the introduction of "attention score" reflects the innate "attention mechanism" characteristics of human beings. The simulation of this mechanism makes the recommender system's logic closer to the user's real thinking process, so as to achieve the purpose of improving the recommendation effect.

Starting from the "attention mechanism," more and more improvements to the structure of deep learning models are based on deep observations of user behavior. Compared with academia, which pays more attention to theoretical innovation, recommendation engineers in the industry need to focus more on their understanding of the actual business problem while developing new recommendation models.

3.9 DIEN: Combination of Sequence Model and Recommender Systems

After Alibaba proposed the DIN model, it did not stop the evolution of its recommendation model, and formally introduced an updated version of the DIN model, DIEN [13], in 2019. The application scenario of the DIEN model is exactly the same as that of DIN. So we will not repeat it in this section. The innovation lies in simulating the evolution process of user interest with the sequence model. The main ideas of DIEN and the design of the interest evolution part are introduced in detail next.

3.9.1   Motivation of the DIEN Model

No matter whether it is e-commerce purchase history, video website viewing history, or news application reading history, the historical behavior of a specific user can be always considered as a time sequence. Since it is a time series problem, there must be some level of dependency on the chronological order among the history items. Such chronological information is undoubtedly valuable for the recommendation process. But do all the models introduced earlier in this chapter make use of this sequential information? The answer is negative. Even the AFM or DIN model that introduces the attention mechanism only scores the importance of different actions, which is time-independent and sequence-independent.

Why is sequential information valuable for recommendation? The behavior of a typical e-commerce user can illustrate this point. For a common e-commerce business, the migration of user interests is actually very fast. For example, a user was picking a pair of basketball shoes last week. After he completes his purchase, his shopping interest this week may turn to buying a mechanical keyboard. The importance of sequence information lies in:

(1) It reinforces the influence of recent behavior on the prediction of the next behavior. In the previous example, the probability that the user has recently purchased a mechanical keyboard is significantly higher than the probability of buying another pair of basketball shoes.
(2) Sequential models can learn information about buying trends. In this example, the sequence model can establish the transition probability from "basketball shoes" to "mechanical keyboard" to a certain extent. If this transition probability is high enough in a global statistical sense, recommending a mechanical keyboard will be a good option when users buy basketball shoes. Intuitively, the user groups of the two are likely to be the same.

If the sequence information is abandoned, the model's ability to learn the time-based or trend-based information can be quite weak. The recommendation model without considering sequential dimension just generates a prediction based on the user's overall purchase history, rather than providing a 'next purchase' recommendation. Obviously, from a business point of view, the sequence model is the correct objective of a recommender system.

3.9.2   Network Structure of the DIEN Model

Based on the motivation of introducing "sequential" information, Alibaba has further developed the DIN model and eventually formed the structure of the DIEN model. As shown in Figure 3.25, the model is still composed of an input layer, an embedding layer, a connection layer, a multilayer fully connected neural network, and the final output layer. The colored "interest evolution network" in the figure is considered to be an embedding representation of user interest, and its final output is the user interest vector $h'(T)$. The innovation of the DIEN model is how to build an interest evolution network in a recommendation model.

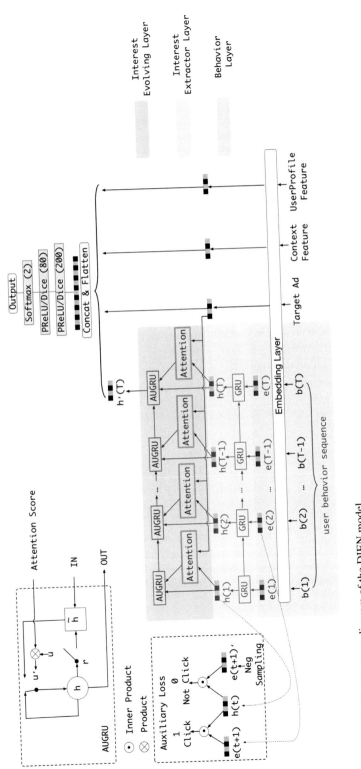

Figure 3.25 The structure diagram of the DIEN model.

The interest evolution network is divided into three layers from bottom to top:

(1) Behavior Layer (color green): converts the original behavior sequence into an embedding behavior sequence;
(2) Interest Extraction Layer (color beige): its main function is to extract user interests by simulating the process of user interest migration;
(3) Interest Evolving Layer (light red): this layer simulates the interest evolution process related to the current target advertisement by adding an attention mechanism based on the interest extraction layer.

In the interest evolution network, the structure of the behavior sequence layer is consistent with the typical embedding layer. The key to simulating the evolution of user interests lies mainly in the interest extraction layer and interest evolution layer.

3.9.3 Interest Extraction Layer

The basic structure of the interest extraction layer is a Gated Recurrent Unit (GRU) network. Compared with the traditional sequence model RNN (recurrent neural network), GRU solves the vanishing gradients problem commonly seen in RNN. Compared with LSTM (long short-term memory network), GRU has fewer parameters and faster training convergence speed. All of the aforementioned reasons result in the final adoption of the GRU network in the DIEN model.

The specific form of each GRU unit is defined as:

$$u_t = \sigma\left(W^u i_t + U^u h_{t-1} + b^u\right)$$
$$r_t = \sigma\left(W^r i_t + U^r h_{t-1} + b^r\right)$$
$$\widetilde{h}_t = \tanh\left(W^h i_t + r_t \circ U^h h_{t-1} + b^h\right)$$
$$h_t = \left(1 - u_t\right) \circ h_{t-1} + u_t \circ \widetilde{h}_t$$

(3.17)

where σ is the sigmoid activation function, $\circ$ is the element-wise product operation, $W^u, W^r, W^h, U^z, U^r, U^h$ are six sets of parameter matrices to be learned. i_t is the input state vector, that is the embedding vector $e(t)$ of each behavior in the behavior sequence layer. h_t is the tth hidden state vector in the GRU network

Following the interest extraction layer with multiple GRUs, the user's behavior vector $b(t)$ is further abstracted to form the interest state vector $h(t)$. In theory, based on the sequence of interest state vectors, the GRU network can already predict the next interest state vector, but why does DIEN further add the interest evolution layer?

3.9.4 Structure of Interest Evolution Layer

The biggest distinction between the interest evolution layer and the interest extraction layer is the addition of an attention mechanism. This mechanism is in the same vein as DIN. It can be seen from the connection of the attention units in

Figure 3.25. The generation process of the attention score of the interest evolution layer is exactly the same as that of DIN, which is the result of the interaction between the current state vector and the target advertisement vector. That is to say, DIEN needs to consider the relevance of targeted advertisements in the process of simulating interest evolution.

This also answers the question at the end of Section 3.9.3. The interest evolution layer is added on top of the interest extraction layer in order to simulate the interest evolution path related to the target advertisement in a more targeted manner. Due to the characteristics of e-commerce such as Alibaba, users are very likely to purchase multiple categories of goods at the same time. For example, while purchasing a "mechanical keyboard," they are still viewing the goods under the "clothing" category. As a result, the attention mechanism is particularly important under such condition. When the target advertisement is an electronic product, the interest evolution path related to the purchase of "mechanical keyboard" is obviously more important than the evolution path of purchasing "clothes." Such distinction logic doesn't exist in the interest extraction layer.

The interest evolution layer achieves application of the attention mechanism by adopting the GRU with Attentional Update gate (AUGRU) structure. AUGRU adds the attention score to the structure of the update gate of the original GRU. The specific form is shown in Eq. 3.18:

$$\tilde{u}_t' = a_t \cdot u_t'$$
$$h_t' = \left(1 - \tilde{u}_t'\right) \circ h_{t-1}' + \tilde{u}_t' \circ \tilde{h}_t' \tag{3.18}$$

Comparing with Eq. 3.17, it can be seen that AUGRU adds the attention score a_t on the basis of the original u_t', where u_t' is the original update gating vector and similar to u_t in Eq. 3.17. The generation method of the attention score is basically the same as that of DIN, which uses the attention activation units.

3.9.5   Inspiration of the Sequence Model to Recommender Systems

This section introduces Alibaba's recommendation model DIEN that incorporates sequence models. Because the sequence model has a strong ability to express time series, it is very suitable for predicting the user's next action after a series of behaviors.

In fact, it is not only Alibaba that has successfully applied the sequence model to its e-commerce recommendation model, but video streaming companies such as YouTube and Netflix have also successfully applied the sequence model to their video recommendation models to predict the user's next streaming preferences (such as next watch).

However, it is necessary to pay attention to the high training cost of the model and the latency in online inferencing caused by serial prediction in a large sequence model. The complexity of sequence model undoubtedly increases the difficulty of its productization. So system optimization turns very important in the engineering implementation. Experiences with implementing a sequence model in production will be discussed in Chapter 8.

3.10 Combination of Reinforcement Learning and Recommender Systems

Reinforcement learning is a very popular research topic in the field of machine learning in recent years. It is originated from the field of robotic studies, and aimed at modeling the decision-making and learning process of an agent in a changing environment. In the learning process of the agent, it will complete the collection of external feedback (Reward), change its own state (State), and then make decisions on the next action (Action) according to its current state, and continue to repeat the cycle. This process is usually referred to as the "action-feedback-state update" cycle.

The concept of agent is very similar to the robots, and the entire reinforcement learning process can be understood by analogizing the robots learning human actions. If the recommender system is viewed as an agent, with its learning and updating process equivalent to the agent's cycle of "action-feedback-state update," then applying reinforcement learning concepts to recommender systems becomes much more intuitive.

In 2018, the reinforcement learning model DRN [14] was firstly proposed by researchers from Penn State University and Microsoft Research Asia. This was an attempt to apply reinforcement learning knowledge to news recommendation.

3.10.1 Deep Reinforcement Learning Recommender Systems Framework

The deep reinforcement learning recommender systems framework is proposed based on the classic process of reinforcement learning. Readers can use the specific scenarios of the recommender system to further familiarize themselves with the concepts of agent, environment, state, action, and feedback in reinforcement learning. As shown in Figure 3.26, the diagram clearly shows the various components of the deep reinforcement learning recommender systems framework and the iterative process of the entire reinforcement learning. The specific explanation of each element in the recommender systems scenario is as follows:

- **Agent:** The recommender system itself, which includes a recommendation model based on deep learning, an exploration strategy, and related data storage (memory);
- **Environment:** The external environment of the entire recommender system consisting of news websites or apps, and users. In the environment, the user receives the recommended results and makes corresponding feedback;
- **Action:** For a news recommender system, an action refers to the system pushing ranked news to the user;
- **Feedback:** After the user receives the recommendation result, the user will give positive or negative feedback. For example, click behavior is considered to be a typical positive feedback, while impression but nonclick is a negative feedback

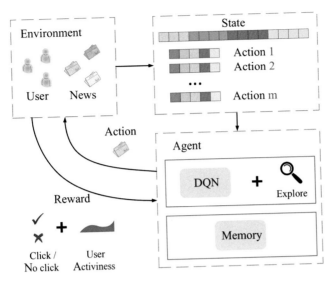

Figure 3.26 Deep reinforcement learning recommender systems framework.

signal. In addition, the user's activity level and the interval between the app opening are also considered as valuable feedback signals;

- **State:** State refers to the description of the environment and its current specific situation. In the news recommendation scenario, the state can be viewed as a feature
vector representation of all actions and feedback received, as well as all relevant
information about the user and news. From the perspective of traditional machine
learning, "state" can be seen as the collection of all the data that has been received
and can be used for training.

Under such a reinforcement learning framework, the learning process of the model
can be iterated continuously. The iterative process mainly includes the following
steps:

(1) Initialize the recommender system, which is the agent in this case.
(2) The recommender system ranks news (actions) based on the currently collected
data (state) and pushes them to the website or app (environment).
(3) The user receives the recommendation list and clicks or ignores (feedback) the
recommendation result.
(4) The recommender system receives feedback and updates the current state or
updates the model through model training.
(5) Repeat the tasks from Step 2.

Readers may have realized that reinforcement learning models have an advantage over
traditional deep models in that they can perform online learning. In other words, the
reinforcement learning models can constantly update themselves with newly learned
knowledge, and make timely adjustments and feedback. This is one of the advantages
of applying reinforcement learning to recommender systems.

3.10.2   Deep Reinforcement Learning Recommendation Models

The agent part is the core of the reinforcement learning framework. For the recommendation agent, the model is the "brain" of the system. In the DRN framework, the role of the "brain" is the Deep Q-Network, DQN for short, where Q is the abbreviation of "Quality." It means that by evaluating the quality of the action, the utility score of the action is calculated and used for decision-making.

The network structure of DQN is shown in Figure 3.27. The concepts of reinforcement learning – state vector and action vector – are applied in feature engineering. User features and context features are classified as state vectors, because they are action independent. User-news crossing features and news features are treated as action features since they are related to the action of recommending news.

User features and environmental features are fitted by the multilayer neural network on the left to generate a value score $V(s)$. The state vector and action vector are used to generate an advantage score $A(s, a)$. Finally, the score from both parts are combined to obtain the final quality score $Q(s, a)$.

3.10.3   Learning of the DRN Model

The learning process of DRN is the main focus of the entire reinforcement learning recommender systems framework. It is the online learning process that gives the reinforcement learning model more real-time advantages than other "static" deep learning models. Figure 3.28 vividly depicts the learning process of DRN in chronological order.

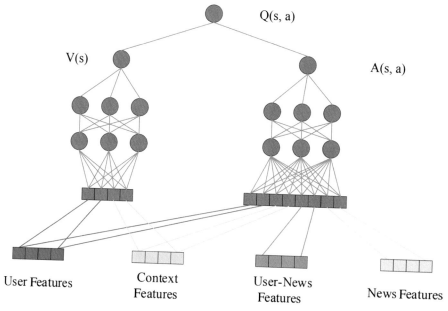

Figure 3.27 The model structure of the DQN model.

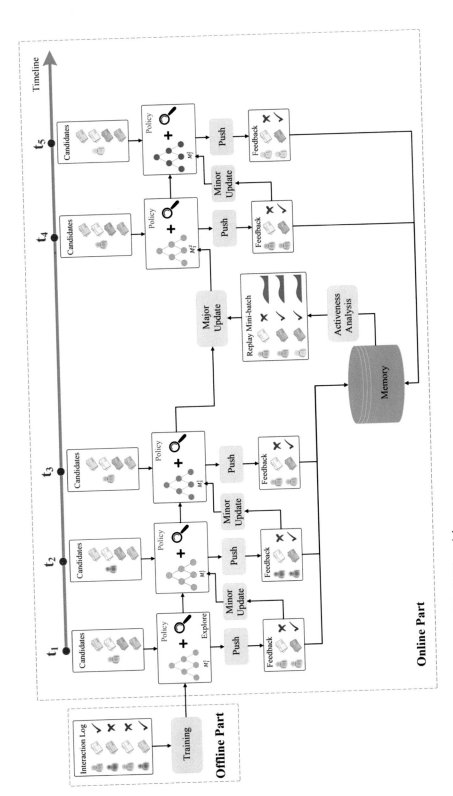

Figure 3.28 The learning process of the DRN model.

The important steps in the DRN learning process are illustrated in chronological order from left to right in Figure 3.28:

(1) In the offline part, the DQN model is trained according to the historical data as the initialization model of the agent;
(2) At the stage $t_1 \rightarrow t_2$, the initial model is used to power the recommendation in the push service for a period of time to accumulate feedback data;
(3) At the time point t_2, the user click data accumulated in the $t_1 \rightarrow t_2$ stage is used to perform a minor update of the model;
(4) At the time point t_4, a major update of the model is performed using the user click data and user activity data in the $t_1 \rightarrow t_4$ stage;
(5) Repeat Steps 2–4.

The model main update operation in Step 4 can be understood as retraining using historical data to replace the existing model with the trained model. So how does the minor update in Step 3 work? This involves a new online training method used by DRN – Dueling Bandit Gradient Descent Algorithm.

3.10.4 Online Learning of the DRN Model: Dueling Bandit Gradient Descent Algorithm

The flow of DRN's dueling bandit gradient descent algorithm is shown in Figure 3.29. The main steps are as follows:

(1) For the current network Q that has been trained, add a small random perturbation ΔW to its model parameter W to obtain a new model parameter $\widetilde{W}$. Here the network corresponding to $\widetilde{W}$ is called the exploration network $\tilde{Q}$;
(2) The recommendation lists L and $\tilde{L}$ are generated respectively with current network Q and the exploration network $\tilde{Q}$. Then, the two recommendation lists are combined into one recommendation list by interleaving (described in detail in Section 7.5) and pushed to the user.
(3) Collect user feedback in real-time. If the feedback of the content generated by the exploration network $\tilde{Q}$ is better than the current network Q, replace the current network with the exploration network and enter the next iteration, otherwise keep the current network

In the first step, the exploration network $\tilde{Q}$ is generated from the current network Q, and the formula for generating random disturbance is shown in Eq. 3.19,

$$\Delta W = \alpha \bullet \text{rand}(-1,1) \bullet W \tag{3.19}$$

where α is the exploration factor, which determines the degree of the exploration. $\text{rand}(-1,1)$ means a random number between $[-1,1]$.

The online learning process of DRN utilizes the idea of "exploration," and the granularity of the model updates can be refined to once per feedback. This process is very similar to the idea of stochastic gradient descent. Although the results of one sample may produce random disturbances, as long as the total decent trend is correct,

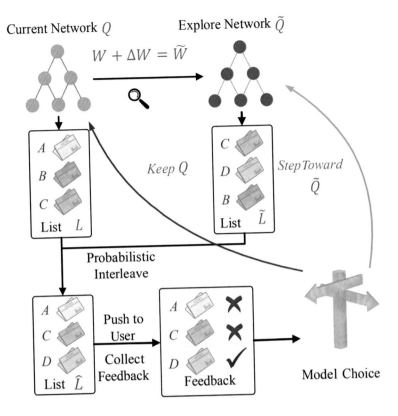

Figure 3.29 The online learning approach of the DRN model.

the optima can be finally reached through a large number of attempts. In this way, DRN keeps the model synchronized with the "freshest" data at all times, and integrates the latest feedback information into the model in real-time.

3.10.5 Inspiration of Reinforcement Learning for Recommender Systems

The application of reinforcement learning in recommender systems once again opens the world of recommendation models from a different angle. The difference between this and the other deep learning models mentioned earlier is that it changes the learning process from static to dynamic, which brings the importance of model real-time learning to a prominent position.

It also brings us a question worth thinking about – should we build a heavy-weight, "perfect" model with a large update delay, or should we build a lightweight and simple model that can be trained in real-time? Of course, there are no assumptions or conjectures in engineering systems, we can only tell which approach is better through actual experiment results. Also, the relationship between "weight" and "real-time" is by no means antagonistic, but before finalizing a technical solution, plenty of evaluation and experiments are necessary for this kind of real-world problem.

3.11   Applications of BERT in a Recommendation Model

Bidirectional Encoder Representations from Transformers (BERT) is a powerful natural language processing model that was introduced by Google in 2018 [15] and achieved state-of-the-art performance in multiple NLP tasks. Like the attention mechanism introduced in Section 3.8, the BERT model was also borrowed into the recommendation world after its demonstrated success in the NLP field. Part of the application of the BERT model in recommender systems is still utilizing its ability to process and understand the natural languages and capture the semantic interpretations for the text data, which will not be covered in this section. In this section, we will mainly walk through two BERT-based recommendation models, the BERT for Recommendation (BERT4Rec) model [16] and User-News Matching BERT (UNBERT) model [17], which adopt the BERT model structure in the sequential recommendation scenarios.

Before introducing the BERT4Rec and UNBERT models, let us briefly review some foundations of the BERT – the Transformer model and self-attention mechanism.

Basics: The Transformer Model and Self-Attention Mechanism

The Transformer model is a revolutionary deep learning architecture that has had a significant impact on NLP tasks, and it builds a foundation for the development of many succeeding language models. Two well-known succeeding language models are the BERT model and the GPT model. The Transformer model was introduced in the famous paper titled "Attention is All You Need" by Vaswani et al. in 2017 [16]. Compared to the traditional RNN (Recurrent Neural Networks) and LSTM (Long Short-Term Memory Networks), the Transformer model has demonstrated state-of-the-art performance in various NLP tasks as well as increasing model training efficiency by increasing the training parallelism.

Now, we will briefly introduce the structure of the Transformer model (as depicted in Figure 3.30).

The transformer model consists of an encoder component (left in Figure 3.30) and a decoder component (right side in Figure 3.30).

Both the encoder and decoder are composed of a stack of N identical layers. On the encoder side, each layer has two sub-layers, one a multihead self-attention mechanism layer and one position-wise fully connected feed-forward layer. The output of each sub-layer is followed by a layer normalization and connected with the residual connections. On the decoder side, in addition to the multihead attention layer and feed-forward sublayer, there is a third sublayer to connect the output of the encoder stack with a multihead attention module.

To better understand the encoder and decoder structures, we need to grasp several key components and features first.

Self-Attention Mechanism: Unlike the attention mechanism introduced in Section 3.8, the self-attention mechanism is used to encode the sequence directly.

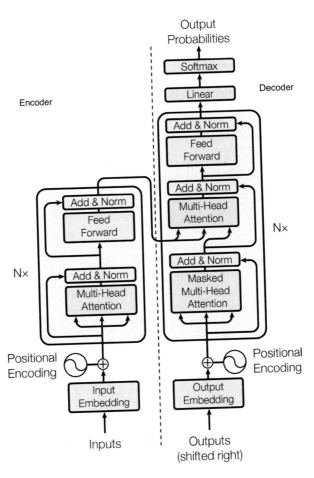

Figure 3.30 The Transformer model architecture [18].

It allows the Transformer model to weigh the importance of each token in the sequence with respect to all other tokens in the same sequence. The attention matrix (as shown in Figure 3.31(a)) is defined as

$$\text{Attention}(Q, K, V) = \text{soft max}\left(\frac{QK^T}{\sqrt{d_k}}\right)V \qquad (3.20)$$

where matrices Q, K, and V are corresponding to "Query," "Key," and "Value," respectively. These matrices don't have actual physical meanings in the Transformer model; rather, they are borrowed from information retrieval contexts to help understanding.

Multihead Attention: The Transformer model adopted a multihead attention mechanism in both the encoder and decoder. The multihead attention layer is depicted in Figure 3.31(b). Compared to a single-head attention structure, the multihead attention mechanism leverages different linear projects to learn

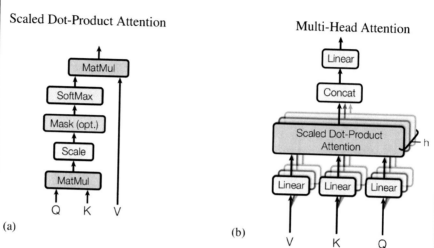

Figure 3.31 (a) Scaled dot-production attention unit; (b) illustration of multihead attention layer [18].

different relationships from training data. The multihead attention function can be described as:

$$\text{Multihead Attention}\left(Q, K, V\right) = \text{Concat}\left(head_1, \ldots, head_2\right)W^O$$
$$\text{where } head_i = \text{Attention}\left(Q_i, K_i, V_i\right) \quad\quad (3.21)$$

where Q_i, K_i, and V_i are query, key, and value matrices for $head_i$.

One benefit of the multihead attention mechanism is that each head attention matrices can be computed in parallel, which significantly improves training efficiency.

Positional Encoding: Unlike the traditional sequence models, the Transformer does not understand the positional order of different tokens in a sequence. In order to solve this problem, a positional encoding function is added to the input embeddings at the beginning of both encoder and decoder tasks. In the original paper, authors used the sine and cosine functions of different frequencies as follows,

$$PE_{\left(pos, 2i\right)} = \sin\left(pos / 1000^{2i/d_{model}}\right)$$
$$PE_{\left(pos, 2i+1\right)} = \cos\left(pos / 1000^{2i/d_{model}}\right) \quad\quad (3.22)$$

where pos is the position and i is the dimension. According to the authors, these positional encoding functions were chosen because they could allow the model to easily learn to attend by relative positions.

There are some other key components in the Transformer model structure, like layer normalization, masking, and so on. These contents won't be discussed in detail; readers can refer to the original paper for more information.

3.11.1   Relationship between BERT and Transformer

The BERT model is a specific implementation of the Transformer architecture, so it is actually one type Transformer model. But compared with the original Transformer model proposed in the "Attention is All You Need" paper [18], the BERT model has the following differences:

- **Model Structure:** Instead of using both encoder and decoder stacks, BERT just used a stack of encoders in the model structure.
- **Training:** The training steps of a BERT model in an NLP application usually involve two steps of training – pre-training and fine-tuning. BERT uses Masked Language Model (MLM) objectives and task-specific objectives in the fine-tuning task. In pre-training, the MLM objective enables the BERT model to fuse both left and right contexts. This is also where "bi-directional" is from, in the BERT model name.
- **Model Usage:** As the BERT model only includes encoder stacks, its direct output are vectors. As a result, the major applications of BERT model are embedding generations and classifications. However, the major use case for the Transformer model is sequence-to-sequence generation.

The following section mainly focuses on the BERT model's applications and its derivatives in recommender systems.

3.11.2   BERT4Rec: BERT for Recommendation Model

After the success of the BERT model in the NLP fields, people started to wonder if the BERT model structure could be also applied to some other fields to handle some other sequential machine learning tasks. In 2019, the BERT4Rec model was introduced, and it successfully transferred the BERT model approaches to sequential recommendations. Section 3.9 introduces a sequence recommendation model, DIEN, which uses an RNN to represent the user's historical behaviors and demonstrates the benefits of a sequential model in the next-item predictions. In contrast to the conventional RNN-based sequential model (as shown in Figure 3.32), the benefits of the BERT4Rec model structure mainly include:

(1) It can gather the learning from both previous and future items during the training.
(2) The multihead attention structure can make overall learning more efficient.

As with many other sequential models, the BERT4Rec model also targeted solving the next-item prediction problem, which can be described as predicting the interaction probability of each item in the candidate pool given the interaction history S_u for user u, The BERT4Rec model architecture is depicted in Figure 3.32(b). It consists of multiple stacks of transformer layer. The details in the Transformer units are illustrated in Figure 3.32(a). As with its predecessor, the BERT4Rec model only used the encoder in the Transformer units. For the output layer, a two-layer

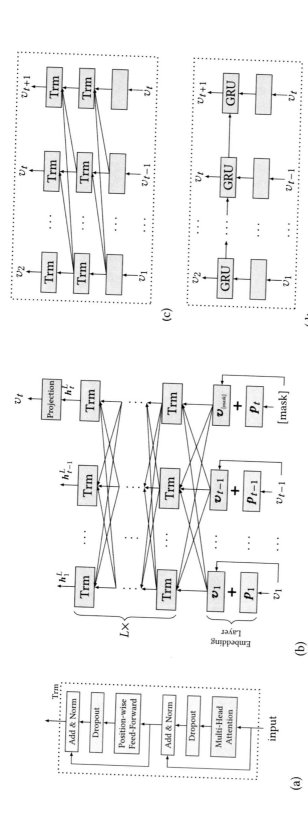

Figure 3.32 (a)Transformer layer, and its differences comparing with (b) BERT4Rec model architecture with the (c) unidirectional model SASRec and (d) conventional RNN-based sequence model [16].

Input: $[v_1, v_2, v_3, v_4, v_5] \xrightarrow{\text{randomly mask}} [v_1, [\text{mask}]_1, v_3, [\text{mask}]_2, v_5]$

Labels: $[\text{mask}]_1 = v_2$, $[\text{mask}]_2 = v_4$

Figure 3.33 Randomly masked interaction sequence and training data generation.

feed-forward network with GELU activation to generate the probability distribution of all the candidate items,

$$P(v) = \text{softmax}(\text{GELU}(h_t^L W^P + b^P)E^T + b^O \qquad (3.23)$$

where W^P is the learnable projection matrix, b^P and b^O are the bias terms, and $E \in \mathbb{R}^{|V| \times d}$ is the embedding matrix for the item set V.

In the model training, BERT4Rec model adopted the same objective as the original BERT model, Masked Language Model objective, in the sequence recommendation to avoid information leaking. The items in the user behavior sequence were randomly masked as shown in Figure 3.33, and the correspondingly generated hidden vectors are passed into the output layer to generate the softmax matrix for training.

The negative log-likelihood of the masked targets is defined as the loss function for each masked input,

$$\mathcal{L} = \frac{1}{|S_u^m|} \sum_{v_m \in S_u^m} -\log P\left(v_m = v_m^* \mid S_u'\right) \qquad (3.24)$$

where S_u' is the masked version for user behavior history S_u, S_u^m is the random masked items in the user behavior history, and v_m^* is the true item for the masked item v_m.

For model inference, the special token "[mask]" is appended to the user interaction history, and then the entire input sequence is fed into the model to generate the predicted probabilities that the user interacts with each item. The item with the maximum probability will be the next recommended item. To make the BERT4Rec model output cover the target sequential recommendation task (that is, predicting the next item after a sequence of interacted items), the authors also added training samples that only mask the last item in training data.

3.11.3 UNBERT: A BERT-Based Model Combining Sequential Recommendation and NLP

The BERT4Rec model only borrows the model structure from BERT and transfers it to a sequential recommendation model. It does not have the advantage of the original BERT model's natural language understanding capabilities. This section introduces the UNBERT model (User-News Matching BERT model), which combines both language understanding and sequential recommendations in the same piece.

The application scenario of UNBERT mode is given a user u with a sequence of clicked news $[n_1^u, n_2^u, \ldots, n_{|n_u|}^u]$ and a set of candidate news $V_u = \{v_1, v_2, \ldots, v_{|V_u|}\}$. The objective of this model is to predict the click probability on the i-th candidate news v_i by user u. The probability score can be denoted by $\hat{y} = f(u, v_i)$.

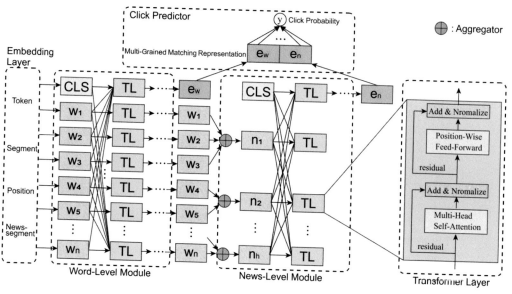

Figure 3.34 The overall architecture of the UNBERT model [17].

The model structure is depicted in Figure 3.34. The UNBERT model is mainly composed of two key modules – word-level module and news-level module, each of which can be considered a separate "BERT module." Each module consists of multiple layers of Transformer stack, including a multihead self-attention sublayer and a position-wise feed-forward layer.

Input Sequence and Embedding Layer

The input sequence construction and embedding layers are illustrated in Figure 3.35. It includes "News Sentence" and "User Sentence," where the News Sentence is simply the text description of the candidate news item, and the User Sentence is the concatenation of the news sequence that the user clicked in the history. The historical news items are separated by a special segment token (NSEP). Each clicked news is also represented by some text-based descriptions. The News Sentence and User Sentence are separated by another special token (SEP). Additionally, a classification token (CLS) is added at the beginning of concatenated sequence to help generate the classification embedding e_w as shown in Figure 3.34.

There are four layers of embeddings generated for each token – token embedding, segment embedding, position embedding, and news segment embedding. The token, segment, and position embeddings are trained using masked LM, and segment embedding is randomly initialized and further updated in the fine-tuning task. The final input token representation E_t is constructed by summing all four embeddings.

Word-Level Module

The word-level module (WLM) mainly applies the Transform Layers to the concatenated input sequence and generates hidden representations for the input tokens. The conventional encoder structure is adopted in the Transformer unit, including the

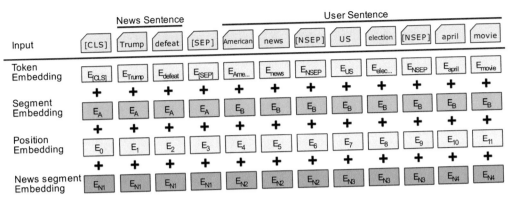

Figure 3.35 UNBERT input sequence construction and embedding layer structures.

multihead self-attention layer, the position-wise feed-forward layer, plus the residual connections and layer normalization between the two layers.

News-Level Module

The news-level module (NLM) aggregates the word's hidden representations of each news from the world-level module and feeds the aggregated vectors to multiple transformer layers to generate the final news representations and matching signal at the news level.

Three different aggregations were studied:

(1) The NSEP Aggregator directly used the generated embeddings of special tokens (NSEP) from the WLM output.
(2) The Mean Aggregator averages the word embeddings for each news segment.
(3) Attention Aggregators apply a lightweight attention network. The attention network applied a fully connected neural network with a *tanh* activation function. Then it connects with another fully connected neural network to generate the combination weights f. The weights then are applied in the linear combination of word embeddings as in Eq. 3.25,

$$n_j = \sum_{i \in S_j} f_i w_i \bigg/ \sum_{i \in S_j} fi \tag{3.25}$$

where the w_i is the word embeddings from WLM for i-th word and S_j is the j-th news representation.

Click Predictor

The click predictor module takes the word-level matching signal e_w from WLM and news-level matching signal e_n from NLM to generate the user click probability of each item. The prediction function is as follows,

$$y = \text{softmax}\left(\left[e_w; e_n\right]W^c + b^c\right) \tag{3.26}$$

In the UNBERT training, the pre-trained *bert-base-uncased* model weight is used directly to initialize the word-level module. Then, the entire model was fine-tuned using the MIND datasets – a real-world news recommendation dataset collected from MSN News logs.

Since the UNBERT model has used a pre-trained BERT model as the foundation model, so it can capture some generalized knowledge outside the fine-tuning data-set. As a result, the UNBERT model has proved excellent performance on cold-start items. This strength is very beneficial for News recommender systems as there are tons of new news generated every day. Considering the importance of news freshness to the user, it is very important that the model can pick up new news items from the candidate pools and recommend to the relevant user in a timely way.

3.11.4   Inspiration of BERT Applications in Recommender Systems

The BERT model's application in recommender systems provides another efficient way of handling sequential input data in both text form and user behavior sequence form. The multihead self-attention mechanism lets the model capture the contexts from long-ranged surrounding items. Besides, it can provide the hidden representations of text-based features, which inherent the original use case of BERT model in NLP tasks.

3.12   LLM: The New Revolution in AI and Its Application in Recommender Systems

Since the introduction of ChatGPT by OpenAI in 2022, it has had a profound impact on the AI field. An example conversation with ChatGPT is shown in Figure 3.36. At the beginning of the conversation, the user provides an input text or instruction to ini-tiate the request for information or assistance. This input text is usually referred to as a "prompt" in the ChatGPT context. ChatGPT will generate the response corresponding to the prompt provided by the user. As we can see in this example, ChatGPT presents astonishing capabilities of reasoning and understanding, as well as the ability to gen-erate more human-like dialogs based on given contexts and questions.

The success of ChatGPT pushes Large Language Models (LLM) to the front of stage and attracts tremendous interest. The LLM is not just limited to the models that support ChatGPT; it is rather a general term to represent a bunch of different language models with large parameter size and based on some neural network structures (for example, the Transformer structure as introduced in Section 3.1). It is usually pre-trained with massive text corpuses from the public sources such as articles, Wikipedia, books, and some other Q&A-type conversational data. From the pretraining step, LLMs can learn numerous generalized knowledge from the public domain and trans-fer the learnings to the downstream tasks. Sometimes, LLMs are also fine-tuned to let them pick the knowledge within specific domains to improve their performance on corresponding tasks. Thanks to LLMs' powerful performance, it has opened up new possibilities of using them in many different domains outside NLP fields.

One of the extensions is adapting the LLM to recommender systems for model per-formance and user experience improvements. In this section, we will follow a recently published literature survey [19] to explore "where" and "how" an LLM can be applied in recommender systems. The high-level scheme is illustrated in Figure 3.37.

Could you tell me how LLM can be used in the recommender system?   Prompt

ChatGPT Responses

Large Language Models (LLMs) like GPT-3.5 can be used in recommender systems to improve user recommendations in various ways. Here are some ways LLMs can be integrated into a recommender system:

1. **Content Generation**: LLMs can generate personalized recommendations by understanding and generating content that matches a user's preferences. For example, if a user is browsing for books, the LLM can generate book summaries or reviews tailored to the user's interests.

2. **Natural Language Understanding**: LLMs can analyze and understand user queries and reviews in natural language. This helps in better understanding user intent and preferences. When a user provides feedback or asks questions, the LLM can parse the text and provide more accurate recommendations based on the context.

3. **Contextual Recommendations**: LLMs can take into account the context of a user's previous interactions and provide recommendations that are relevant to their current situation. For instance, if a user is watching a movie, the LLM can generate suggestions for similar movies or provide trivia about the movie being watched.

Figure 3.36 An example of a conversation with ChatGPT.

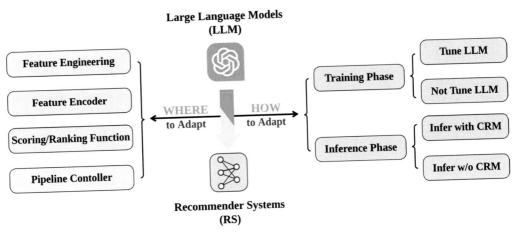

Figure 3.37 The decomposition of "where" and "how" to adapt the LLM in the recommender systems.

3.12.1   Where to Adapt LLM

In the survey, authors abstracted the following key components and elaborated on the applications of LLM in each of these key areas:

- Feature engineering
- Feature encoder

- Scoring/ranking function
- Pipeline Controller

3.12.1.1   LLM in Feature Engineering

In the feature engineering application, LLM mainly generates the auxiliary textual features based on original input data (for example, user profiles, item descriptions, and so on) to augment the input features. During the feature generation, the strength of LLM in reasoning, understanding, and summarization can be leveraged to make the generated text-based features more accurate and concise than the original output.

One example of a feature engineering application is the MINT framework introduced in [20]. MINT is an approach that targets the narrative-driven recommendation (NDR), where the user gives a verbose query including contextual information and requests, and the recommender system recommends the item based on the user's query and interacted item history. One challenge of NDR model training is that it always lacks training data. MINT is designed to mainly generate synthetic training data pairs utilizing InstructGPT for final retrieval model training. The synthetic data generation and model training are depicted in Figure 3.38.

In the MINT approach, authors used InstructGPT model to generate the narrative queries. The prompt examples are shown in Figure 3.39. The few-shot strategy was adopted in the query generation task with a few examples are provided in the prompt. It is expected that InstructGPT will follow the examples provided in the prompt, capture the relationship between different parts of the example, and then finally generate the synthetic queries to complete the target task. User's historical interacted items, past review and actual user narrative query are provided in each few-shot example. The intention is to let LLM capture the interests and preferences from past activities and then artificially generate the corresponding queries, mimicking what a user may ask in a query.

The synthetic queries are then collected and paired with all the interacted items. Since the synthetic queries may only capture part of the interests, not all the items are relevant to the synthetic queries. So the authors used a filter model to filter low-relevance pairs. Finally, these synthetically generated data pairs are then used as the training samples for a retrieval model based on a bi-encoder structure.

This work provides an example of how LLM is being used to generate the synthetic data or input features to help with the model training. Through this approach, the general

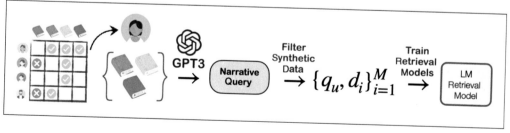

Figure 3.38 The illustration of the MINT approach to generate the narrative queries for set items liked by a user with an LLM. The generated queries will be paired with the item to form a training sample for an LM-based retrieval model.

> **Three Few-Shot Examples:**
>
> **A user likes these recommendations:** Mission BBQ in Deptford Township, Keswick Tavern in Glenside ...
> **The user wrote these reviews:** This place is always packed! Keswick Tavern is a go to if you're looking for great food and large alcohol/beer selection ...
> **In response to the request on Reddit:** Hi Philadelphia area friends, I will be moving Philadelphia soon and I am looking for some popular local restaurants I can turn into my staples ...
>
> **Target Completion For LLM:**
>
> **A user likes the following recommendations:** Rue De La Course in New Orleans, Swirl Wine Bar & Market in New Orleans ...
> **The user wrote the following reviews:** The wide variety of tea is impressive. On Fridays they offer free wine tastings ...
> **In response to the request on Reddit:** LLM completion ...

Figure 3.39 Prompts used in InstructGPT to generate narrative queries.

knowledge and reasoning abilities from the LLM can be carried over to text generation tasks, which can provide additional latent signals into the text input features.

3.12.1.2 LLM as Feature Encoder

In this application, LLM is used as a feature encoder to encode the textual features and use the encoded representations in the recommendation model. The benefits of using a LLM as a feature encoder are:

(1) Enriching the user or item representations with more semantic meanings.
(2) Transferring generalized knowledge from a pretrained LLM foundation model for cross-domain or cold start recommendations.

The UNBERT model introduced in Section 3.11.2 falls within this bucket. In the UNBERT model, a pre-trained BERT is adopted in the Word Level Module to encode the concatenated texts for target news and user-interacted news. Readers can refer to Section 3.11.2 for more details.

3.12.1.3 LLM as Scoring/Ranking Function

In this application, LLM is used to directly generate (1) the rating for the candidate item, (2) the recommendation list of the items, and (3) both rating and recommendation lists with a multitask setup.

In this section, we will briefly introduce one work by the Google team [21] and present an example of using LLM to finish the scoring task. In this work [21], authors explored the LLM's ability to generate ratings with zero-shot, few-shot, and fine-tuned settings. The task is to predict users' ratings based on their viewing history.

The prompt design for zero-shot and few-shot are presented in Figure 3.40 (a) and (b), respectively. In the zero-shot prompt, the user's interaction history is just listed down with the user rating, whereas a few rating prediction examples are included in

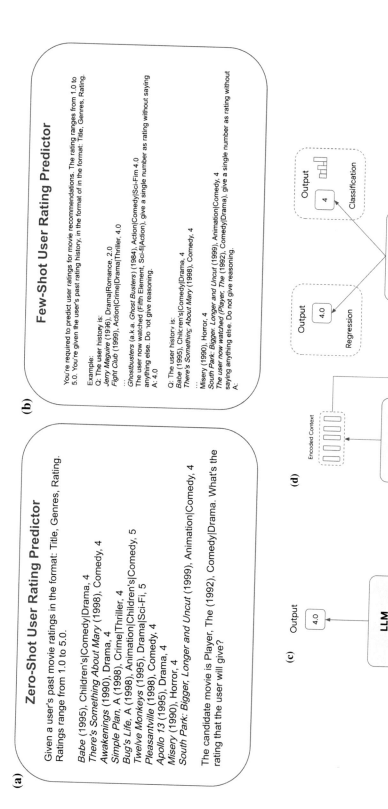

(a)

Zero-Shot User Rating Predictor

Given a user's past movie ratings in the format: Title, Genres, Rating. Ratings range from 1.0 to 5.0.

Babe (1995), Children's|Comedy|Drama, 4
There's Something About Mary (1998), Comedy, 4
Awakenings (1990), Drama, 4
Simple Plan, A (1998), Crime|Thriller, 4
Bug's Life, A (1998), Animation|Children's|Comedy, 5
Twelve Monkeys (1995), Drama|Sci-Fi, 5
Pleasantville (1998), Comedy, 4
Apollo 13 (1995), Drama, 4
Misery (1990), Horror, 4
South Park: Bigger, Longer and Uncut (1999), Animation|Comedy, 4

The candidate movie is Player, The (1992), Comedy|Drama. What's the rating that the user will give?

(b)

Few-Shot User Rating Predictor

You're required to predict user ratings for movie recommendations. The rating ranges from 1.0 to 5.0. You're given the user's past rating history, in the format of in the format: Title, Genres, Rating.

Example:
Q: The user history is:
Jerry Maguire (1996), Drama|Romance, 2.0
Fight Club (1999), Action|Crime|Drama|Thriller, 4.0

...
Ghostbusters (a.k.a. *Ghost Busters*) (1984), Action|Comedy|Sci-Fim 4.0
The user now watched (Fifth Element, Sci-fi|Action), give a single number as rating without saying anything else. Do not give reasoning.
A: 4.0

Q: The user history is:
Babe (1995), Children's|Comedy|Drama, 4
There's Something About Mary (1998), Comedy, 4

...
Misery (1990), Horror, 4
South Park: Bigger, Longer and Uncut (1999), Animation|Comedy, 4
The user now watched (Player, The (1992), Comedy|Drama), give a single number as rating without saying anything else. Do not give reasoning.
A:

(c) Output

4.0 ← **LLM Decoder** ← Input

(d)

Encoded Context ← **LLM Encoder** ← Input

Output 4.0 ← Regression

Output 4 ← Classification

LLM Decoder

Figure 3.40 (a) A zero-shot example; (b) a few-shot example; (c) a decoder-only fine-tuning model; (d) an encoder-decoder-based fine-tuning model for the rating task.

the prompt in the few-shot setting. Throughout the experiment, the authors found LLM can be very sensitive to the provided prompt and doesn't always follow instructions.

Then, the authors adopted fine-tuning and fine-tuned several models in the Flan-T5 model families. In both decoder-only (Figure 3.40(c)) and encoder-decoder models (Figure 3.40(d)), a projection layer is added to generate the output for either the classification task or the regression task. Then, the model is fine-tuned with training samples to better fit the prediction task.

Through the experiments, the authors concluded that zero-shot and few-shot LLM approaches have lower performance than the fully supervised methods. Fine-tuned LLMs can help close the gap and bring benefits in (1) higher training data efficiency (that is, smaller training data size is needed), (2) much easier feature processing and modeling, and (3) new capabilities expansion with conversational recommendations.

3.12.1.4   LLM as Pipeline Controller

It has been proven that LLM doesn't only understand textual information, but also presents strong capabilities for in-context learning and logical reasoning. As a result, it could also play a role as a controller to decide where logic flow should go in the entire recommendation pipeline.

In a recent work [22], the CHAT-REC system was introduced to bridge the recommender systems and LLMs. This system consists of several key components: the prompt constructor, the LLM (ChatGPT), and the conventional recommender system. The workflow of the CHAT-REC is depicted in Figure 3.41. We will use a pseudo example to illustrate how the system works:

(1) The user sent a query, "Could you recommend some action movies to me?"
(2) The **prompt constructor** collects different contexts to generate the prompt. The contexts' sources include user raw query, recommender system interfaces, user profile, user-item history, and dialog history.
(3) The generated prompt is then fed into the **LLM (ChatGPT)** module to generate the output. In the output, ChatGPT will decide if the conventional **recommender system** will be called.
(4) In the first pass, the **LLM** decides to call the **recommender system** to generate the candidate set. Then the recommender system will generate the candidate sets and send them back to the **prompt constructor**.
(5) The **prompt constructor** then generates the new prompt with the recommended candidate set, and sends it to the **LLM module**.
(6) The **LLM** decides that no recommendation call is needed, and then conducts the reranking to pick the top five candidates to return to the user.
(7) If he user asks for an explanation, the user query and other contexts will repeat the process from Step (1). The **LLM module** can determine that no recommendation call is needed and generate the responses to the user directly.

From this example workflow, we can see that the LLM model is being used as an orchestrator in the entire system by leveraging its excellent ability of reasoning and understanding and drives the interaction between the user and recommender systems.

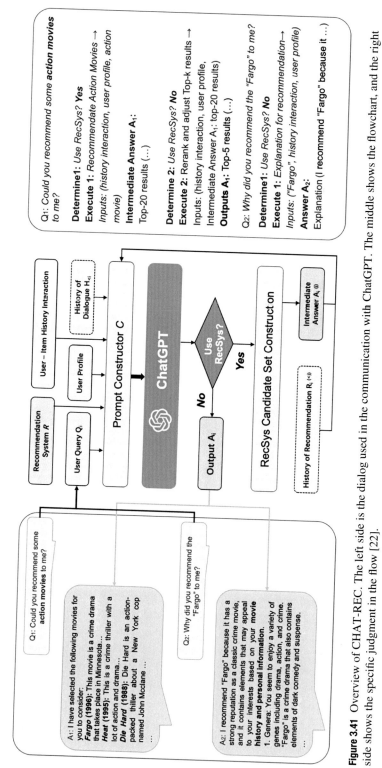

Figure 3.41 Overview of CHAT-REC. The left side is the dialog used in the communication with ChatGPT. The middle shows the flowchart, and the right side shows the specific judgment in the flow [22].

3.12.2 How to Adapt LLM

In this survey paper [19], the authors divided the usage of LLM in recommender systems into four quadrants, as shown in Figure 3.42. The four quadrants were:

(1) Tuned LLM
(2) Not tuned LLM
(3) Infer with conventional recommendation model (CRM)
(4) Not infer with conventional recommendation model (CRM)

In Figure 3.42, we can see the overall research development trajectory starts from tuned-LLM + infer with CRM and firstly moves toward the not-tuned LLM + infer w/o CRM quadrant. In this trajectory, the model size is significantly increased. As there is no model training in this quadrant, it is very fast for the model development, but the performance is sacrificed as a trade-off consequence. Then, the researchers start to diverge in both directions to two other quadrants – not tuned LLM + CRM and tuned LLM + w/o CRM. The main motivations are to achieve better model performance as well as reduce the model size for faster training and inferencing.

As we have introduced one model in each quadrant in the previous section to show the adaptations of LLM with recommender systems, we will not expand to cover the other models here. Interested readers can follow the references from this survey paper [19] to continue exploring this new tide of revolution.

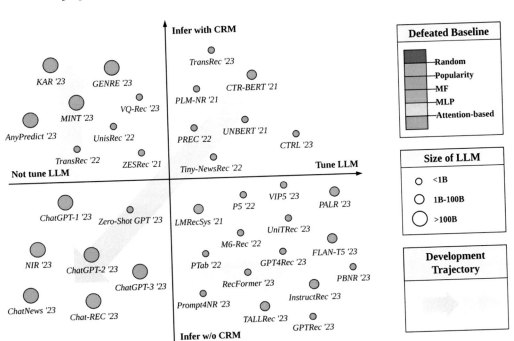

Figure 3.42 Four quadrant classification about how to adapt LLM to recommender systems. Circle size denotes the model size and the colors indicate the best benchmarking model that each model can beat. The light-colored arrows show the overall development trajectory.

3.12.3   Inspiration and Challenges of LLM Adaptation in Recommender Systems

The recent developments of LLMs have not only attracted the world's attention to the AI field, but also opened a new "gate" for recommender systems. The LLMs' astonishing understanding and reasoning abilities give us a new angle on building recommender systems, and also add a new powerful tool to our toolbox. However, we also need to acknowledge the challenges that we are facing in the LLM world.

At the end of the survey [19], the authors summarized the challenges from three aspects: (1) efficiency, (2) effectiveness, and (3) ethics:

(1) **Efficiency:** This includes both training and inference latency. As the model becomes bigger, it requires more training data to train the model effectively. Both the larger model size and larger training data can significantly increase the training efficiency. Also, the increased model parameter amount makes it challenging to finish the inferencing task under the limited time constraints in the online service.

(2) **Effectiveness:** Even though many researchers have demonstrated the powerfulness of the LLMs, still the LLM can have its own shortcomings and limitations. Two examples are limited context window size and ID feature understanding. From past studies, we can see LLMs show a reduction of understanding ability when the input texts are too long in the prompt. For the other limitation, since the ID features are not semantically meaningful, so it will be quite hard for the LLMs to understand and differentiate the IDs in the model input.

(3) **Ethics:** This is a quite common topic in recommender systems. The practitioners in the recommendation field have been studying many approaches for removing bias from recommender systems. It has also been found that LLMs can present certain biases originating from the pre-training corpus and could potentially generate harmful or offensive content.

Luckily, numerous researchers and engineers have been working on each aspect of these challenges and to create solutions to solve them. The reader can refer to the references in the survey to get more details about those solutions, to inspire research and actual implementations.

3.13   Summary: The Deep Learning Era of Recommender Systems

This section describes the relevant knowledge of state-of-the-art deep learning recommendation models, echoing the evolution diagram of deep learning models at the beginning of the chapter. In this section, we will summarize the key knowledge of deep learning recommendation models (as shown in Table 3.2).

With so many deep learning recommendation model options, the premise for readers not to get lost is to be familiar with the relationship between each model and its applicable scenarios. It needs to be clear that in the era of deep learning, no specific model can be competent for all business scenarios, and it can be seen from Table 3.2 that the characteristics of each model are different.

Table 3.2 Key points of deep learning recommendation models

Model Name	Mechanisms	Characteristics	Limitations
AutoRec	Based on the auto-encoder, encode users or items, and use the generalization ability of the auto-encoder to make recommendations	The single hidden layer neural network has a simple structure, enabling fast training and deployment	Limited expressivity
Deep Crossing	Utilizing the classic deep learning framework of "Embedding layer + multihidden layer + output layer," automatically finish the deep crossover of the features	Classic deep learning recommendation model framework	Use fully connected hidden layers for feature crossing, lacks specificity
NeuralCF	Replace the dot product operation of the user vector and the item vector in the traditional matrix factorization with the interoperation of the neural network	Expressive enhanced version of matrix factorization model	Only the ID features of users and items are used, and no other features are added
PNN	For cross operations between different feature domains, define multiple product operations such as "inner product" and "outer product"	Improving the feature crossover on the top of classic deep learning framework	The "outer product" operation is approximated, which affects its expressivity to a certain extent.
Wide&Deep	Use the wide part to strengthen the "memorization" of the model, and use the deep part to strengthen the "generalization" of the model	Pioneered the construction method of the ensembled model, which has a significant impact on the subsequent development of the deep learning recommendation model	The wide part requires manual feature cross selection
Deep and Cross	Replacing the wide part in the Wide&Deep model with a cross network	Solved the problem of manual feature interaction in the Wide&Deep model	The complexity of the feature cross network is high
FNN	Use the parameters of FM to initialize the parameters of the embedding layer of the deep neural network	Use FM to initialize the parameters to speed up the convergence of the entire network	The main structure of the model is relatively simple, and there is no objective-oriented feature crossover layer
DeepFM	On the basis of Wide&Deep model, replace the original linear wide part with FM	Enhanced the feature interactions of the wide part	No significant structural difference with the classic Wide&Deep model
NFM	Replace the operation of second-order hidden vector crossover in FM with a neural network	Compared with FM, NFM has stronger expressivity and feature intersection ability	Very similar to the structure of the PNN model

(continued)

Table 3.2 (cont.)

Model Name	Mechanisms	Characteristics	Limitations
AFM	On the basis of FM, an attention score is added to each crossed result after the second-order hidden vector cross, and the attention score is learned through the attention network	Different crossed features have different importance	The training process of the attention network is complicated
DIN	Based on the traditional deep learning recommendation model, an attention mechanism is introduced. The attention score is calculated by using the correlation between user behavior history items and target advertising items	Make more targeted recommendations given different advertising items	Not take advantage of the other features other than "historical behavior"
DIEN	Combine the sequence model with the deep learning recommendation model, and use the sequence model to simulate the evolution process of users' interests	The sequence model enhances the system's ability to express the changes of user interests, so that the recommender system begins to consider the valuable information in the time-related behavior sequences	The training of the sequence model is complicated, and the latency of the online inferencing is relatively large. It requires engineering optimization in production.
DRN	Apply the idea of reinforcement learning to the recommender system, and conduct online real-time learning and updating of the recommendation model	The ability of the model to utilize the real-time data is greatly enhanced	The online inferencing is more complicated, and the engineering implementation is more difficult
BERT4Rec and UNBERT	The applications of BERT model in recommender systems provide an efficient way to handle the sequential input data in both text form and user behavior sequence form	The multihead self-attention mechanism lets the model capture the contexts from long-ranged surrounding items. Besides, it can provide the hidden representations of text-based features, which inherent the original use case of BERT model in NLP tasks	The model complexity and online serving resources is much higher than other recommendation model
LLM	Rebuild recommender system with LLM	The LLMs' astonishing understanding and reasoning abilities give us a new angle to build the recommender system, and also add a new powerful tool to our toolbox	It's a totally new domain to combine LLM with recommender system. There are still lots of new challenges that we are facing in the LLM world

For this reason, this chapter does not list any model performance benchmarking, because it is impossible to form authoritative test results with different datasets, different application scenarios, different evaluation methods and evaluation indicators. In the actual application process, it is also necessary for the engineers to select the most suitable deep learning recommendation model after sufficient parameter tuning and comparison based on their own business data.

The deep learning recommendation model has never stopped its development. From Alibaba's multimodal and multiobjective deep learning model, to YouTube's session-based recommendation model, to the LLM revolution, the deep learning recommendation model not only evolves faster and faster, but also has been applied to wider application scenarios. The following chapters introduce the application of deep learning models in recommender systems from different perspectives. We also hope that readers will continue their exploration into the latest development of deep learning recommendation models based on the knowledge introduced in this chapter.

References

[1] Suvash Sedhain, et al. Autorec: Autoencoders meet collaborative filtering. Proceedings of the 24th International Conference on World Wide Web, May 18, 2015 (pp. 111–112).

[2] Ying Shan, et al. Deep crossing: Web-scale modeling without manually crafted combinatorial features. Proceedings of the 22nd ACM SIGKDD international conference on knowledge discovery and data mining, August 13, 2016 (pp. 255–262).

[3] Kaiming He, et al. Deep residual learning for image recognition. Proceedings of the IEEE conference on computer vision and pattern recognition, June 27–30, 2016 (pp. 770–778).

[4] Xiangnan He, et al. Neural collaborative filtering. Proceedings of the 26th international conference on world wide web. International World Wide Web Conferences Steering Committee, April 3, 2017 (pp. 173–182).

[5] Yanru Qu, et al. Product-based neural networks for user response prediction. IEEE 16th International Conference on Data Mining (ICDM), December 12, 2016 (pp. 1149–1154).

[6] Heng-Tze Cheng, et al. Wide & deep learning for recommender systems. Proceedings of the 1st workshop on deep learning for recommender systems, September 15, 2016 (pp. 7–10).

[7] Ruoxi Wang, et al. Deep & cross network for ad click predictions. Proceedings of the ADKDD'17, August 14, 2017 (pp. 1–7).

[8] Weinan Zhang, Tianming Du, Jun Wang. Deep learning over multi-field categorical data – a case study on user response prediction. Advances in Information Retrieval: 38th European Conference on Information Retrieval, March 20–23, 2016 (pp. 45–57).

[9] Huifeng Guo, et al. DeepFM: A factorization-machine based neural network for CTR prediction: arXiv preprint arXiv:1703.04247 (2017).

[10] Xiangnan He, Tat-Seng Chua. Neural factorization machines for sparse predictive analytics. Proceedings of the 40th International ACM SIGIR Conference on Research and Development in Information Retrieval, August 7, 2017 (pp. 355–364).

[11] Jun Xiao, et al. Attentional factorization machines: Learning the weight of feature interactions via attention networks: arXiv preprint arXiv: 1708.04617 (2017).

[12] Guorui Zhou, et al. Deep interest network for click-through rate prediction. Proceedings of the 24th ACM SIGKDD International Conference on Knowledge Discovery & Data Mining, July 19, 2018 (pp. 1059–1068).

[13] Guorui Zhou, et al. Deep interest evolution network for click-through rate prediction. Proceedings of the AAAI Conference on Artificial Intelligence, 33(1), 2019: 5941–5948.

[14] Guanjie Zheng, et al. DRN: A deep reinforcement learning framework for news Recommender. Proceedings of the 2018 World Wide Web Conference. International World Wide Web Conferences Steering Committee, April 23, 2018 (pp. 167–176).

[15] Jacob Devlin, et al. Bert: Pre-training of deep bidirectional transformers for language understanding: arXiv preprint arXiv:1810.04805 (2018).

[16] Fei Sun, et al. BERT4Rec: Sequential recommendation with bidirectional encoder representations from transformer. Proceedings of the 28th ACM International Conference on Information and Knowledge Management, November 3, 2019 (pp. 1441–1450).

[17] Qi Zhang, et al. UNBERT: User-news matching BERT for news recommendation. *IJCAI*, 21, 2021: 3356–3362.

[18] Ashish Vaswani, et al. Attention is all you need. *Advances in Neural Information Processing Systems*, 30, 2017.

[19] Jianghao Lin, et al. How can recommender systems benefit from large language models: A survey: arXiv preprint arXiv:2306.05817 (2023).

[20] Sheshera Mysore, Andrew McCallum, Hamed Zamani. Large language model augmented narrative driven recommendations. Proceedings of the 17th ACM Conference on Recommender Systems, September 14, 2023 (pp. 777–783).

[21] Wang-Cheng Kang, et al. Do LLMs understand user preferences? Evaluating LLMs on user rating prediction: arXiv preprint arXiv:2305.06474 (2023).

[22] Yunfan Gao, et al. Chat-rec: Towards interactive and explainable LLMs-augmented recommender system: arXiv preprint arXiv:2303.14524 (2023).

4 Application of Embedding Technology in Recommender Systems

In the deep learning framework, the application of embedding technology is very extensive, especially in the internet industries with recommendation, advertising, and search as the main business use case. It is not an exaggeration to call the embedding technique the "basic core operation" of deep learning.

The embedding operation has been mentioned many times in the previous chapters. Its main function is to convert sparse vectors into dense vectors for further processing by the upper-layer deep neural network. However, the role of embedding technology is far more than that. Its application scenarios are very diverse, and the implementation methods are also different.

In academia, embedding technology itself, as a popular direction in the field of deep learning research, has experienced a rapid evolution from processing sequence samples, to processing graph samples, and then to processing heterogeneous multifeature samples. In industry, embedding technology has almost become the most widely used deep learning technology due to its ability to integrate information and easy online deployment. The introduction to embedding technology in this chapter will focus on the following aspects:

(1) Introduction to the basics of the embedding concept;
(2) Introduction to the evolution of embedding methods from the classic Word2vec, to the popular graph embedding, and then to the multifeature fusion embedding technology;
(3) Introduction to the specific application of embedding technology in recommender systems and the method of online deployment and fast inferencing.

4.1 What Is Embedding?

Generally speaking, embedding uses a low-dimensional dense vector to represent an object. The object here can be a word, a product, a movie, and so on. The meaning of "represents" is that the embedding vector can express some characteristics of the corresponding object, and the distance between two vectors reflects the similarity between two objects.

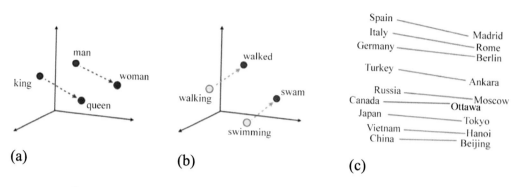

Figure 4.1 Examples of word vectors. (a) Male–female. (b) Part of speech. (c) Country–capital.

4.1.1 Examples of Word Vectors

The popularity of the embedding method started from research on the problem of word vectors in the field of natural language processing. Here we take the word vector as an example to further explain the meaning of embedding.

Figure 4.1(a) shows the mappings of the embedding vectors of several words (with implicit relationships on genders) encoded by the Word2vec method in the embedding space. It can be seen that the distance vector from Embedding(king) to Embedding(queen) is parallel with that from Embedding(man) to Embedding(woman). This example indicates that the operation between word embedding vectors can even contain semantic-relationship information between words. Similarly, the part-of-speech example shown in Figure 4.1(b) also reflects this feature of word vectors. The distance vectors from Embedding(walking) to Embedding(walked) and Embedding(swimming) to Embedding(swam) are similar, which indicates that the part-of-speech relationship between walking–walked and swimming–swam is similar.

Under the premise of a large amount of corpus input, embedding technology can even mine some more general knowledge. As shown in Figure 4.1(c), Embedding (Madrid) – Embedding (Spain) ≈ Embedding (Beijing) – Embedding (China). This shows that the operation between embeddings can mine general relational knowledge like "capital-country."

From these examples, it is clear that in the word vector space, even if the word vector is not known at all, it can still be inferred by the semantic relationship and the word vector operation. This is how embedding describes the items in a specific vector space and at the same time reveals the potential relationship between items. In a sense, the embedding method even has an ontological and philosophical significance.

4.1.2 Expansion of Embedding Application in Other Fields

Now that embedding can vectorize words, it can also generate vectorized representations for the items in other application domains in some way.

For example, if embedding is applied to movie items, the distance between Embedding(The Avengers) and Embedding(Iron Man) should be very close in the embedding vector space, while the distance between Embedding(The Avengers) and Embedding(Gone with the Wind) will be relatively far.

In the same way, if the product is embedded in the e-commerce scenarios, the vector distance between Embedding(keyboard) and Embedding(mouse) should be relatively close, while the distance between Embedding(keyboard) and Embedding(hat) will be relatively far.

Unlike word vectors that use a large text corpus for training, the training samples in different fields are different. For example, video recommendation often uses the user's streaming sequence to embed movies, while e-commerce platforms use the user's purchase history as training samples.

4.1.3 Importance of Embedding Technology for Deep Learning Recommender Systems

Going back to the deep learning recommender system, why is embedding technology so important for model learning, or even the "basic core operation" of deep learning recommender systems? There are three main reasons:

(1) In the recommendation applications, one-hot encoding is widely used to encode categorical and ID-type features, resulting in extremely sparse feature vectors. Plus, the structural characteristics of deep learning make it unfavorable for the processing of sparse feature vectors. Therefore, almost all deep learning recommendation models include the embedding layer, which is responsible for converting high-dimensional sparse feature vectors into low-dimensional dense feature vectors. Therefore, mastering various embedding technologies is the basic step for building a deep learning recommendation model.

(2) Embedding itself is an extremely important feature vector. Compared with the feature vectors generated by traditional methods such as MF, embedding has stronger expressivity. After the graph embedding technology is introduced, embedding can introduce almost any information for encoding, so that it contains a lot of valuable information. On this basis, the embedding vector is often connected with other recommender systems' features and then fed into the subsequent deep learning network for training.

(3) Utilizing embeddings to calculate the similarity between an item and a user is a commonly adopted approach in the retrieval layer technology for recommender systems. After fast nearest-neighbor search techniques such as locality-sensitive hashing are applied to the recommender systems, embedding is more suitable for rapid "preliminary screening" of massive candidate items, filtering out hundreds to thousands of items. The filtered candidate list is then handed over to the deep learning network for finer ranking.

Therefore, embedding technology plays an extremely important role in deep learning recommender systems. Familiarity with and mastering various popular embedding methods is a powerful tool for building successful deep learning recommender systems.

4.2   Word2vec: The Classic Embedding Method

When it comes to embedding, we have to mention Word2vec. This has made word vectors popular again in the field of natural language processing. But, more importantly, since Google proposed Word2vec in 2013 [1,2], embedding technology has been extended from the field of natural language processing to many other application fields of deep learning such as advertising, searching, recommendation, and so on. It has become an indispensable technique in the deep learning knowledge framework. As a result, being familiar with Word2vec is crucial to understanding all the embedding-related technologies and concepts.

4.2.1   What Is Word2vec?

Word2vec is short for "word to vector." As the name suggests, Word2vec is a model that generates a vector representation for words.

In order to train the Word2vec model, a corpus consisting of a set of sentences needs to be prepared. Suppose one of the sentences of length T is $w_1, w_2, \ldots, w_T$, and assume that each word is closely related to its adjacent word, that is, each word is determined by the adjacent words (the main principle of the continuous bag of words (CBOW) model in Figure 4.2) or determines its adjacent words (the main principle of the Skip-gram model in Figure 4.2). As shown in Figure 4.2, the input of the CBOW model is the words around ω_t, and the predicted output is ω_t, while Skip-gram is the opposite. Empirically, Skip-gram works better; thus, we will use Skip-gram as the framework to explain the details of the Word2vec model in this section.

4.2.2   Training Process of the Word2vec Model

In order to generate training samples for the model based on the corpus, we select a sliding window with a length of $2c + 1$, which includes c words before and after the target word and target word itself. Then we extract a sentence from the corpus and move the sliding window from left to right. The phrases in the window then form a training sample.

With the training samples generated, it is time to define the optimization objective function. Given that each word w_t determines the adjacent word w_{t+j} and based on the method of maximum likelihood estimation, the training process will maximize the product of the conditional probability $p(w_{t+j} | w_t)$. With the logarithmic probability applied here, the objective function of Word2vec becomes as shown in Eq. 4.1.

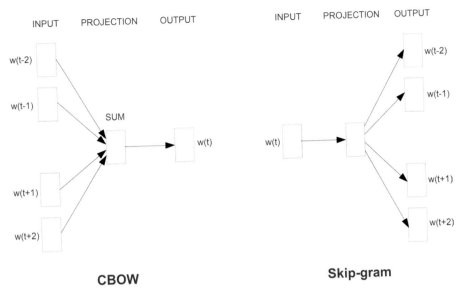

Figure 4.2 Structures of two Word2vec models (CBOW and Skip-gram).

$$\frac{1}{T}\sum_{t=1}^{T}\sum_{-c<j<c,\,j\neq0}\log p\left(w_{t+j}\mid w_{t}\right)\qquad(4.1)$$

The next main problem is how to define the conditional probability $p(w_{t+j} \mid w_t)$. As a multiclassification problem, the most direct method is to use the softmax function. The goal of Word2vec is to use a vector v_w to represent the word w and to use the inner product $v_i^T v_j$ of any two word vectors to represent the degree of semantic similarity. Then the definition of the conditional probability $p\left(w_{t+j} \mid w_t\right)$ can be intuitively given, as shown in Eq. 4.2,

$$p\left(W_O \mid W_I\right)=\frac{\exp\left(V_{w_O}'^{\,T}V_{w_I}\right)}{\sum_{w=1}^{W}\exp\left(V_w'^{\,T}V_{w_I}\right)}\qquad(4.2)$$

where w_o represents w_{t+j}, which is called the output word, and w_I represents w_t, which is called the input word.

Given this conditional probability formula, it is easy to ignore the fact that w_t is used to predict w_{t+j} in the Word2vec Skip-gram model. However, the vector representation of these two vectors is not in the same vector space. As shown in the earlier conditional probability formula, V_{w_o} and V_{w_I} are the output vector representation and input vector representation of word w, respectively. So what are the input vector representation and the output vector representation? Here, the neural network structure diagram of Word2vec (as shown in Figure 4.3) is used for further explanation.

According to the definition of conditional probability $p(w_{t+j} \mid w_t)$, the product of the two vectors can be put in the form of a softmax to convert it into the neural

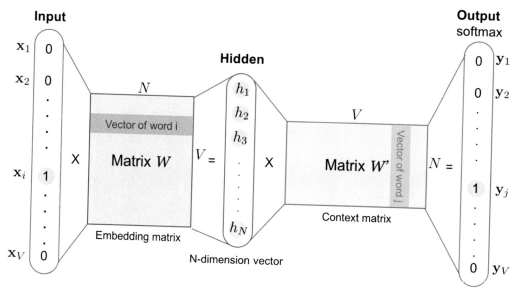

Figure 4.3 Neural network structure diagram of Word2vec.

network structure, as shown in Figure 4.3. After the model architecture of Word2vec is represented by a neural network, the model parameters can be solved by gradient descent during the training process. The input vector representation is the weight matrix $W_{V \times N}$ from the input layer to the hidden layer, and the output vector representation is the weight matrix $W'_{N \times V}$ from the hidden layer to the output layer.

After obtaining the input vector matrix $W_{V \times N}$, the weight vector corresponding to each row is the "word vector" in the general sense. So this weight matrix is naturally converted into a lookup table of Word2vec (as shown in Figure 4.4). For example, if the input vector is a one-hot vector composed of 10 000 words and the hidden layer dimension is 300, then the weight matrix from the input layer to the hidden layer has a dimension of 10 000 × 300. After being converted into a word vector lookup table, the weight of each row becomes the embedding vector of the corresponding word.

4.2.3 Negative Sampling in Word2vec Training

In fact, it is not very feasible to completely follow the training method as described in Section 4.2.2, which treats the original Word2vec as a multiclass structure. Assuming that the number of words in the corpus is 10 000, it means that there are 10 000 neurons in the output layer. When updating the weights from the hidden layer to the neurons in the output layer each iteration, the prediction errors of all 10 000 words in all dictionaries need to be calculated [3]. The training system can hardly bear such a huge amount of computation in the actual training process.

In order to reduce the training costs of Word2vec, negative sampling is often adopted. Compared with the original method, which calculates the prediction error of

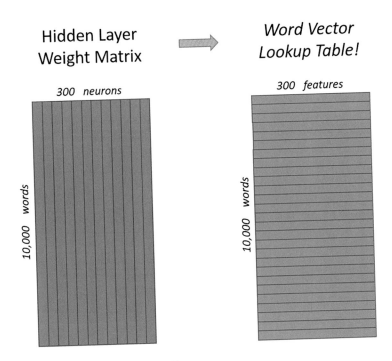

Figure 4.4 Lookup table of Word2vec.

all words in all dictionaries, the negative sampling method only needs to calculate the prediction error for a few negative samples. In this case, the optimization objective of the Word2vec model degenerates from a multiclassification problem to an approximate binary classification problem [4], as shown in Eq. 4.3.

$$E = -\log\sigma\left(v'_{w_o}{}^T h\right) - \sum_{w_j \in W_{neg}} \log\sigma\left(-v'_{w_j}{}^T h\right) \tag{4.3}$$

where v'_{w_o} is the output word vector for a positive sample, h is the hidden layer vector, W_{neg} is the set of negative samples, and v'_{w_j} is the negative sample word vector. Since the size of the negative sample set is very limited (usually less than 10 in practical applications), the computational complexity can be reduced by at least 1/1000 (assuming a vocabulary size of 10 000) in each iteration of gradient descent.

In fact, the hierarchical softmax method can also be used to speed up the training speed of Word2vec. But the implementation is more complicated, and the final performance is not significantly better than the negative sampling method, so it is less used. Interested readers can refer to Reference [3], which contains details of the hierarchical softmax derivation process.

4.2.4   Importance of Word2vec to Embedding Technology

Word2vec was officially proposed by Google in 2013. In fact, it did not entirely originate from the Google paper. The research on word vectors can be traced back to 2003 [5], or even earlier. But it was Google's successful application of Word2vec that allowed word vector technology to be rapidly promoted in the industry, and then made embedding a hot research topic. It is no exaggeration to say that Word2vec is of fundamental significance to research on embedding in the deep learning era.

From another perspective, the model structure, objective function, negative sampling method, and objective function in negative sampling proposed in the research of Word2vec have been reused and optimized many times in subsequent research. Mastering every detail in Word2vec has become the basis for studying embedding. In this sense, mastering the contents of this section is very important.

4.3   Item2vec: The Extension of Word2vec in Recommender Systems

After the birth of Word2vec, the idea of embedding quickly spread from the field of natural language processing to almost all fields of machine learning, one of which is recommender systems. Since Word2vec can embed the words in the word sequence, there should also be a corresponding embedding method for the user's purchase sequence and streaming sequence. This is the basic idea of Item2vec model [6].

4.3.1   Fundamentals of Item2vec

As mentioned in the matrix factorization section (Section 2.3), the user latent vector and the item latent vector are generated through matrix decomposition. Viewing the matrix factorization model from the perspective of embedding, the user latent vector and the item latent vector are one type of user embedding vector and item embedding vector, respectively. Due to the popularity of Word2vec, more and more embedding methods can be directly used to generate item embedding vectors, while user embedding vectors are more often calculated by averaging or clustering item embeddings in the user's action history. Using the similarity between the user vector and the item vector, the candidate set can be quickly obtained directly in the retrieval layer of the recommender system, or directly used in the ranking layer to get the final recommendation list. Following this idea, Microsoft proposed a method, Item2vec, to calculate the embedding vector of items in 2016.

Compared with Word2vec, which uses word sequence to generate the embedding vectors, Item2vec utilizes the sequence of actions from a user's browsing, purchasing, and other histories.

Assuming that a sentence of length T in Word2vec model is $w_1, w_2, \ldots, w_T$, the loss function can be expressed as shown in Eq. 4.1. Similarly, assuming the user's action sequence of length K is $\omega_1, \omega_2, \ldots, \omega_K$, the loss function of Item2vec is then as follows,

$$\frac{1}{K}\sum_{i=1}^{K}\sum_{j\neq i}^{K} \log p\left(w_j | w_i\right) \tag{4.4}$$

By comparing the difference between Eqs. 4.1 and 4.4, it can be found that the only difference between Item2vec and Word2vec is that Item2vec abandons the concept of time window and considers that any two items in the sequence are related. Therefore, in the loss function of Item2vec (Eq. 4.4), the loss is the sum of the log probabilities of item pairs, instead of the log probabilities of items within the time window.

After the optimization target is defined, the remaining training process of Item2vec and the generation process of the final item embedding are consistent with Word2vec. The lookup table of the final item vector is analogical to the lookup table of the word vector in Word2vec. Readers can refer to the relevant content of Word2vec in Section 4.2 for more training details.

4.3.2   Item2vec in Generalized Form

In fact, the techniques of using embedding to vectorize items are much more than Item2vec. Generally speaking, any method capable of generating an item vector can be called Item2vec. A typical example is the two-tower model that has been successfully applied in companies such as Baidu and Facebook (as shown in Figure 4.5).

In the two-tower model depicted in Figure 4.5, the components on the advertising items side actually implement the generations of item embeddings. Given this model structure is called "two tower," the structure on the advertising side is also referred to as the "item tower." Then, the role of the "item tower" is essentially to generate the feature vector for an item. After the multilayer neural network structure in the item tower, a multidimensional dense vector is finally generated. From the perspective of embedding, this dense vector is actually the embedding vector of the item, but the embedding model has changed from Item2vec to a more complex but more flexible "item tower" model. The input features are one-hot encoded feature vectors based on the item list in user behavior sequences. It turns out to

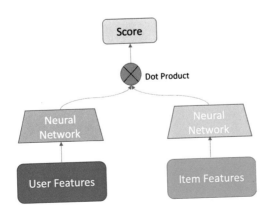

Figure 4.5 Two-tower model.

be a comprehensive item feature vector, which can contain more information. The ultimate purpose of both Item2vec and the "item tower" is to convert the original features of the item into a dense vector representation of the item embedding, so no matter what the model structure is, this kind of model can be called a "generalized" Item2vec class model.

4.3.3   Characteristics and Limitations of Item2vec

As an extension of the Word2vec model, Item2vec can theoretically use any sequence data to generate the embedding vector of an item, which greatly expands the application scenarios of Word2vec. The Item2vec model in a broad sense is actually a general term for item vectorization methods, which can use different deep learning network structures to embed the item features.

The Item2vec method also has its limitations. Since it can only use sequence data, Item2vec often meets constraints when dealing with graph structured data of internet, which is why graph embedding technology emerged.

4.4   Graph Embedding: Introducing More Structural Information

Word2vec and its derived Item2vec are the basic methods of embedding technology, but both are based on sequence samples (such as sentences and user action sequences). In the online use cases, it is more natural to represent the online data in the graph structures. A typical scenario is an item relationship graph generated from user behavior data (as shown in Figures 4.6(a) and (b)) and a knowledge graph composed of attributes and entities (as shown in Figure 4.6(c)).

When faced with the graph structure, the traditional sequence embedding method seems powerless. In this context, graph embedding represents a new research direction and has gradually become more popular in the field of deep learning recommender systems.

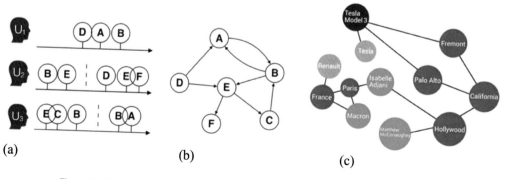

Figure 4.6 Item relationship graph and knowledge graph. (a) User behavior sequence. (b) Item relation graph. (c) Knowledge graph.

Graph embedding is a method of encoding for nodes in a graph structure. The final node embedding vector generally contains the structural information of the graph as well as the local similarity information of nearby nodes. Different graph embedding methods have different principles and different ways of retaining graph information. The following introduces several state-of-the-art graph embedding methods, and their differences and similarities.

4.4.1 DeepWalk: The Basic Graph Embedding Method

In the early days, the most influential graph embedding method was DeepWalk [7], which was proposed in 2014. Its main idea is to perform random walks on the graph structure composed of items to generate a large number of item sequences, then use these item sequences as the training samples fed into Word2vec for training, and finally get the item embeddings. Therefore, DeepWalk can be viewed as a transition method connecting sequence embedding and graph embedding. The algorithm flow of DeepWalk was adopted in the paper "Billion-scale commodity embedding for e-commerce recommender in Alibaba" [9], as shown in Figure 4.7.

The process of generating the item embeddings using the DeepWalk method is as follows:

(1) Collect original item sequences that users interact with (Figure 4.7(a));
(2) Build an item relational graph based on these user behavior history sequences, as shown in Figure 4.7(b). It can be seen that the edge between items A and B is because user U1 purchased item A and item B successively. If multiple identical directed edges are subsequently generated, the weights of the directed edges are accumulated. After all user behavior sequences have been converted into edges in the item relation graph, the global item relational graph is established;
(3) Randomly select the starting point and then populate the new item sequences by randomly walking on the relationship graph, as shown in Figure 4.7(c);
(4) Feed the item sequences generated here into the Word2vec model – as shown in Figure 4.7(d) – to generate the final item embedding vectors.

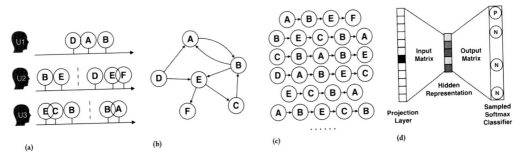

Figure 4.7 The algorithm flow of DeepWalk. (a) Users' behavior sequences. (b) Item graph construction. (c) Random walk generation. (d) Embedding with skip-gram.

In the algorithm flow of DeepWalk, the only thing that needs to be formally defined is the transition probability of random walk, that is, the probability of traversing the adjacent point v_j of v_i after reaching the node v_i. If the item relational graph is a directed weighted graph, then the probability of jumping from node v_i to node v_j is defined as

$$P\left(v_j\middle|v_i\right) = \begin{cases} \dfrac{M_{ij}}{\sum_{j \in N_+(v_i)} M_{ij}}, & v_j \in N_+\left(v_i\right) \\ 0, & e_{ij} \notin \varepsilon \end{cases} \tag{4.5}$$

where ε is the set of all edges in the item relational graph, $N_+(v_i)$ is the set of all outgoing edges of node v_i, and M_{ij} is the weight of the edge from node v_i to node v_j. This shows the transition probability of DeepWalk is the ratio of the current edge's weight against the sum of all the outgoing edge weights.

If the item relational graph is an undirected and unweighted graph, then the transition probability will be a special case of Eq. 4.5, that is, the weight M_{ij} will be a constant 1, and $N_+(v_i)$ should be the set of all thredges of node v_i, rather than the set of all the outgoing edges.

4.4.2 Node2vec: Trade-Offs between Homophily and Structural Equivalence

In 2016, researchers from Stanford University went a step further on the basis of DeepWalk and proposed the Node2vec model [8], which enables the graph embedding method to balance between the network homophily and structural equivalence.

Specifically, the "homophily" of the network means that the embeddings of nodes with similar distances should be as similar as possible. As shown in Figure 4.8, the embedding expressions of node U and its connected nodes s_1, s_2, s_3, and s_4 should be close to each other, which is the embodiment of network homogeneity.

"Structural equivalence" means that the embedding of structurally similar nodes should be as similar as possible. In Figure 4.8, node U and node s_6 are the central nodes of their respective local area networks. They are similar in structure, and their embedding expressions should also be similar. This type of similarity is referred to as structural equivalence.

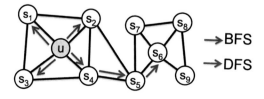

Figure 4.8 Schematic diagram of breadth-first search (BFS) and depth-first search (DFS) of the network.

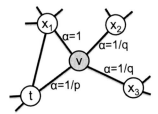

Figure 4.9 The illustration of transition probability in Node2vec.

In order to make the results of graph embedding express the "structure" of the network, in the process of random walk, it is necessary to make the node jumping more inclined to breadth-first search (BFS). BFS will traverse more in the neighborhood of the current node, and this process is equivalent to a "local scan" of the network structure around the current node. Whether the current node is a local center node, an edge node, or a connectivity node, the number and order of nodes contained in the generated sequence starting from such nodes must be different so that the final embedding captures more structural information.

In addition, in order to express network "homophily," it is necessary to make the process of random walk more inclined to depth-first search (DFS), because DFS is more likely to walk to distant nodes through multiple jumps. However, in any case, the walk of DFS is more likely to stay within a large cluster, which makes the embedding of nodes within a cluster or community more similar. Thus, it can express the "homophily" of the network better.

So in the Node2vec algorithm, how do we control the balance between BFS and DFS? The answer is that it is controlled mainly through the transition probability between nodes. Figure 4.9 shows the transition probability of Node2vec algorithm jumping from node t to node v, and then jumping from node v to the surrounding points.

The probability of jumping from node v to the next node x is $\pi_{vx} = \alpha_{pq}(t,x) \cdot \omega_{vx}$, where ω_{vx} is the weight of edge connecting node v and x, and $\alpha_{pq}(t,x)$ is defined as in Eq. 4.6,

$$\alpha_{pq}(t,x) = \begin{cases} \dfrac{1}{p}, & \text{if } d_{tx} = 0 \\ 1, & \text{if } d_{tx} = 1 \\ \dfrac{1}{q}, & \text{if } d_{tx} = 2 \end{cases} \tag{4.6}$$

where d_{tx} refers to the distance from node t to node x, and parameters p and q jointly control the tendency of random walk. The parameter p is called the return parameter. The smaller p is, the greater the probability of random walking back to node t. In this case, Node2vec emphasizes more the structural equivalence of the network. The parameter q is called the in-out parameter. The smaller q is, the more likely it is to randomly walk to the distant nodes, and then Node2vec will capture more network homophily.

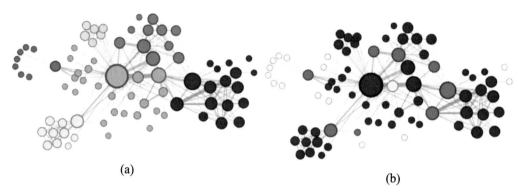

Figure 4.10 Visualization of Node2vec results with more emphasis on (a) homophily and (b) structural equivalence.

Node2vec's flexibility for balancing network homophily and structural equivalence was validated by experiments with different hyper-parameters p and q. Figure 4.10(a) shows a visualization with Node2vec reflecting more homophily. It can be seen that the colors of nodes with similar distances are closer. Figure 4.10(b) depicts the structure when Node2vec captures more structural equivalence, where the nodes with similar structural characteristics have the same colors.

The concepts of the homophily and structural equivalence of the network in Node2vec can be intuitively explained in recommender systems. Items with the same homophily are likely to be products of the same category or attributes, or frequently purchased together, while items with the same structural equivalence are those with similar trends or similar structural properties, such as the most popular items in each category, the best "always-buy-together" items in each category, and so on. There is no doubt that both are very important feature expressions in recommender systems. Due to the flexibility of Node2vec and the ability to explore different graph features, it is even possible to feed both the embedding with training emphasis on structural equivalence and the homogeneous embedding into the subsequent deep learning network, so as to retain different graph feature information of items.

4.4.3   EGES: A Comprehensive Graph Embedding Method from Alibaba

In 2018, Alibaba published its embedding method – Enhanced Graph Embedding with Side Information (EGES) [9] applied in Taobao.com. The basic idea was to introduce supplementary information based on the graph embedding generated by DeepWalk.

Embedding of the item can be generated by simply using the item related graph generated by user behavior. But if you encounter a newly added item or a "long tail" item without much interactive information, the recommender systems will have a serious cold start problem. In order to obtain a "reasonable" initial embedding for cold start products, the Alibaba method enriches the source of embedding information by introducing more side information, so that products without historical behavior records can obtain a more reasonable initial embedding.

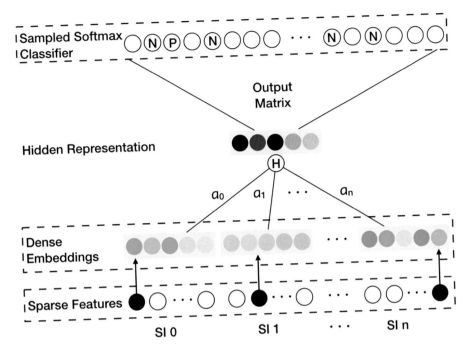

Figure 4.11 EGES model.

The first step in generating graph embedding is to generate an item relationship graph. This graph can be generated through the sequence of user behaviors. It is also possible to use information such as same attribute and same category to establish edges between items to generate a content-based knowledge graph. The item vector generated based on the knowledge graph can be called the supplementary information embedding vector. Of course, there can be multiple supplementary information embedding vectors according to different types of supplementary information.

How does one fuse multiple embedding vectors of an item to form the final embedding of the item? The easiest way is to add an average pooling layer to the deep neural network and take the average of different embeddings. In order to prevent the loss of useful embedding information caused by simple average pooling, the Alibaba team has strengthened it on top of average pooling by adding weights to each embedding (similar to the attention mechanism of the DIN model), as shown in Figure 4.11. The EGES model assigns different weights $a_0, a_1, ..., a_n$ to the embedding vectors corresponding to each type of feature. The hidden representation layer in Figure 4.11 is the layer that performs a weighted average operation on different embeddings. The weighted average embedding vector is input into the softmax layer, and the weight of each embedding $a_0, a_1, ..., a_n$ is obtained through gradient back propagation.

In the actual model, Alibaba uses e^{a_j} instead of a_j as the weight of the corresponding embedding vector. We think there may be two main reasons for this: one is to avoid the zero-valued weight; the other is because e^{a_j} has better mathematical properties in the gradient descent process.

EGES does not have overly complicated theoretical innovations, but it provides an engineering method of integrating multiple embeddings, which reduces the impact of the cold start problem caused by the lack of certain types of information. It is an embedding method that is suitable for practical adoption.

Graph embedding remains a hot topic in research and practice in both industry and academia. In addition to the mainstream methods such as DeepWalk, Node2vec, and EGES introduced in this section, LINE [10], SDNE [11], and other methods are also important graph embedding models. Interested readers can learn about these further by reading the references.

4.5   Integration of Embedding and Deep Learning Recommender Systems

We have introduced the principles and development process of embedding. But in the real implementation of recommender systems, embedding needs to integrate with other parts of the deep learning network to complete the whole recommendation process. As an integral part of the deep learning recommender systems, embedding technology is mainly used in the following three ways:

(1) As an embedding layer in the deep learning network, it converts the input features from high-dimensional sparse vectors to low-dimensional dense feature vectors;
(2) As a pre-trained embedding feature vector, after connecting with other feature vectors, it can serve as an input to the deep learning network for training;
(3) By calculating the similarity between user embedding and item embedding, embedding can be directly used as one of the retrieval layers or retrieval strategies of the recommender system.

In this chapter, we will describe the detailed methods for combining embedding and deep learning recommender systems.

4.5.1   Embedding Layer in Deep Learning Networks

High-dimensional sparse feature vectors are naturally not suitable for training complex multilayer neural networks due to the number of weights. Therefore, if a deep learning model is used to process high-dimensional sparse feature vectors, an embedding layer is almost always added between the input layer and the fully connected layer to complete the mapping of the high-dimensional sparse feature vector to the low-dimensional dense feature vectors. This technique is adopted in most of the recommendation models introduced in Chapter 3. The embedding layers of the three typical deep learning models Deep Crossing, NerualCF, and Wide&Deep are circled in red in Figure 4.12.

It can be clearly seen that the embedding layers of the three models use the one-hot encoded vectors of categorical features as input, and then output the low-dimensional embedding vectors. So structurally, the embedding layer in the deep neural network is a direct mapping of a high-dimensional vector to a low-dimensional vector (as shown in Figure 4.13).

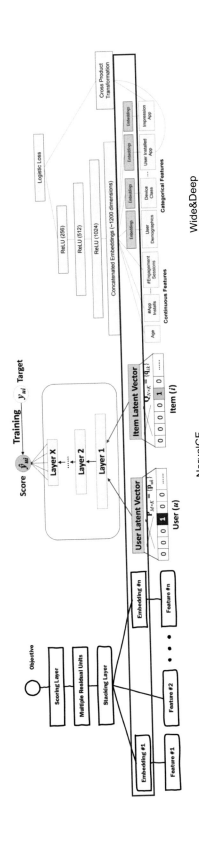

Figure 4.12 Embedding layers in the Deep Crossing, NeruaICF, and Wide&Deep models.

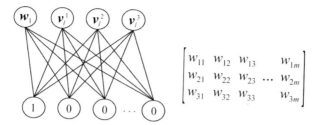

Figure 4.13 Graphical and matrix representation of the embedding layer.

After expressing the embedding layer in the form of a matrix, the embedding mapping is essentially a process of solving a weight matrix of $m \times n$, where m is the dimension of the input high-dimensional sparse vector and n is the dimension of the output dense vector. If the input vector is a one-hot encoded feature vector, the column vector in the weight matrix is the embedding vector of the one-hot feature at the corresponding dimension.

It is theoretically optimal to integrate the embedding layer with the entire deep learning network for training, because the upper-layer gradient can be directly back-propagated to the input layer, and the model as a whole is self-consistent. However, the disadvantage of this structure is obvious. The dimension of the input vector of the embedding layer is often very large, resulting in a huge number of parameters of the entire embedding layer. Therefore, the addition of the embedding layer will slow down the convergence speed of the entire neural network. This has been discussed in Section 3.7.

4.5.2   Pre-Training Method for Embedding

In order to solve the problem of the huge training cost in the embedding layer, the training of embedding is often performed independently of the deep learning network. After the dense representation of the sparse features is obtained, it is then fed into the neural network together with other features for training the deep learning network.

A typical model using the embedding pre-training method is the FNN model introduced in Section 3.7. This uses each feature latent vector obtained by the FM model training as the initialization weight of the embedding layer, thereby accelerating the convergence speed of the entire network.

In the original implementation of the FNN model, the entire gradient descent process will still update the weight of the embedding. If you want to further speed up the convergence speed of the network, you can also fix the weight of the embedding layer and only update the weight of the upper neural network, which makes the training efficient.

To extend this, the idea of embedding is to establish a mapping from high-dimensional vectors to low-dimensional vectors. The mapping method is not limited to neural networks, but can be any heterogeneous model. For example, in the

GBDT+LR combination model introduced in Section 2.6, the GBDT part is essentially an embedding operation. The GBDT model is used to complete the embedding pre-training, and then the generated embedding vectors are input into the single-layer neural network (that is, logistic regression) for CTR prediction.

Since 2015, with the development of graph embedding technology, the expressivity of embedding itself has been further enhanced, and all kinds of supplementary information can be integrated into embedding. This makes embedding a very valuable feature of recommender systems. Usually, the training process of graph embedding can only be performed independently of the recommendation model, which makes the pre-training approach a more popular embedding training practice in the field of deep learning recommender systems.

It is true that separating the embedding training from the training process of the deep neural network will lead to loss of information but the independence of the training process also brings an improvement of training flexibility. For example, the embedding of an item or user is relatively stable, since the user's interest and the attributes of the item usually do not change dramatically within a few days. So the embedding model refreshing does not need to be very high, and can even be as low as weekly. However, in order to grasp the latest overall trend in the data as soon as possible, the upper-layer neural network often requires more frequent training or even online learning. Using different training frequencies to update the embedding model and the neural network model is the optimal solution after a trade-off between training overhead and model freshness.

4.5.3   Application of Embedding in the Retrieval Layer of Recommender Systems

The enhancement of embedding's expressivity makes it a feasible choice in the direct use of embedding to generate recommendation lists. Therefore, the application of embedding in the retrieval layer to compute the similarity of representation vectors has gradually become popular in many recommender systems. Among them, the solution of the YouTube recommender systems retrieval layer (as shown in Figure 4.14) is a typical method of using embedding to retrieve the candidate items.

Figure 4.14 illustrates the structure of the retrieval layer model in the YouTube recommender systems. The input layer features of the model are all user-related features. From left to right are the embedding vector of the user's viewing history video, the embedding vector of the user's search word, the embedding vector of the user's geographic attribute feature, the age of the user (sample), and the gender-related features.

The output layer of the model is a softmax layer. This model is essentially a multiclass classification model. The prediction objective is to guess which video the user will watch. Therefore, the input of the softmax layer is the user embedding generated by the three-layer ReLU fully connected layer, and the output vector is the user watching probability distribution for each video. Since each dimension of the output vector corresponds to a video, the column vector of the softmax layer corresponding

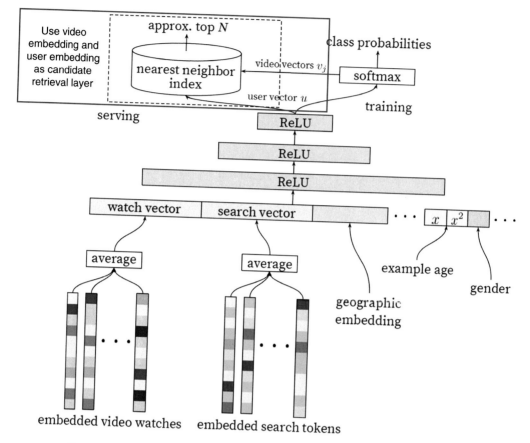

Figure 4.14 Structure diagram of the retrieval layer model in YouTube recommender systems.

to this dimension can be used as the item embedding. Through offline training of the model, each user's embedding and item embedding can be finally obtained.

With the model deployment in production, it is not necessary to deploy the entire deep neural network to complete the prediction process from the original feature vector to the final output. It is necessary only to store the user and item embeddings in the online memory database. Through the inner production of user and item embeddings, we can compute the similarity between the user and the candidate item. After sorting by the similarity score, we can get the Top N most relevant items from the candidate set for the next steps. This is the process of utilizing embedding technique to retrieve the relevant candidate items.

This process takes $O(n)$ time complexity to traverse all the items in the candidates set, where n is the candidate pool size. In many web applications, the overall candidate set size n can easily reach millions, so even an $O(n)$ level operation can take a lot of computing time, resulting in a high latency in the online inference process. Is there an indexing method to make this candidate retrieval process faster? The answer is revealed in Section 4.6.

4.6 Locality Sensitive Hashing: A Fast Search Method for Embedding-Based Searching

As mentioned, one of the most important uses of the embedding technique is to retrieve similar items from the candidate set in recommender systems. The main function of the retrieval layer of recommender systems is to quickly reduce the candidate set size from a large scale (for example, millions) to a smaller, manageable scale (for example, thousands or hundreds). This can prevent sending all candidate items directly into the subsequent deep learning model which avoids leading to the waste of computing resources and high online inferencing latency.

Compared with traditional rule-based candidate retrieval methods, embedding technology is more suitable for solving the retrieval problem for recommender systems because of its ability to synthesize a variety of information and features in the similarity prediction. In practical application, the key to the embedding productionization is how the embedding technique can quickly process hundreds of thousands or even millions of candidates, so as to satisfy the overall end-to-end latency constraints in the entire recommendation process.

4.6.1 Fast Nearest Neighbor Search with Embedding

The traditional calculation method of embedding similarity is to apply the inner product operation between user and item embedding vectors. This means that in order to retrieve a user's Top N relevant items, it is necessary to traverse all the items in the candidate set. Assuming that the embedding space has k dimensions and the candidate set size is n, then the time complexity of traversing all the items in the candidate set is $O(kn)$. In a practical recommender system, the total number of candidate items n can easily reach the order of millions. So the time complexity of this traverse step is unbearable and will lead to significant latency in the online model inferencing process.

Let's think about this process from a different angle. Since the embedding of the user and the item is in the same vector space, the process of retrieving the most relevant item to the user using the embedding vector is actually a process of searching for the nearest neighbor in this vector space. If you can find a way to quickly search for the nearest neighbors in a high-dimensional space, then the embedding fast search problem can also be solved.

The nearest neighbor search by establishing a k-dimension tree (that is, k-d tree) structure is commonly used for the fast nearest neighbor search method, and the time complexity can be reduced to $O(\log_2 n)$. However, the structure of the k-d tree is more complex, and it often needs backtracking when searching for the nearest neighbors to ensure the results are always the closest, which makes the search process more complicated. Moreover, the time complexity of $O(\log_2 n)$ is not ideal. So is there a way with lower time complexity and easier operation? Next, we introduce the state-of-the-art fast nearest neighbor search method for the embedding space in practical recommender systems – Locality Sensitive Hashing (LSH) [12].

4.6.2   Fundamentals of Locality Sensitive Hashing

The basic idea of LSH is to let adjacent points fall into the same "bucket," so that when performing a nearest neighbor search, only one bucket or several adjacent buckets need to be searched. Assuming the number of elements in each bucket is a constant, the time complexity of the nearest neighbor search can be reduced to the $O(1)$ level. Then, how are "buckets" created in LSH? Next, we take the nearest neighbor search based on Euclidean distance as an example to explain the process of constructing an LSH "bucket."

First of all, let us clarify one question regarding the distance in different spaces. If a point in a high-dimensional space is mapped to a low-dimensional space, can its Euclidean relative distance be maintained? As shown in Figure 4.15, there are four colored dots in the middle of a two-dimensional space. When the dots in the two-dimensional space are mapped to three one-dimensional spaces a, b, and c through different angles, it can be seen that the close dots in the original two-dimensional space remain close in all one-dimensional spaces. However, the green dot and red dot that were originally far away become close in one-dimensional space a, but far away in space b.

Thus, we can draw a qualitative conclusion – in Euclidean space, when the points in the high-dimensional space are mapped to the low-dimensional space, the originally close point must still be close in the low-dimensional space, but the originally far away points have a certain probability of becoming close.

After realizing that the low-dimensional space can retain the close-distance information from the high-dimensional space, we can construct the LSH "bucket" based on this knowledge.

For embedding vectors, inner product operations can be used to build the LSH buckets. Suppose v is an embedding vector in a k-dimensional space, and x is a randomly generated k-dimensional mapping vector. As shown in Eq. 4.7, the inner product operation can map v to a one-dimensional space and become a scalar value.

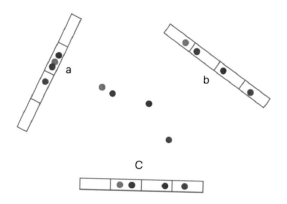

Figure 4.15 Mapping the dots in high-dimensional space to low-dimensional space.

$$h(v) = v \cdot x \tag{4.7}$$

It can be seen from these conclusions that one-dimensional space can partially preserve the approximate distance information of high-dimensional space. Therefore, bucketing can be performed by applying the hash function $h(v)$ defined as follows,

$$h^{x,b}(v) = \left\lfloor \frac{v \cdot x + b}{w} \right\rfloor \tag{4.8}$$

where $\lfloor \ \rfloor$ is a round-down operation, w is the width of the bucket, and b is a uniformly distributed random variable between 0 and w to avoid the solidification of the bucket boundary.

The distance information is partially lost in this mapping and bucketing operation. If only one hash function is used for bucketing, there must be some prediction errors for similar points. An effective solution is to use m hash functions for simultaneous bucketing. If two points fall into the same bucket with m hashing functions, the probability that the two points are, in fact, similar is significantly increased. In this way, the approximate Top K nearest neighbors of the target point can be found by traversing the reduced candidates in the same or adjacent hashing buckets.

4.6.3   Multi-Bucket Strategy for Locality Sensitive Hashing

If multiple hash functions are used for bucketing, there is a problem to be solved – whether to use an AND operation or an OR operation to generate the final candidate set. If the candidate set is generated by an AND operation (for example, "point A and point B are in the same bucket of hash function 1" and "point A and point B are in the same bucket of hash function 2"), then the accuracy of getting the nearest neighbors in the candidate set will be improved. The reduction of the size of the traversed candidate set will reduce the amount of traversal calculation and thus reduce the overall calculation overhead. But some neighboring points (such as points near the boundary of the bucket) could be still missing. On the other hand, if an OR operation is used to generate the candidate set (for example, "point A and point B are in the same bucket of hash function 1" or "point A and point B are in the same bucket of hash function 2"), the recall rate of the nearest neighbors in the candidate set is improved. But the size of the candidate set increases and the computational cost increases. After all, it requires trade-offs between precision and recall while deciding how many hash functions are used, and whether to use an AND operation or an OR operation.

This is the LSH method of inner product operation in Euclidean space. If cosine similarity is used as the distance standard, what method should be used for bucketing?

Cosine similarity measures the size of the angle between two vectors, and the vector with the smaller angle is the "nearest neighbor." Therefore, the vector space can be divided into different hash buckets by using a fixed-spaced hyperplane. Likewise, the precision or recall of LSH methods can be improved by choosing different sets of hyperplanes. Of course, the methods of evaluating the distance are far more than Euclidean distance and cosine similarity; they also include many other approaches such as Manhattan distance, Chebyshev distance, Hamming distance, and so on. The method of LSH could be also different based on different distance definitions. However, the general idea of using LSH bucketing to retain partial distancing information by reducing the candidate item size is common regardless of the distance-defining approach.

4.7   Summary: Core Operations of Deep Learning Recommender Systems

This chapter introduces the core operation of deep learning – embedding technology. From the original Word2vec, to Item2vec, and then to graph embedding which integrates more structural information and supplementary information, the application of embedding in recommender systems is getting deeper and deeper, and

Table 4.1 Key points of the embedding methods and related techniques

Embedding Method	Mechanisms	Characteristics	Limitations
Word2vec	Use the correlation of words in sentences to build the model; use single hidden layer neural network to obtain the embedding vector of words	Classic embedding method	Can only be trained on word sequence samples
Item2vec	Extend the idea of Word2vec to any sequence data	Extend Word2vec to the recommendation domain	Can only be trained on sequence samples
DeepWalk	Perform random walks on the graph structure; generate sequence samples, and use the idea of Word2vec	Easy-to-use graph embedding method	Not objective oriented
Node2vec	On the basis of DeepWalk, the results of graph embedding can balance the homophily and structural equivalence by adjusting the weight of random walk	Controllable tuning to emphasize on different graph pattern	Need more hyper-parameter tuning
EGES	Generate the final embedding by integrating embeddings corresponding to the embeddings from different information domains	Integrate a variety of supplementary information to solve the cold start problem of embedding	No major academic innovation, but more from an engineering perspective to solve the problem of multiembedding integration
LSH	Fast embedding vector nearest neighbor search using the principle of locality sensitive hashing	Solve the problem of fast candidate retrieval using embedding	There is a small probability of missing the nearest neighbor, which requires more hyper-parameter fine tuning

the applied methods are becoming more and more diverse. After LSH is applied to the search for similar candidate items, embedding technology is becoming more mature in terms of theory and engineering practice. Table 4.1 summarizes the basic mechanisms, characteristics, and limitations of the embedding methods mentioned in this chapter.

Starting from Chapters 2 and 3, we introduce the evolution of state-of-art recommendation models. In this chapter, we focus on the embedding technology related to deep learning recommendation models. Now we complete the introduction to the relevant knowledge of recommendation models in this book.

The recommendation model is the engine that drives recommender systems to achieve personalization. It is also the key area where all the recommendation teams invest the most efforts. You must have sensed the rapid development and evolution of recommendation models in academia and industry from the contents of previous chapters. It should be noted that for a mature recommender system, in addition to recommending models, we also need to consider retrieval strategies, cold start, exploitation and exploration, model evaluation, online service, and many other issues.

In the following chapters, we view recommender systems from some different perspectives and introduce the cutting-edge technologies of different modules of recommender systems. The following contents complement the recommendation model and constitute the main framework of the deep learning recommender systems.

References

[1] Tomas Mikolov, et al. Distributed representations of words and phrases and their compositionality. *Advances in Neural Information Processing Systems*, 26, 2013.

[2] Tomas Mikolov, et al. Efficient estimation of word representations in vector space: arXiv preprint arXiv:1301.3781 (2013).

[3] Xin Rong. Word2vec parameter learning explained: arXiv preprint arXiv:1411.2738 (2014).

[4] Yoav Goldberg, Omer Levy. Word2vec explained: Deriving Mikolov et al.'s negative-sampling word-embedding method: arXiv preprint arXiv: 1402.3722 (2014).

[5] Yoshua Bengio, et al. A neural probabilistic language model. *Journal of Machine Learning Research*, 3, 2003: 1137–1155.

[6] Oren Barkan, Noam Koenigstein. Item2vec: Neural item embedding for collaborative filtering. 2016 IEEE 26th International Workshop on Machine Learning for Signal Processing (MLSP), Salerno, Italy, September 13–16, 2016.

[7] Bryan Perozzi, Rami Al-Rfou, Steven Skiena. DeepWalk: Online learning of social representations. Proceedings of the 20th ACM SIGKDD International Conference on Knowledge Discovery and Data Mining, New York, USA, August 24–27, 2014.

[8] Aditya Grover, Jure Leskovec. node2vec: Scalable feature learning for networks. Proceedings of the 22nd ACM SIGKDD International Conference on Knowledge Discovery and Data Mining, San Francisco, USA, August 13–17, 2016.

[9] Jizhe Wang, et al. Billion-scale commodity embedding for e-commerce recommender in Alibaba. Proceedings of the 24th ACM SIGKDD International Conference on Knowledge Discovery and Data Mining, London, UK, August 19–23, 2018.

[10] Jian Tang, et al. Line: Large-scale information network embedding. Proceedings of the 24th International Conference on World Wide Web. International World Wide Web Conferences Steering Committee, Florence, Italy, May 18–22, 2015.

[11] Daixin Wang, Peng Cui, Wenwu Zhu. Structural deep network embedding. Proceedings of the 22nd ACM SIGKDD International Conference on Knowledge Discovery and Data Mining, San Francisco, USA, August 13–17, 2016.

[12] Malcolm Slaney, Michael Casey. Locality-sensitive hashing for finding nearest neighbors [lecture notes]. *IEEE Signal Processing Magazine*, 25(2), 2008: 128–131.

5 Recommender Systems from Multiple Perspectives

While building a recommender system, a good recommendation model is important, but only having a good model is not enough. In fact, recommender systems need to solve complex problems, and all technical details are essential to the final recommendation performance. This requires machine learning engineers to examine the system from multiple perspectives, not only to grasp the core of the model, but also to think about the recommender system holistically.

This chapter will dive deeper into recommender systems from seven different angles. We hope to present a comprehensive walkthrough for the relevant knowledge in recommender systems. The contents include:

(1) How do recommender systems select and process features?
(2) What are the popular strategies of the retrieval layer in recommender systems?
(3) Why is it important to have real-time recommender systems? How to improve the real-time performance of the model?
(4) How to choose the best optimization objective for the recommendation model based on specific scenarios?
(5) How to improve model structure based on user intent?
(6) How to solve the cold start problem in recommender systems?
(7) What is the "exploration vs. exploitation" problem? What are the common solutions?

There is no logical relationship among these problems, but they are all essential components of recommender systems besides the recommendation model. Only by understanding these problems can we build a recommender system with comprehensive capabilities and robust architecture.

5.1 Feature Engineering of Recommender Systems

In this section, we will look into recommender systems from a feature engineering perspective. "Garbage in garbage out" is a phrase often mentioned by machine learning engineers. The boundary of the machine learning model's capability lies in the fitting and generalization of the data. Thus, the data and the features determine the upper limit of machine learning performance. Therefore, feature engineering is irreplaceable in the performance improvement of recommender systems. In order to conduct a high-quality feature engineering study, three problems need to be solved in sequence:

(1) What are the principles we should follow while working on feature engineering?
(2) What are the commonly used feature categories?
(3) How to process the original input features to generate feature vectors for model training and inferencing?

5.1.1   Feature Engineering in Recommender Systems

In recommender systems, the core of features represents the relevant information about certain behaviors. While making recommendations, behaviors must be converted into numerical values before they can be learned by the machine learning model. Therefore, the information from these behaviors must be extracted into features, and use multidimensional features to represent the behavior.

Information loss is inevitable during the process of converting the actual behavior to some abstract features. Firstly, in the actual recommendation scenario, there is usually a large amount of information, including contexts, images, and status. It is impossible to store all this information due to its massive data volume. Secondly, lots of this information is redundant and unusable. Taking excessive unrelated information into the model can inhibit the generalization ability of the model. Because of these two reasons, feature engineering in recommender systems needs to obey the following principle:

The goal of feature engineering is to extract a set of features so that it retains as much useful information as possible while eliminating redundant information in the behavior.

For example, while making a movie recommendation, how should the features be extracted to model the behavior of "the user clicks on a movie"?

To answer this question, let's put ourselves in the user's shoes. What factors could influence our choice to click on a certain movie while viewing a list of movies? Here, we came up with this list of six factors ranked by their importance:

(1) Preferences on the movie genres.
(2) Popularity of the movie.
(3) Whether there is a favorite actor or director in the movie.
(4) Attractiveness of the movie poster.
(5) Whether watched the movie before.
(6) Mood at the moment.

Following the principle of "retaining as much of the useful information as possible," when extracting features for a movie recommendation, the features should be able to retain the information of these six factors as much as possible. Table 5.1 shows the factors and their corresponding useful information and features.

It is worth mentioning that in the process of feature extraction, it is inevitable to lose some information. For example, the factor of "mood at the moment" is discarded. For another example, inferring the user's preferences from his/her viewing history

Table 5.1 Factors, useful information, and features

Factors	Useful Information	Features
Preferences on the movie genres	List of movies watched	Features of the movie id, or further generate interest embedding features
Popularity of the movie	Popularity score of the movie	Popularity features
Whether there is a favorite actor or director in the movie	Metadata of the movie	Labels in the metadata
Attractiveness of the movie poster	Image of the movie poster	Image features
Whether watched the movie before	Movie watching history	Boolean values for "watched or not"
Mood at the moment	N/A	N/A

will also lead to information loss. Therefore, it is a realistic engineering practice to retain useful information based on available data to the fullest extent.

5.1.2 Common Features in Recommender Systems

This section covers the commonly used feature categories based on the principle of feature engineering in recommender systems. Readers may refer to this list when building their own feature engineering.

5.1.2.1 User Behavior Data

User behavior data is the most commonly used and critical data for recommender systems. The user's potential interest and true evaluation of the item are all included in the user's behavior history. In recommender systems, user behaviors are generally divided into explicit feedback and implicit feedback, which are reflected in different forms under various business scenarios. Table 5.2 shows examples of user behavior data in different business scenarios.

The use of user behavior data often involves an understanding of the business. Different behaviors have different weights when extracting features, and some user behaviors that are strongly related to business characteristics need to be discovered by machine learning engineers through their own observations.

In the current feature engineering of recommender systems, implicit feedback behaviors are becoming more and more important. This is mainly because the collection of explicit feedback behaviors is too difficult and the amount of data is small. With the increasing requirements of data volume in deep learning models, using only explicit feedback data is not enough to support the final convergence of the model training. Therefore, the implicit feedback that can reflect the characteristics of user behavior is the focus of feature mining at present.

For processing user behavior features, two methods are commonly considered. One is to convert the list of user behavior into a multi-hot vector and use it as a feature vector; the other is to pre-train the item embedding (referring to the embedding method

Table 5.2 Examples of user behavior data in different business scenarios

Business Scenario	Explicit Feedback	Implicit Feedback
E-commerce site	Rating of products	Click, add to cart, purchase, and so on
Video website	Ratings, likes, and so on, on the video	Click, play, playing time, and so on
News website	Likes, dislikes, and so on	Clicks, comments, and so on
Music website	Rating of songs, artists, albums	Click, play, favorite, and so on

Figure 5.1 Diversity of social network relationships.

in Chapter 4), and then generate the historical behavior embedding vector by taking the average or using a method similar to the attention mechanism of the DIN model (referring to Section 3.8), and use it as a feature vector.

5.1.2.2   User Relationship Data

The internet is essentially the connection between people and information. If user behavior data is a log of "connection" between people and things, then user relationship data records connections among people. In the age of the internet, one common phrase that people say is "birds of a feather flock together." User relationship data is undoubtedly valuable information for recommender systems to utilize.

User relationship data can also be divided into "explicit" and "implicit" types, or called "strong relationship" and "weak relationship." As shown in Figure 5.1, users can establish a "strong relationship" through "following," "friendship," and other connections, and they can also be in a "weak relationship" by "liking each other," "being in the same community," or even "watching a movie together."

In recommender systems, there are many ways to utilize user relationship data. It can be used in the retrieval layer to retrieve items; it can also be used to establish a

Table 5.3 Classification and sources of attributes and labels

Subject	Category	Source
User	Demographic attributes (gender, age, address, and so on)	User registration information, third-party DMP (Data Management Platform)
Item	Label of user interest	User choices
	Label of the item	Added by user or system administrator
	Item attributes (product category, price; movie category, year, actor, director, and so on)	Background entry, third-party database

relationship graph, and generate embedding of users and items through graph embedding methods. Another utilization is to create new attribute features for users through the characteristics of their "friends" directly from relationship data. It is even possible to build a social recommender system with user relationship data.

5.1.2.3 Attributes and Tags

In our discussion, attributes and tags are considered the same thing, because essentially, they both directly describe the characteristics of the user or the item. The subject of attributes and tags can be a user or an item. Their sources are very diverse. Table 5.3 summarizes the main categories of these data.

User attributes, item attributes, and tags are the most important descriptive features. Mature companies often establish a tagging system for users and items, which is maintained by a dedicated team. A typical example is the product classification system of an e-commerce company; there may also be tags added by the users through crowdsourcing methods.

In recommender systems, attributes and tags are generally converted into feature vectors by multi-hot encoding. Some important attributes and tag features can also be converted into embedding first, and then input into the recommendation model.

5.1.2.4 Content Data

Content data can be regarded as an extension of the attribute and tag features. They are also descriptions of the item or the user. But compared with label features, content data are often large pieces of descriptive text, pictures, or even videos.

Generally speaking, content data cannot be directly converted into features that can be "digested" by the recommender system. It is necessary to extract key features through natural language processing, computer vision, and other technical means, and then input them into the recommender system. For example, while making recommendations for pictures, videos, or other visual content, computer vision models are often used to detect objects, extract features (as shown in Figure 5.2), and then convert these features (elements) into tags for the recommender system.

Figure 5.2 Using computer vision model for target detection and extracting image features.

5.1.2.5   Contextual Information

Context is the information describing the environment in which the action of recommendation is generated. The most commonly used contextual information is "time" and GPS-based "location." Depending on the recommendation use cases, the contextual information has a very wide range, including but not limited to time, location, season, month, whether it is a holiday, weather, air quality, major social events, and so on.

The purpose of integrating contextual information is to preserve the information of the environment where the recommendation occurs as much as possible. Here is a typical example: in a movie recommendation, users tend to watch relaxed and romantic movies in the evening, and mystery and thriller movies in the middle of the night. Without contextual features, recommender systems will not be able to capture valuable information related to these scenarios.

5.1.2.6   Statistical Features

Statistical features refer to features calculated by statistical methods, such as historical CTR, historical CVR, item popularity, and so on. Statistical features are generally continuous features, which can be directly input into the recommender system for training with standardization and normalization.

Statistical features are essentially some coarse predictors. For example, in the CTR prediction problem, the historical average CTR of an item can be viewed as the simplest prediction model, but the prediction ability of this model is very weak, so the historical average CTR is often only used as one of the features of a complex CTR model. Statistical features usually have a strong correlation with the final target, therefore they are an important feature category that should never be ignored.

5.1.2.7 Combined Features

Combined features refer to new features generated by combining multiple features. The most common example is the population segmentation composed of "age + gender." In early recommender systems, recommendation models (such as logistic regression) often do not have the ability to combine features. However, with the development of deep learning recommender systems, the combined features no longer need to be manually selected and screened, but can be handed over to the model for automatic processing.

5.1.3 Common Methods for Feature Processing

For recommender systems, the input to the model is often numerical feature vectors. For many of the feature categories mentioned in the previous section, there are numerical features like "age," "playing time," and "historical CTR," which can naturally become a dimension in the feature space. However, for many other features, such as the user's gender or viewing history, how are they transformed into numerical feature vectors? This next section discusses common feature processing methods for both continuous and categorical features.

5.1.3.1 Continuous Features

Typical examples of continuous features are the aforementioned numerical features such as user age, statistical features, item release time, and video playback duration. For the processing of such features, the most commonly used methods include normalization, discretization, and adding nonlinear functions.

The main purpose of normalization is to unify the dimensions of each feature and normalize continuous features to the [0,1] interval. You can also do 0-mean normalization, that is, normalize the original dataset to a dataset with a mean of 0 and a variance of 1.

Discretization is the process of dividing the original continuous values into buckets by determining the quantiles, and finally forming discrete values. The main purpose of discretization is to prevent overfitting caused by continuous values and uneven distribution of values. The discretized continuous features are converted into feature vectors for the recommendation model, just like the one-hot encoded categorical features.

Adding a nonlinear function is to directly transform the original feature through a nonlinear function, and then add both the original feature and the transformed feature to the model for training. Commonly used nonlinear functions include

$$x^a, \log_a(x), \log\left(\frac{x}{1-x}\right).$$

The purpose of adding a nonlinear function is to better capture the nonlinear relationship between the feature and the optimization objective, and enhance the nonlinear expressivity of this model.

5.1.3.2   Categorical Features

Typical examples of category features are users' historical behavior data, attributes, and label data, and so on. Its original form is often a category or an id. The most common processing method for this type of feature is to use one-hot encoding to convert it into a numerical vector. The "Basics" of Section 2.5 introduces one-hot encoding

---

Basics: What Is Multi-Hot Encoding?

For data such as historical behavior and label features, users often interact with multiple items, or are labeled with multiple tags of the same category. In this case, the most commonly used method is multi-hot encoding.

For example, an e-commerce website has a total of 10 000 products, and the user has purchased 10 of them, then the user's historical behavior data can be converted into a 10 000-dimensional numerical vector, of which only 10 of the purchased products correspond to the dimension of 1, the other dimensions are 0. This is multi-hot encoding.

---

in detail. On the basis of one-hot encoding, when encountered with multiple category selections for the same feature, multi-hot encoding can also be used.

The main problems of one-hot or multi-hot encoding of categorical features are that the dimension of the feature vectors is too large, the features are too sparse. This can easily lead to underfitting of the model, and the model has too many weight parameters, which leads to slow convergence of the model. Therefore, with the maturity of the embedding technology, it is widely used in the processing of categorical features. The categorical features are firstly encoded into dense embedding vectors, and then combined with other features to form the final input feature vectors.

5.1.4   Feature Engineering and Business Understanding

So far in this section, we introduced the types of features and main processing methods of feature engineering for recommender systems. In the era of deep learning, the recommendation model itself undertakes a lot of feature selection and combination work, and machine learning engineers do not need to spend a lot of time on feature engineering as before. However, the powerful feature processing capabilities of deep learning models do not mean that we can abandon our understanding of business data. On the contrary, feature engineering itself has become a part of the deep learning model when recommendation models and feature engineering tend to be fused together nowadays.

For example, in the Wide&Deep model, machine learning engineers need to have a deep understanding of the business application in order to determine which features to "feed" to the Wide part for memory strengthening. In the DIEN model, the feature extraction of user behavior is deeply coupled within the model structure, and the complex sequence model structure is used to embed the user behavior sequence.

In this sense, the traditional work of artificial feature combination and filtering no longer exists, and it is replaced by a deep learning model that combines feature engineering and model structure with unified thinking and overall modeling. What remains unchanged is that only by deeply understanding the business and the user's thinking and behavioral motives in business use cases can the most valuable features be accurately extracted and successful deep learning models be constructed.

5.2 The Main Strategy of the Retrieval Layer in Recommender Systems

Section 1.2 depicts a technical architecture diagram of recommender systems, in which two main stages of a recommendation model – the retrieval stage and the ranking stage – are clearly described. The retrieval stage is responsible for quickly reducing the massive candidate set to a scale of hundreds to thousands; and the ranking stage is responsible for ranking the reduced candidate set. The recommendation models in Chapters 2 and 3 are mainly used in the ranking stage. This section focuses on the main strategies of the retrieval layer.

5.2.1 Functional Characteristics of the Retrieval Layer and the Ranking Layer

The main reason for the recommendation model dividing into a retrieval layer and a ranking layer is because of engineering considerations. In the ranking stage, complex models and high-dimensional features are generally used to create accurate sorting. In this process, if the candidate set is of millions of magnitudes which are directly inferred one by one, the computing resources and latencies are unbearable for an online service process. Therefore, the retrieval layer is added, and a small number of features and simple models or rules are used to quickly screen candidate sets (as shown in Figure 5.3), reducing the overhead of the precise ranking stage.

If we consider the original design of the retrieval layer and the ranking layer, and combine them with the system structure shown in Figure 5.3, then we can summarize the following characteristics of the retrieval layer and the ranking layer:

- **Retrieval layer:** Large candidate set, fast speed, simple model, and few features. It tries to ensure that the items of interest to the user are quickly retrieved at this stage, that is, to ensure the retrieval rate of related items.
- **Ranking layer:** The primary goal is to get accurate ranking results. Since the number of items to be processed is small, more features and more complex models can be used.

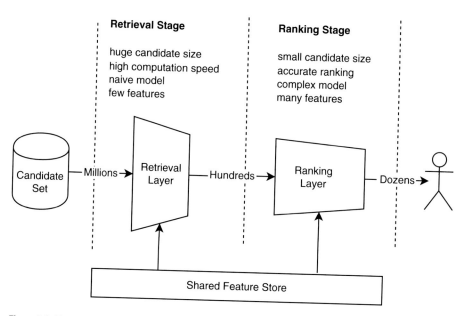

Figure 5.3 Two stages of a recommender system.

When designing the retrieval layer, "calculation speed" and "retrieval rate" are actually two contradictory indicators. In order to improve the "calculation speed," the retrieval strategy needs to be as simple as possible; but to improve the "retrieval rate" the retrieval strategy needs to construct an effective candidate set, which in turn requires a not-too-simple retrieval strategy, so that the retrieved items will meet the requirements of the ranking model.

After balancing the calculation speed and retrieval rate, the current mainstream retrieval method in the industry is a "multichannel retrieval strategy" that combines multiple simple strategies.

5.2.2 Multichannel Retrieval Strategy

A "multichannel retrieval strategy," as its name suggests, refers to a strategy that combines multiple strategies, features, or simple models to retrieve a part of a candidate set, and then mix the candidate sets together for the subsequent ranking model.

Clearly, the "multichannel retrieval strategy" is the result of a trade-off between "computation speed" and "retrieval rate." Each simple strategy ensures the fast retrieval of the candidate set, and combining strategies designed from different angles ensures that the retrieval rate is close to the ideal state, so as not to offset the ranking stage.

Figure 5.4 shows an example for an information flow to illustrate the commonly used multichannel retrieval strategies, including "hot news," "interest tags," "collaborative filtering," "recent trends," "friends likes," and other retrieval methods. It includes some simple models with high computational efficiency (such as collaborative filtering); also includes some retrieval methods based on a single feature (such as

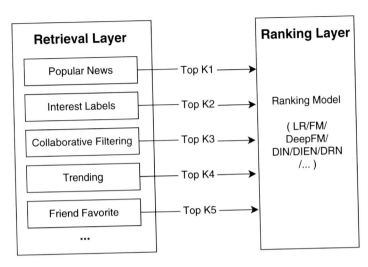

Figure 5.4 Common multichannel retrieval strategies.

interest tags), and some pre-processed retrieval strategies (such as hot news, recent trends, and so on).

In fact, the choice of retrieval strategies is strongly related to business. For video recommendations, the retrieval strategy can be "hot videos," "director retrieval," "actor retrieval," "recently released," "popular trends," "genre retrieval," and so on.

Each retrieval strategy will pull back K candidate items. For different retrieval strategies, the K value can be different. The K value here is a hyperparameter. Generally, a reasonable range of values needs to be determined by offline evaluation and online A/B testing.

Although multichannel retrieval is a practical engineering method, manual adjustment is required from strategy selection to the setting of candidate set size parameters. The information between strategies is also fragmented, and the impact of different strategies on an item cannot be comprehensively understood. So is there a retrieval method with strong comprehensiveness and computational speed that can meet these needs? The retrieval method based on embedding gives a feasible solution.

5.2.3   Embedding-Based Retrieval Method

Section 4.5 explains the method of using a deep learning network to generate embeddings and apply them in the retrieval layer of YouTube's recommender system. Coupled with the fact that locality-sensitive hashing can be used for fast embedding nearest neighbor calculation, the retrieval method based on embedding is not inferior to multichannel retrieval in effect and speed.

In fact, information such as "interest tags," "popularity," "popular trends," and "item attributes" used in multichannel retrieval can be incorporated into the final embedding vector as side information in the embedding retrieval method (a typical example is the EGES embedding method introduced in Section 4.4). Using embedding retrieval is equivalent to considering multiple strategies of multichannel retrieval.

Another advantage of embedding retrieval is the continuity of ratings. The similarity, popularity, and other scores generated by different retrieval strategies in multichannel retrieval are not comparable, which makes it impossible to determine the size of the candidate set for each retrieval strategy based on these scores. Embedding retrieval, however, can use the similarity between embeddings as the only criterion, and hence the size of the retrieved candidate set can be freely determined.

The method of generating embedding is by no means unique. In addition to the methods such as Item2vec and Graph Embedding introduced in Chapter 4, simple models such as matrix factorization and a factorization machine can also derive the embedding vectors of users and items. In real-world applications, the optimal embedding generation method for the retrieval layer can be determined based on its effectiveness.

5.3   Real-Time Performance of Recommender Systems

There is a famous quote in the movie *Kung Fu*: "In the world of Kungfu, speed defines the winner." If the recommendation model's architecture is the invincible Kungfu, then the real-time capability of the system is what makes it "fast and unbreakable." This section discusses the importance of the recommender system's real-time capability, and how to improve the real-time performance of the system.

5.3.1   Why Are Real-Time Recommendations Important?

Before trying to improve the real-time performance of recommender systems, we first consider whether it is truly an important factor affecting the recommendation results. In order to prove the importance of real-time performance to the recommender system and the recommendation effect, Facebook has used the "GBDT+LR" model to conduct experiments (as shown in Figure 5.5). We will use this data as an example to illustrate the importance of real-time performance.

In Figure 5.5, the horizontal axis represents the time (in days) between the end of the model training and model testing, and the vertical axis is the relative value of the loss function's normalized entropy. As shown in the figure, whether it is the "GBDT+LR" model or a simple tree model, the value of the loss function has a positive correlation with the model update delay. That is, the longer it takes for the model to update, the less effective it will be; conversely, when the model is updated frequently, it will have better real-time performance and smaller loss, which means better recommendations.

Let's consider user experience. Users of personalized news applications would expect to quickly find articles that match their interests. Users of short-form video services would expect to quickly "scroll" to something they are interested in. Similarly, when shopping online, people expect to find their favorite items quickly. As long as the recommender system can perceive user feedback and meet the user's expectations in real-time, the recommendation's effectiveness is improved. This is an intuitive manifestation of the "real-time" role of recommender systems.

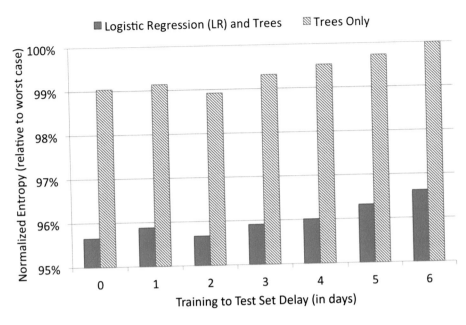

Figure 5.5 Facebook's real-time model experiment.

On the other hand, from the perspective of machine learning, the importance of real-time recommender systems is reflected in the following two aspects:

(1) A fast-updated recommender system means the features representing the user's recent habits and preferences are changing rapidly, which enables more timely recommendations for the user.
(2) A quickly updated recommender system makes it easier for the model to discover the latest data patterns, and quickly capture the latest trends.

These two reasons directly match the two parts of the recommender system's real-time capability: real-time features and real-time model.

5.3.2   Real-Time "Features" of Recommender Systems

The real-time features of recommender systems refer to collecting and updating the input features of the model in "real-time," so that the system can always have the latest features for prediction and recommendation.

For example, in a short-form video app, a user watched an entire video of 10-minute "Badminton Teaching." No doubt the user was interested in the topic "Badminton." The system would hope to continue recommending videos related to "Badminton" for the user immediately. However, due to the lack of real-time features of the system, the user's viewing history was not sent back to the recommender system immediately. As a result, the system only learned that the user had watched the video "Badminton Teaching" 30 minutes later, and the user already logged off and would no longer see any recommendations by then. This is an example of recommendation failure due to poor real-time performance.

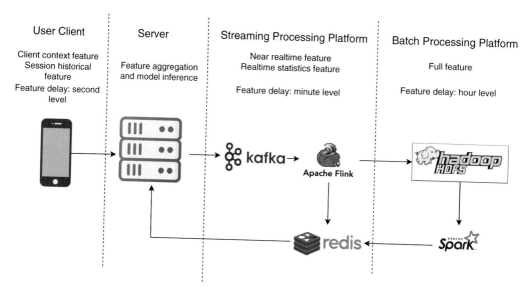

Figure 5.6 Data flow architecture of recommender systems.
Apache Kafka, Kafka, the Apache Kafka Logo, Apache Hadoop, Hadoop, the Apache Hadoop Logo, Apache Flink, Flink, the Apache Flink Logo, Apache Spark, Spark, the Apache Spark Logo and Apache are either registered trademarks or trademarks of the Apache Software Foundation. Redis is a registered trademark of Redis Ltd. Any rights therein are reserved to Redis Ltd. Any use by Cambridge is for referential purposes only and does not indicate any sponsorship, endorsement or affiliation between Redis and Cambridge.

Truly, when the user logs in to the app next time, the recommender system could use the previous user history and continue to recommend videos related to "Badminton." But undoubtedly, it has lost the most likely opportunity to increase user stickiness and retention.

In order to illustrate the method of enhancing the real-time performance of "features," we will describe the three main stages that affect the real-time capability of "features" on the data flow architecture diagram of recommender systems (as shown in Figure 5.6).

5.3.2.1   Client Real-Time Features

The client is the closest link to the user and is where the user's in-session behavior and all contextual characteristics can be collected in real-time. In a classic recommender system, it is a common way to request recommendation results by using the client to collect contextual features such as time, location, and recommendation scenarios, and then sending these features to the server along with the http request. But it is easily overlooked that the client is also where the user's behavior within the session can be collected in real-time.

In the case of a news app, the user clicks and reads three articles in one session (assuming a three-minute session). These three articles are crucial to the recommender system because they represent the user's immediate interests. If the recommendation results can be changed in real-time based on the user's immediate interests, it will be a good user experience for a news app.

If a traditional streaming computing platform (Flink in Figure 5.6) or even a batch computing platform (Spark in Figure 5.6) is used, due to latency issues, the system may not be able to retrieve and store the in-session behavior into a feature database (such as Redis) within three minutes. As a result, the user's recommendation list will not be immediately affected by the in-session behavior, and thus cannot achieve a real-time update of the recommendation results.

If the client can cache the in-session behavior and transmit it to the server in real-time like the context features, then the model can obtain the in-session behavior in real-time and make recommendations based on it. This is the advantage of using client real-time features for timely recommendations.

5.3.2.2 Quasi-Real-Time Feature Processing of Stream Computing Platform

With the increasing maturity of a number of excellent stream computing platforms such as Storm, Spark Streaming, and Flink, the use of stream computing platforms for quasi-real-time feature processing has almost become the standard configuration of current recommender systems. The stream computing platform is a platform that stream processes the logs in mini batches. Due to the nature of waiting and processing a small batch of logs each time, the stream computing platform is not exactly a real-time platform, but the advantage is that it can perform some simple calculation of statistical features within the time window, such as the number of impressions and clicks of an item, the distribution of clicked topics by a user, and so on.

The features calculated by the stream computing platform can be immediately stored in the feature database for the recommendation model to use. Although it is not designed to change the user's recommendation list in real-time according to the user's behavior, a few minutes' delay can basically ensure that the users' recent behaviors are incorporated into the recommender system in quasi-real-time.

5.3.2.3 Full Feature Processing of Distributed Batch Processing Platform

As the data eventually reaches the distributed storage system dominated by HDFS, distributed batch computing platforms such as Spark can finally calculate and extract full features. This stage also focuses on data manipulations such as joining multiple data sources and merging delayed signals.

The user's impression, click, and conversion data often arrive at HDFS at different times. The conversion data of some game apps can even be delayed by several hours. Therefore, full data batch processing is the only stage that can handle the extracting and merging of all features and corresponding labels. Higher-order feature combination is also a task that requires the readiness of all features, which is often impossible on client or streaming computing platforms.

Here are some main uses of the computing results from the distributed batch processing platform:

(1) Model training and offline evaluation.
(2) The features are stored in the feature database for subsequent online recommendation models.

From data generation to complete loading into HDFS, along with the calculation delay of Spark, the total delay of this process often takes hours, and will by no means meet the requirement of "real-time" recommendation. Therefore, it can only provide more accurate recommendations when the user logs in next time.

5.3.3 Real-Time "Model" of the Recommender Systems

Compared with the real-time requirements of "features," the real-time requirements of "model" are often considered from a more global perspective. The real-time features try to describe users, items, and the context with more accuracy, so that the recommendation results generated by the system can be more relevant and fit the scene at that moment. The real-time model, however, is to quickly capture new data patterns at the global level and discover new trends and correlations.

For example, an e-commerce website holds promotional activities for a major online shopping event. The real-time features will quickly discover products that users may be interested in based on their recent behavior, but it will never find a hot product that has just become popular, a promotion that has just started, or the latest preferences of people similar to this user. To discover such global data changes, the recommendation model needs to be updated in real-time.

The real-time performance of the model is closely related to the training method of the model. As shown in Figure 5.7, the real-time performance increases as the training methods move from full update to incremental update, and then to online learning.

5.3.3.1 Full Update

"Full update" means that the model uses all training samples in a certain period of time for training. Full update is the most commonly used model training method, but it requires all the training data to be "displaced" (recorded in big data storage systems such

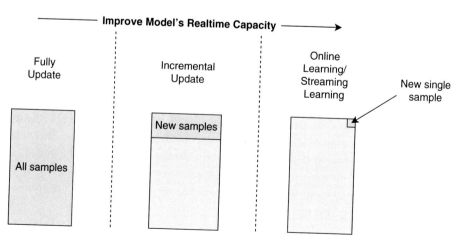

Figure 5.7 The relationship between the real-time performance of the model and the training method.

as HDFS), and it often takes a long time to train full samples. Therefore, full update has the worst real-time performance compared to other model update methods. In contrast, the "incremental update" method can effectively improve the training efficiency.

5.3.3.2 Incremental Update

Incremental update only "feeds" the newly added samples to the model for incremental training. Technically, deep learning models often use the stochastic gradient descent (SGD) method and its variants for learning. The learning of incremental samples by the model is equivalent to continuing to input incremental samples for gradient descent based on the original samples. The disadvantage of incremental update is that the model of incremental update is often unable to find the global optimal point. Therefore, in the actual application, the combination of incremental update and global update is often used. After several rounds of incremental updates, global update is performed when the business volume is small to correct the errors accumulated in the model during those incremental updates.

5.3.3.3 Online Learning

Online learning is the main method for real-time models, that is, to update the model as soon as a new sample is obtained. Like incremental update, online learning is also technically implemented through SGD training. However, due to the need for model training in an online environment and the updating and storage of a large number of model-related parameters, the engineering requirements are higher.

Another problem of online learning is that the lack of sparsity of the model. For example, in a model with several millions of input features, if the model is sparse, the majority of the feature weight coefficients can be set to zero without affecting the accuracy of the model. This way, a small online model can be used with only a very small portion of nonzero weighted features (because all features with a weight of 0 can be discarded), which is conducive to speeding up the entire model service process. However, if SGD is used to update the model, compared with the batch method, it is prone to generate a large number of small-weighted features, which increases the size of the model. This leads to increased difficulty of model deployment and update. In order to balance the accuracy and model sparsity in the online learning process, a lot of related research are conducted, including a few famous ones such as FOBOS [1] from Microsoft and FTRL [2] from Google.

Another direction of online learning is to combine reinforcement learning with the recommender system. In Section 3.10, we introduced the reinforcement learning recommendation model DRN, which adopted a competitive gradient descent algorithm. It performs online learning by exploring new parameters randomly, and adjusting parameters based on real-time feedback. This can be an effective way to improve a model's real-time performance in reinforcement learning.

5.3.3.4 Partial Update

Another idea to improve a model's real-time performance is to perform a partial update. The general idea is to reduce the update frequency of the part with low training efficiency and increase the update frequency of the part with high training efficiency. The representative of this approach is the "GBDT+LR" model from Facebook.

Section 2.6 has introduced the model structure of "GBDT+LR." The model uses GBDT for automatic feature engineering, and uses LR to fit the optimization target. GBDT is serial and needs to train each tree sequentially, so the training efficiency is low and the update cycle is long. If the entire model of "GBDT+LR" is trained every time, the inefficiency of GBDT will slow down the update of LR speed. In order to utilize the feature processing capability of GBDT and the ability of LR to quickly fit the optimization target, the deployment method adopted by Facebook is to train the GBDT model once a day. After the GBDT model is fixed, the LR model is trained in real-time to quickly capture the overall changes in the data. Through a partial update of the model, the balance between GBDT and LR capabilities is achieved.

The method of "partial update of the model" is mostly used in the deep learning model with an embedding layer and neural network. Since the parameters of the embedding layer takes up most of the parameters of the deep learning model, its training process will slow down the overall convergence speed of the model. Therefore, in real application, it often adopts a mixed strategy: pre-training the embedding layer and frequently updating the model above the embedding layer. This is another application of the "partial update."

5.3.3.5   Real-Time Update of the Client Model

Earlier in this section, we mentioned the real-time methods of "features" on the client. Since the client is the part closest to users and has the best real-time capability, can we update the model on the client based on the newly generated user behavior?

Real-time client model update is still in the exploratory stage in the recommender system industry. For some computer vision problems, lightweight models can be generated through model compression and deployed on the client, but for "heavyweight" models like recommendation models, it is often dependent on the server where relatively powerful computing resources and rich feature data are available. Nonetheless, the client can often save and update some parameters and features of the model, such as the current user's embedding vector.

The logic and motivation here is that in the deep learning recommender system, the model often needs to take two critical feature vectors: user embedding and item embedding. For the update of item embedding, global data is generally required, so it can only be updated on the server; for user embedding, however, it relies more on the user's own data. Therefore, moving the user embedding update to the client, which can reflect the user's latest behavior to the user embedding, so that the recommendation results can be updated in real-time on the client.

Here is a simple example to illustrate the process. If the user embedding is obtained by averaging the item embeddings clicked by the user, then the client, as the first to obtain the latest item information clicked by the user, can update the user embedding in real-time based on these items, and save the embedding. When making the next recommendation, the updated user embedding is sent to the server, and the server can return real-time recommendation content according to the latest user embedding.

5.3.4 Using the "Wooden Bucket Theory" to Look at the Iterative Update of Recommender Systems

This section introduced the main methods to improve the "feature" real-time and "model" real-time performance of recommender systems. Since there are many aspects that affect the real-time performance of a recommender system, the engineers need to adopt a strategy that focuses on one point and improve before moving on to the next. But how to accurately find this key point is a problem requires us to look at it with the "wooden bucket theory," that is, finding the shortest piece of plank that slows down the real-time performance of the recommender system, replace or improve it, so that the bucket of "recommender system" can hold more "water."

Looking at the iterative update of the entire recommender system from a higher perspective, the "wooden bucket theory" is also applicable. The model part and engineering part of the recommender system are always alternately optimized. When the attempt to improve the recommendation results by improving the model is hindered or the cost is too high, the direction of optimization can be focused on the engineering part, so as to achieve the goal of spending less effort and achieving more significant results.

5.4 How to Set the Optimization Goals in Recommender Systems

A famous technology company CEO once said: "Don't use diligence in tactic to cover up laziness in strategy." This quote also applies to the technology innovation and application. If a technology itself is novel and advanced, but the direction of application deviates from its actual demand, then the achievements of this technology cannot be significant. In recommender systems, if the optimization goal of your model is inaccurate, no matter how good the evaluation metric is, it will deviate from the actual goal you want to achieve. Therefore, making no strategic mistakes and reasonably setting the optimization goals are the focus for every machine learning engineer before they start building a recommender system.

To set a "reasonable" optimization goal for a recommender system, you first need to establish a "reasonable" principle. For a company, in most cases, the goal is to achieve a certain business target, so formulating the optimization goal according to the company's business targets should be a "reasonable" choice. This is further illustrated next with the examples of recommender systems for YouTube and Alibaba.

5.4.1 The Rationality of YouTube Taking Viewing Duration as the Optimization Goal

Section 1.1 used YouTube's recommender system [3] as an example, emphasizing the key role of recommender systems in achieving the growth of a company's business goals.

YouTube's main business model is the advertising revenue brought by free videos. Its in-video ads will appear periodically before and during video playback, so its advertising revenue is directly proportional to the user's viewing time. In order to achieve the company's business targets, the optimization goal of YouTube's recommender system is not CTR estimations, such as click-through rate or playback rate, but the user's playback time.

It is undeniable that indicators such as click-through rate are correlated with user playback time, but there are still some differences in "optimization motivation" between the two. If the click-through rate is the optimization goal, then the recommender system will tend to recommend short-form videos with a "clickbait title" and a "surprising preview image." And if the playback time is the optimization goal, then the recommender system should take into account the length of the video, the quality of the video, and other characteristics. It may be a better choice to recommend a high-quality "movie" or "series" for this goal. Differences in recommendation goals will lead to differences in the propensity of the recommender system, which in turn affects whether the business goal of "increasing the user's viewing time" can be achieved.

In the ranking model of YouTube's recommender system (as shown in Figure 5.8), playback duration is set as the optimization goal in a very clever way.

The ranking model originally treated the recommendation problem as a classification problem, that is, predicting whether a user clicks on a certain video. Since it is a classification problem, it would be difficult to predict the playback time (predicting time duration should be what a regression model does). However, YouTube cleverly converts the playback time into the weight of positive samples. The output layer is trained using weighted logistic. While making the prediction, the odds of the sample is calculated using e^{Wx+b}. This probability is the prediction of the model's playback time. (The argument here is not rigorous. The inference of the YouTube ranking model will be further discussed in Section 8.3.)

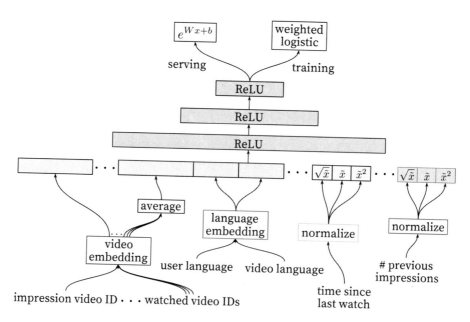

Figure 5.8 The output layer of the YouTube recommendation model.

YouTube's prediction of playback time is in line with its advertising-based profit model and business interests. Formulating a reasonable optimization goal is critical to achieve the business goals of the recommender system.

Unlike video companies, for Alibaba and other e-commerce companies, an indicator such as playback time naturally does not exist. So what are the key factors that Alibaba considers when designing the optimization goals for its recommender system?

5.4.2   Unity of the Scenarios for Model Optimization and Application

The formulation of optimization goals should also consider the unity of model optimization scenarios and application scenarios. In this regard, Alibaba's multiobjective optimization model gives a good example.

When making recommendations on e-commerce websites such as Amazon and Taobao, the process from login to purchase can be abstracted into two steps:

(1) Product impression, user browses the product details page.
(2) User makes a purchase.

Different from the video websites such as YouTube, for e-commerce websites, the company's business goal is to have users make more purchases through recommendations. Because "the optimization goal should be consistent with the company's business goals," the e-commerce recommendation model should be a CVR estimation model.

Since the conversion, the purchase behavior happens in the second step, when training the CVR model, it is intuitive to use click data plus conversion data (data in the gray and dark gray areas in Figure 5.9) to train the CVR model. When using the CVR model, because what the user directly sees after logging in is not the specific product details page, but the homepage or list page, the CVR model needs to make a prediction in the stage of product impression (the data in the outermost circle in Figure 5.9). This leads to the problem that the training scenario is inconsistent with the prediction scenario. In this situation, the model will most likely produce biased prediction results, which will lead to the loss of application benefits.

Here, let's solve the problem in another way. Firstly, we can build a CTR prediction model for the first step scenario; then we build a CVR prediction model for the second step scenario. This way, each application scenario will have its corresponding prediction model, and this is indeed a practice often used by e-commerce or

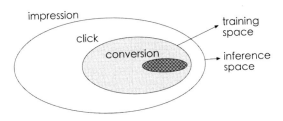

Figure 5.9 Inconsistency between training and prediction scenarios.

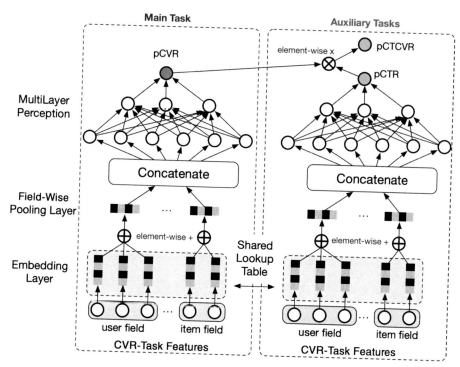

Figure 5.10 Alibaba's multiobjective optimization model ESMM.

advertising companies. But the shortcoming of this solution is that the CTR model is out of touch with the final optimization goal, because the final goal of the whole problem is "conversion to purchase," not "click." Only utilizing click data in the first step is obviously not the best scheme to optimize the conversion rate globally.

In order to simultaneously optimize the CTR and CVR models, Alibaba proposed a multiobjective optimization model ESMM (Entire Space Multi-task Model) [4]. ESMM can be regarded as a model that simultaneously simulates the two stages of "impression to click" and "click to conversion."

From the model structure (as shown in Figure 5.10), the underlying embedding layer is shared by the CVR part and the CTR part. The purpose of sharing the embedding layer is mainly to solve the problem of sparse positive samples of the CVR task and use CTR data to generate more accurate feature representations for users and items.

The middle layer is that the CVR part and the CTR part each use a completely isolated neural network to fit their own optimization goals – pCVR (post-click conversion rate) and pCTR (post-view click-through rate). Finally, pCVR and pCTR are multiplied to obtain pCTCVR.

The relationship between pCVR, pCTR and pCTCVR is shown in Equation 5.1:

$$\underbrace{p(y=1, z=1|x)}_{\text{pCTCVR}} = \underbrace{p(y=1|x)}_{\text{pCTR}} \times \underbrace{p(z=1|y=1,x)}_{\text{pCVR}} \tag{5.1}$$

pCTCVR refers to the probability of a click-conversion sequence after impression.

ESMM also integrates pCVR, pCTR, and pCTCVR into a unified model, so the model can obtain the values of all three optimization objectives in one run. In model application, the appropriate objective can also be selected according to the corresponding application scenario. For this reason, Alibaba has solved the two key problems of "inconsistency between training scenario and prediction scenario" and "utilization of both click and conversion data for global optimization" by building a multiobjective optimization model – ESMM.

Whether it is YouTube or Alibaba, although the model structures of their recommender systems are quite different, when designing the optimization goals, they both fully consider the real business goals and application scenarios, and try to "simulate" the prediction scenarios while training the model. This is the first principle for designing successful recommender systems.

5.4.3 Multi-Task Learning in Recommender Systems

The situation faced by Alibaba and other e-commerce companies are not unique. Many business situations require modeling in multiple steps and thus need multi-task learning techniques. Aside from ESMM, industry has various methods of multi-task learning. In this section, we will introduce some of the typical methods.

5.4.3.1 Weighted Loss Function

To solve multi-task learning problems, the most straightforward approach is to create a weighted loss function. This approach is essentially combining multiple tasks into one task. It is easy to train and deploy, and the outcome is favorable by improving the outcome of the additional tasks without compromising the primary task. However, the weights of the additional tasks can be hard to determine and may require AB testing.

The loss function is shown in Equation 5.2:

$$\text{Loss} = -\frac{1}{n}\sum_{i=1}^{n} w_i \times y_i \times \log(p_i) + w_i \times (1 - y_i) \times log(1 - p_i) \tag{5.2}$$

5.4.3.2 Shared-Bottom Multi-Task Model

Another basic approach for multi-task learning is the shared-bottom multi-task model (as illustrated in Figure 5.11(a)). The neural network, denoted as function $f(x)$, follows the input layer and is shared by multiple tasks. Built upon the output of this shared-bottom network are the K tower networks, denoted as h^k, where $k = 1, 2, \ldots, K$ for each subtask, respectively. The output of each subtask is $y_k = h^k(f(x))$.

The advantage of this model is that the parameters for each task complement each other in the shared bottom, which enhances the learning efficiency. The model performs best when the tasks are highly correlated with each other. But when they are not, this hard parameter sharing will actually harm model prediction.

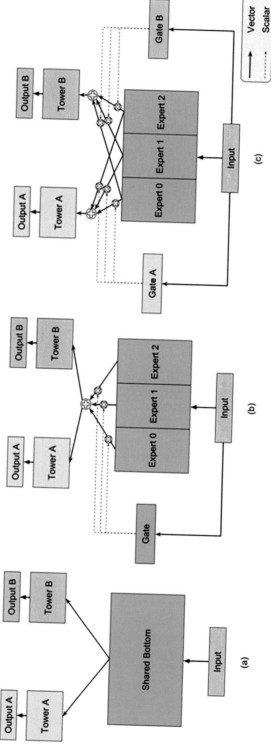

Figure 5.11 (a) Shared-bottom model. (b) One-gate MoE model. (c) Multi-gate MoE model.

5.4.3.3 Mixture-of-Experts

To solve this problem for less correlated tasks, the concept of soft parameter sharing is proposed, and Mixture-of-Experts (MoE) is a main method of soft parameter sharing [5]. For this approach (as shown in Figure 5.11(b)), a network constitutes a set of experts replaces the shared bottom, where each expert is a forward-feeding network. In addition, a gating network is used to control which of the experts should be used for each training case. MoE can be formulated as:

$$y_k = h^k \left(f^k (x) \right) \tag{5.3}$$

$$f^k (x) = \sum_{i=1}^{n} g(x)_i f_i (x) \tag{5.4}$$

Here, y_k is the output of the kth subtask, f_i $(i = 1,\ldots,n)$ are the n expert networks, and $g(x)_i$ is the ith logit of the output of $g(x)$ with $\sum_{i=1}^{n} g(x)_i = 1$. Here, g is the gating network, represented by a SoftMax layer of linear transformations from the input:

$$g(x) = \text{Softmax}\left(W_g x\right) \tag{5.5}$$

The function g generates probability distribution for the n experts, and outputs a weighted sum of all the experts. MoE can be regarded as an ensemble of multiple independent models.

5.4.3.4 Multi-gate Mixture-of-Experts

Google scientists and engineers continued to advance this algorithm and created Multi-gate Mixture-of-Experts (MMoE) model [6]. MMoE uses as many gating networks as there are tasks (as shown in Figure 5.11(c)). This way, the weights for the expert networks are tailored individually to each task and therefore achieved selective utilization of experts. Consequently, the model becomes better equipped to capture the correlations and differences among subtasks.

Specifically, MMoE can be formulated as:

$$y_k = h^k \left(f^k (x) \right) \tag{5.6}$$

$$f^k (x) = \sum_{i=1}^{n} g^k (x)_i f_i (x) \tag{5.7}$$

Here, g^k is the gating network for the kth subtask, and it can be expressed as:

$$g^k (x) = \text{softmax}\left(W_{gk} x\right) \tag{5.8}$$

MMoE has largely improved the modeling process for multiple tasks, but it still has prominent shortcomings. First of all, the experts are shared by all tasks, and therefore cannot capture more complicated relationships between tasks and can bring noises for some tasks. In addition, the lack of interaction between experts can diminish the model's performance. To solve some of these problems, scientists and engineers from Tencent proposed another novel model for multi-task learning – Progressive Layered Extraction (PLE) [7].

5.4.3.5 Progressive Layered Extraction

Compared to the corresponding single-task models, one conundrum for multi-task learning is the difficulty of improving the performance of all tasks simultaneously.

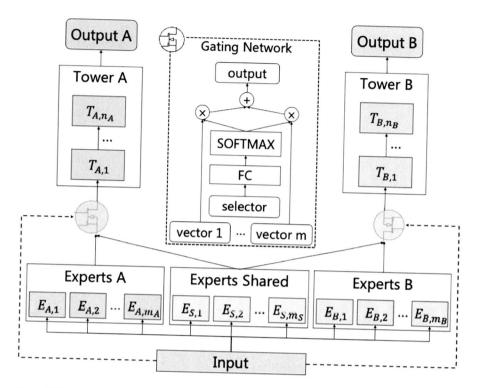

Figure 5.12 Customized gate control model.

The improved prediction of some tasks usually comes at the cost of the performance of other tasks. PLE was built to address this problem with a customized sharing structure design.

As illustrated in Figure 5.12, PLE assigns an expert for each task, while also keeping a shared expert for all tasks. The gating network uses a selector to determine the expert used for each task, so as to achieve a more flexible balance between tasks.

The output of the kth task is:

$$y^k \left(x \right) = t^k \left(g^k \left(x \right) \right) \tag{5.9}$$

where t^k is the tower network of the kth task and g^k is the gating network, which is denoted as:

$$g^k \left(x \right) = w^k \left(x \right) S^k \left(x \right) \tag{5.10}$$

Here, w^k is the weights for all experts in the selector S^k, and S^k is consisted of the shared experts and the experts specific for the kth task.

In order to incorporate interactions between experts, the customized gate control model can be generalized with PLE (as shown in Figure 5.13). In PLE, multilevel extraction networks are used to extract higher-level shared information. Besides gates for task-specific experts, a gating network is also employed in the extraction network for shared experts to combine knowledge from all experts in this layer. As a result, the

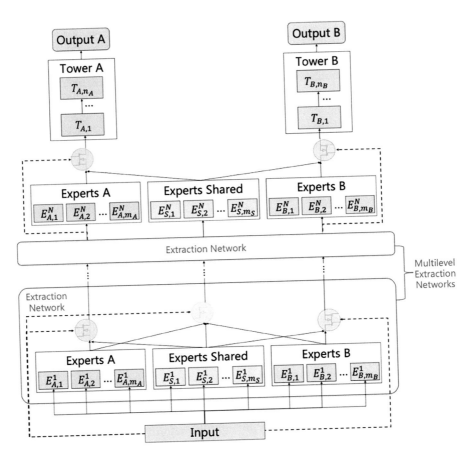

Figure 5.13 Progressive layered extraction model.

parameters are progressively separated in upper layers, which enabled more efficient and flexible joint representation learning and sharing.

From the inception of straightforward weighted loss functions and shared-bottom multi-task models to the sophisticated domains of MoE, MMoE, and PLE, driven by the relentless progression of techniques, companies have artfully devised multi-task learning models. These models aim to discover optimal solutions adeptly suited for addressing a multitude of tasks, ultimately realizing intricate business objectives. Such an accomplishment stands as a testament to the importance of grounding these approaches in real-world business applications and aligning them closely with the overarching business goals.

5.4.4 Setting the Optimization Goal Is a Collaborative Work with Other Teams

Regarding the topic of "optimization goals," the third point we want to emphasize is not a technical issue, but a teamwork effort. Building a successful recommender system is a complex and systematic problem that cannot be accomplished by the technical team alone. Instead, it requires the coordination of the product team, operation team, and content editing team to jointly achieve the business goals.

During the coordination process, the technical team complains about the product team's frequent modification of the requirements, and the product team complains about the technical team's lack of understanding of their design intentions. There are often structural contradictions between the two. If you are looking for the best entry point to decouple the work between the product team and the technical team, then it would be the setting of the optimization goal for the recommender system.

Only by setting appropriate optimization goals can the technical team focus on model improvement and structural adjustment, and avoid exposing too much of the complicated and obscure technical details to the outside world. On the other hand, for the product team, only by setting reasonable optimization goals can the recommender system serve the company's overall business interests and product design targets. To be honest, conflicts, compromises, and trade-offs among the teams are indispensable in this process. But only by negotiating the optimization goals before solving the problems can we avoid strategic mistakes, prevarication, and rework as much as possible, and maximize the business interests of the company and the productivity of the teams.

5.5   What Is More Important than Model Structure in Recommender Systems?

The previous chapters of this book focus on the technical aspects of recommender systems, introduced the model structures as well as deep learning techniques such as embedding. In this section, we discuss one question: Besides the technical problems, are there other more important factors that affect the effectiveness of a recommender system?

5.5.1   Is There a "Silver Bullet" to Solve All Recommendation Problems?

While communicating with peers in the recommendation industry, one question is often asked: "Which recommendation model is better?" It is true that model structure is critical to the final recommendation performance, but is there really a model structure that is the "silver bullet" to solve all recommendation problems?

To answer this question, we can start with analyzing a model – the recommendation model DIEN proposed by Alibaba in 2019. The details of DIEN model were introduced in Section 3.9, and we will briefly review in this section. The overall structure of the DIEN model is a GRU sequence model, and it simulates the evolution of user interests through the sequence model. The interest evolution part first converts item ID to item embedding based on the user behavior sequence from the behavior layer. The interest extraction layer uses the GRU sequence model to simulate the user interest evolution and extracts the interest embedding vector. The interest evolution layer combines the attention mechanism with the AUGRU sequence model to simulate the interest evolution process associated with targeted advertising.

Since the model was proposed, due to Alibaba's huge influence in the industry, many practitioners believe that they have found a "silver bullet" to solve the recommendation problem. However, many problems emerge from the actual application, and people tend to look into the model itself for solutions to these problems. For example, "Is the dimension of the embedding layer not enough?" "Is it necessary to increase the number of states in the interest evolution layer?" and so on.

The point is, anyone who raised such questions defaulted to a premise, that is, the DIEN model that can improve the performance in Alibaba's recommendation scenarios should be equally effective in other application scenarios. However, is this assumption really reasonable? Is the DIEN model the "silver bullet" in the field of recommender systems?

The answer is no.

Let's make a simple analysis. Since the key of DIEN is to simulate and express the evolution of user interest, the premise of model application must be that there is "interest evolution" in the use case. Alibaba's use case is very easy to understand – users' buying interests change at different times. For example, after purchasing a laptop, a user will have a certain probability of purchasing its peripheral products; after purchasing a certain type of clothing, a user may choose some other clothing that matches it. These are intuitive examples of interest evolution.

Another reason why DIEN can be effective in Alibaba's use case is that the user's interest evolution path can be nearly completely preserved in the data flow. As China's largest e-commerce group, Alibaba's product matrix composed of various product lines can almost completely capture the migration of user shopping interest. Of course, users may go shopping on other e-commerce platforms, thus interrupting the evolution of shopping interest in Alibaba. However, statistically speaking, the interest evolution of a large number of users can still be captured by Alibaba's data system.

Therefore, the prerequisite for the DIEN model is that the use case needs to meet two conditions:

(1) There is an "interest evolution" in application scenarios and
(2) The evolution process of user interests can be completely captured by the data.

If either one of the two conditions is not established, then the DIEN model will probably not bring great benefits.

Take the video streaming media recommender system as an example. On a comprehensive streaming media platform (such as a smart TV), users can choose their own channels and content, or choose to watch Netflix, YouTube, or other streaming media channels. Once the user enters Netflix or another third-party application, we cannot get the specific data in the application. In this case, the system can only obtain part of the user's viewing and clicking data. It is not easy to extract the user's points of interest; much less can we talk about building the entire evolution path of the user's interest. Even if the interest evolution path is barely constructed, it is an incomplete or even wrong path.

Based on such characteristics, is DIEN suitable to be the main architecture of the recommendation model? The answer is no. The DIEN model cannot reflect the characteristics of business data and user motivations. In this situation, it would be unwise to think that the poor model performance is due to the parameters not properly adjusted or sample size not large enough. Compared with these technical reasons, it is most important to understand the use case and be familiar with the data characteristics.

At this point, we are ready to give the answer to the question in the title – while building a recommendation model, it is most important to start from the application scenario and follow the characteristics of user behavior and data, and propose a reasonable motivation to improve the model.

In other words, the model structure is not the "silver bullet" for building a good recommender system. The real "silver bullet" is good observations of user behavior and application scenarios. Based on these observations, improve the model structure to best express these characteristics. The following three examples are further illustrations of this statement.

5.5.2   Netflix's Observation on User Behavior

Netflix is one of the largest streaming media company in the United States. Its recommender system generates a list of movies based on user preferences. In addition to the ranking of videos, one factor that has the most impact of the click-through rate is actually the preview image of the movie. For example, for a user who likes Matt Damon, when he sees Matt Damon's profile picture on the poster of the movie, the probability of clicking on the movie will increase significantly. After verifying this through A/B testing, Netflix's data scientists began to optimize the generation of movie preview images [8] to improve the overall click-through rate of the recommendation results.

In the specific optimization process, the model will use different movie preview templates and fill them with different foregrounds, backgrounds, texts, and so on, according to the preferences of different users. By using a simple linear "exploration vs. exploitation" model, it is possible to verify which combination is the most suitable for a certain type of user to personalize the posters.

In this problem, Netflix does not use a complex model, but the effect of CTR improvement is on the order of 10%, far exceeding the benefits of improving the model structure. This is to solve problems from the perspective of users and scenarios. This is also in line with the idea of "wooden bucket theory" proposed in Section 5.3. The most effective way to improve a recommender system is not to persistently improve the already long plank, but to find the shortest plank and improve the overall performance.

5.5.3   Observe User Behavior and Add Valuable User Information to the Model

To give another example, Figure 5.14 is the illustrated home page of a typical video streaming platform, and each row is a category of movies. But for a new user, the system lacks this user's click and playback samples. So for Roku engineers, can they find other valuable information to solve the data sparsity problem?

This requires us to go back to the product, understand the problem from the user's perspective, and discover key signals. For this user interface, if the user is interested in a certain type of movie, they will inevitably slide the mouse or remote control to the right (as indicated by the arrows at the rightmost in Figure 5.14) to browse other movies in this type. Actions are a good indicator of a user's interest in this case.

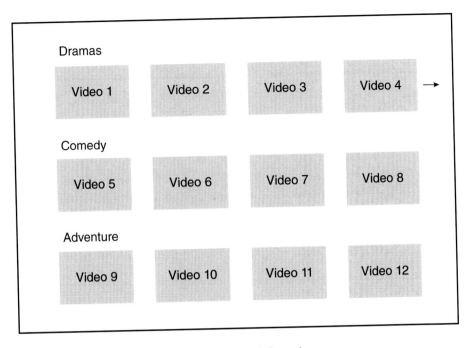

Figure 5.14 Capture user behavior that contains key information.

The introduction of this action will undoubtedly have a positive effect on building user interest vectors, solving the problem of data sparseness, and improving the effectiveness of the recommender system. Broadly speaking, the introduction of new valuable information is equivalent to adding a new "water source" to the recommender system, while improving the model structure is the further mining of the existing "water source." Usually, new water sources bring higher benefits, and with less difficulty comparing to continuous excavation of existing water sources.

5.5.4 Motivation for Improvement of the DIN Model

Back to Alibaba's recommendation model. Section 3.8 details that the predecessor of the DIEN model is DIN, and its basic idea is to combine the attention mechanism with the deep neural network (as shown in Figure 3.24).

Let's have a brief review of the principle of DIN. Based on the classic deep CTR model, DIN adds an activation unit to each type of feature while constructing the feature vector. This activation unit acts like a switch, controlling whether to put this type of feature into the feature vector and the weight when putting it in. Who controls this switch? It is determined by the relationship between the advertised item to be predicted and the features. That is to say, when predicting whether user u likes item i, DIN only takes into account the features related to item i, and the doors of other features will be closed, and they will not be considered at all or have very little weight.

So is it a purely technical consideration when Alibaba's engineers came up with the idea of applying attention mechanisms to deep neural networks?

The author once communicated with the authors of DIN papers, and found that their starting point is also observations of user behavior. As comprehensive e-commerce websites, Tmall and Taobao's collection of historical user behavior records are valuable only if they are related to candidate items. Based on this starting point, the switch and weight structure of related items are introduced, and finally it is found that the attention mechanism happens to be the most suitable technical structure that can explain this motivation. Conversely, if the attention mechanism is applied purely from a technical point of view just to verify whether it will be effective, it is "putting the cart before the horse," because this is not a conventional way of solving problems in the industry, but a tentative technical verification process. This pure "guess work" type of verification will undoubtedly increase the workload.

5.5.5   Machine Learning Engineers Cannot Be Just an "Alchemist"

Many machine learning engineers jokingly refer to their jobs as "parameter tuner" or "alchemists." In the context of deep learning, the selection of hyperparameters is of course an indispensable job. However, if machine learning engineers only focus on whether to add dropout to the network, whether to change the activation function, whether to add regularization items, and modify the depth and width of the network, it is impossible to make targeted improvements that truly meet the application scenario.

Many peers in the industry say that making a recommender system is to "try to figure out people's minds." We do not fully agree with this statement, but it does reflect the theme of this section to a certain extent – thinking about problems and building models from the perspective of users.

If you are reading this book and already have several years of work experience, you may be very familiar with machine learning related technologies. Instead, you should jump out of the technology, stand in the perspective of users, experience their ideas in depth, and discover their preferences and habits, and then when you can use machine learning tools to verify and simulate it, there will be unexpected results awaiting.

5.6   Solutions to Cold Start

Cold start is a problem that recommender systems must face. Any recommender system has to start from scratch, with very few data and features, and gradually grow into rich dataset. So with the lack of valuable data, how to make effective recommendations is the problem of "cold start."

Specifically, the cold start problem is mainly divided into three categories based on how data is lacking:

(1) User cold start: After a new user signs up, how can personalized recommendations be made without historical behavior data?

(2) Item cold start: After a new item (new movie, new product, and so on) is added, how can the item be recommended to users without an interaction record for the item?

(3) System cold start: When the recommender system lacks all relevant historical data at the beginning of its operation.

For different application scenarios, solving the cold start problem requires business insight, and a reasonable strategy based on the opinions of domain experts. Generally speaking, the mainstream cold start strategies can be classified into the following three categories:

(1) Rule-based cold start process;
(2) Enrich available features;
(3) Utilize active learning, transfer learning, and "exploration vs. exploitation" mechanisms.

5.6.1   Rules-Based Cold Start Process

During the cold start process, due to the lack of data, the engine for personalized recommendation cannot work effectively. Naturally, the system can be rolled back to the "pre-recommender system" era and adopt a rule-based recommendation method. For example, in a user cold start scenario, lists such as "hot charts," "recent trends," and "highest ratings" can be used as the default recommendation lists. In fact, most music, video and other applications use this method as the default rule for cold start.

Furthermore, you can refer to domain expert opinions to create some personalized item lists, and make coarse-grained rule-based recommendations based on the limited information of users, such as age, gender, and addresses inferred from IP when registering. For example, use the click-through rate or other similar targets to build a decision tree of user attributes, build a cold start list at the leaf node of each decision tree, and after the new user completes registration, find the corresponding leaf node on the decision tree and use this list to complete the user cold start process.

In the item cold start scenario, other similar items can be found according to some rules, and the cold start process of the item can be completed by using the recommendation logic of similar items. Of course, finding similar items is a strongly business-related task. This section uses Airbnb as an example to illustrate the process.

Airbnb is the world's largest short-term rental platform. When launching a new short-term rental house, Airbnb will designate a "cluster" for the rental house according to its properties, and houses in the same "cluster" will have similar recommendation rules. So the following three rules are relied upon by the designate "cluster" for cold start short-term rental housing:

(1) Same price range.
(2) Similar housing attributes (area, number of rooms, and so on).
(3) The distance to the target house is within 10 kilometers.

To complete cold start for a new short-term rental house in the market, find three similar houses that best meet these rules, and locate the cluster based on the clusters of these three existing houses.

From this example, we can see that the rule-based cold start method is more relied on the business insights from domain experts. When formulating cold start rules, it is necessary to fully understand the company's business characteristics and make full use of existing data in order to make cold start rules reasonable and efficient.

5.6.2 Enrich Available Features

The rule-based cold start process is effective in most cases and is a very practical method. But this process is separate from the "master model" of the recommender system. Is it possible to optimize cold start performance by improving the main recommendation model? The answer is yes. The main method is to use more user or item attributes as features rather than historical behavior features in the model.

In the absence of historical behavior features, the recommender system can still complete coarse-grained recommendations based on the attributes of users and items. These attributes mainly consist of the following categories:

(1) User's registration information, including basic demographic attributes (age, gender, education, occupation, and so on) and geographic information inferred from IP address, GPS information, and so on.

(2) User information provided by a third-party Data Management Platform (DMP). Companies such as BlueKai, Nielsen, and Talking Data all provide such services with a very high matching rate, which can greatly enrich user attributes. These third-party data management platforms exchange data with a large number of applications and websites. They can not only provide basic demographic attributes, but also provide a series of high-level features such as desensitized user interests, income levels, and advertising tendencies.

(3) The characteristics of the item. Introducing content-related features of items into recommender systems is an effective way to solve "item cold start." The characteristics of the item may include the item's classification, label, description text, and so on. In a specific business field, there can also be richer field-related content features. For example, in the field of video recommendation, the content features of a video may include the actors, year of the movie, genre, and so on.

(4) Request user input for cold start features. Some applications request users to enter some information as cold start features when they log in for the first time. For example, some music applications will ask users to select "music style"; some video applications will ask users to select several favorite movies. These are the work of enriching cold start features.

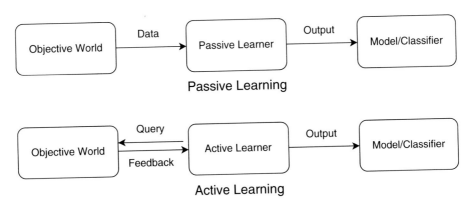

Figure 5.15 Flow chart of passive learning and active learning.

5.6.3   Utilize Active Learning, Transfer Learning, and "Exploration vs. Exploitation" Mechanisms

In addition to the rule-based recommendations and feature engineering, there are many other machine learning tools that can help us complete the "system cold start," including active learning, transfer learning, and "exploration vs. exploitation" mechanisms. They have different methodologies for solving the cold start problem. Some brief descriptions of the basic ideas follow next.

5.6.3.1   Active Learning

Active learning [9] is in relative to "passive learning" (as shown in Figure 5.15). Passive learning is to model on the existing dataset. During the learning process, the dataset will not be changed, nor will new data be added. The learning process is "passive." On the other hand, active learning not only uses existing data for modeling, but also "actively" discovers which data is the most needed, actively sends inquiries to the outside, and obtains feedback, thereby accelerating the entire learning process and generating a more comprehensive model.

Code 5.1 learning process in pseudocode. In each iteration, the system will evaluate each potential "query" to see which query can minimize the loss of the model after adding the query, then send the query to the outside world, and update the model M after receiving feedback.

```
for j = 1,2,…,totalIterations do
     foreach qj in potentialQueries do
           Evaluate Loss(qj)
   end foreach
       Ask query qj for which Loss(qj) is the lowest
       Update model M with query qj and response (qj,yj)
   end for
   return model M
```

Code 5.1 Pseudocode for active learning

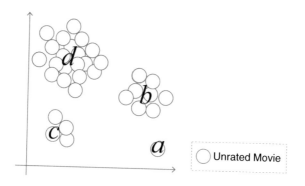

Figure 5.16 Example of active learning in recommender systems.

Here, Loss(q_j) represents E(Loss(M')). M' is a new model generated after adding query q_j to model M, and Loss(q_j) means the expectation of loss of new model M'.

So how does the active learning model play a role in the cold start process of a recommender system? Here is an example to illustrate. As shown in Figure 5.16, the horizontal axis and the vertical axis represent two feature dimensions. Each point in the figure represents an item (for example, a movie for video recommendations), and the shade of the point represents the user's actual rating of the movie. Then, Figure 5.16 shows a cold start scenario, that is, the user has not rated any movies, how should the system make recommendations?

The goal of active learning is to give possible scores for all items as quickly as possible. In this example, all videos are clustered into four categories: a, b, c, and d, and the sizes of the clusters are different. So with active learning, which movie should we choose in the next recommendation?

The answer is that the central node of the largest cluster d should be selected as the recommended movie, because by actively asking the user for the rating of the central node of d, the user's feedback on the largest cluster d can be obtained, which maximizes the benefits of the recommender system. Strictly speaking, the loss function of the recommender system should be defined so as to accurately evaluate the loss reduction benefit obtained by recommending different movies. Here we just use an example to help readers understand the principle of active learning.

The principle of active learning is similar to reinforcement learning. Looking back at the reinforcement learning framework in Section 3.10, we can see that the process of active learning completely follows the reinforcement learning cycle of "action-feedback-state update." Its goal is to let the recommender system go through the cold start state as quickly as possible in repeated iterations, and provide users with more personalized recommendation results.

5.6.3.2   Transfer Learning

As the name implies, transfer learning is the transfer of data or knowledge from other fields when data in a certain field is insufficient. Then, the reason of using transfer learning to solve the cold start problem is straightforward. The cold start problem is essentially caused by insufficient data or knowledge in the field. If knowledge in other fields can be used for recommendations in the current field, then the cold start problem is naturally solved.

Transfer learning is very common in recommender systems. In the ESMM model introduced in Section 5.4, Alibaba uses CTR data to generate embeddings of users and items, and then shares them with the CVR model, which itself is using the idea of transfer learning. This allows the CVR model to use the "knowledge" of the CTR model to complete the cold start process when there is no conversion data.

Another more practical transfer learning method is under the premise that the model structure and feature engineering of domain A and domain B are the same. If the model of domain A has been fully trained, the parameters of domain A model can be directly used as the initial values of the parameters in domain B model. With the continuous accumulation of domain B data, model B is iteratively updated. The purpose of this is to obtain personalized and reasonable initial recommendations even when the data in domain B is insufficient. The limitation of this method is that the features used in domain A and domain B must be basically the same.

The application of transfer learning in recommender systems is also a hot topic in recent years. Due to the length of the article, we will not go into further details here. If interested, readers can use this as an introduction and continue to read other related academic articles.

5.6.3.3   "Exploration vs. Exploitation" Mechanism

The "exploration vs. exploitation" mechanism is another effective idea to solve the cold start problem. Simply put, "exploration vs. exploitation" is a balance between "exploring new data" and "exploiting old data," so that the system can use old data to make recommendations, achieve the business goals, and efficiently explore whether the new item is a "premium" item. This way, the new item will gain its chance of impression and quickly start data collection for cold start.

Here, we use the most classic example of exploration vs. exploitation, Upper Confidence Bound (UCB) [10], to explain the concept of this method.

Equation 5.11 is the formula for calculating the score of each item using the UCB method. Here $\bar{x}_j$ is the observed average return of the jth item (the average return here can be click-through rate, conversion rate, playback rate, and so on), n_j is the number of times the jth item has been exposed to users so far, and n is the total number of impressions of all items so far.

$$\text{UCB}(j) = \bar{x}_j + \sqrt{\frac{2 \ln n}{n_j}} \qquad (5.11)$$

A simple calculation shows that when the average return of an item is high, the score of UCB will be high; in the meantime, when the number of impressions of the item is low, the score of UCB will also be high. That is to say, using the UCB method for recommendation, the recommender system will tend to recommend items with "high return" or "cold start." Then, as the cold start item is recommended with a higher tendency, it quickly collects feedback data, so that it can quickly pass the cold start stage.

In fact, the "exploration vs. exploitation" problem is a very important issue in recommender systems. In addition to solving the cold start problem, it can also tap the potential interests of users and maintain the long-term beneficial state of the system. Section 5.7 will focus on discussing the mainstream methods to solve the "exploration vs. exploitation" problem.

5.6.4   The Dilemma of "Making Bricks without Straw"

As the saying goes, "You can't make bricks without straw." The difficulty of a cold start problem is that there is no straw, and the machine learning engineer has to make bricks. There are two ways to solve this dilemma:

(1) Although there is no straw, it is impossible to have nothing to use. One could first get some clay and grass, and try to make something. This requires the cold start algorithm to use some coarse-grained features, attributes, and even knowledge in other fields for cold start recommendation without accurate historical behavior data.

(2) Collect straws while making bricks, and quickly pass the stage of "no straw." This way of solving the problem is to make some bricks first, sell them for money to buy straws, and make the bricks better and better, and exchange for more and more straws. This is the idea of using active learning, "exploration vs. exploitation" mechanisms, and even reinforcement learning models to solve the cold start problem.

In actual work, these two methods are often used in combination. We hope that all "engineers" can quickly pass through the stage of "no straw," and start making their sturdy bricks as soon as possible.

5.7   Exploration vs. Exploitation

The famous story from Aesop's fable talked about a couple who killed the goose that lays the golden eggs. The moral of the story is to negate the practice of doing things only for short-term interests without long-term plans. We use this analogy for recommender systems. All the historical data of users and items is like a goose. If the recommender system only focuses on getting the golden eggs and does not feed the goose, then one day the goose dies and there will be no more golden eggs.

The behavior of "getting the egg" here refers to the fact that the recommender system blindly uses historical data to make recommendations based on user history, and does not pay attention to discovering new interests and new high-quality items for users. On the other hand, the behavior of "feeding the goose" is naturally that the recommender system actively explores new interests, recommends new items, and discovers potential high-quality items.

The opportunities to make recommendations for users are limited. Both recommending content that users like and exploring new interests of users will occupy valuable recommendation opportunities. How should we balance these two things? That's what "exploration vs. exploitation" is trying to solve.

There are currently three main categories of methods to solve the "exploration vs. exploitation" problem.

(1) Traditional methods: These methods simplify the problem into a multiarmed bandit problem. The algorithms include ε-Greedy, Thompson Sampling and UCB. This type of solution focuses on the exploration vs. exploitation of new items. The methods do not consider factors such as users and contexts, so they are non-personalized methods.

(2) Personalized methods: This type of methods effectively combines the personalized recommendation and the idea of exploration vs. exploitation algorithm. It balances exploration and exploitation while considering factors such as users and context. Therefore, they are considered personalized methods.

(3) Model-based methods: This type of methods integrates the ideas of exploration vs. exploitation algorithm into the recommendation model, and effectively combines with the deep learning model, which has become a hot spot in recent years.

5.7.1 Traditional Exploration vs. Exploitation Methods

The traditional exploration vs. exploitation method is actually a Multiarmed Bandit (MAB) problem.

Basics: The Multiarmed Bandit Problem

A person sees some slot machines (a machine with a lever by the side. Insert a certain amount of money, pull the lever, and there will be a random chance to win a certain amount of money). They look exactly the same, but each slot machine has different expectations for rewards. At first, the person doesn't know the expectation and probability distribution of the rewards of these slot machines. If there are N opportunities, what is the best order to select slot machines so that the rewards can be maximized? This is the multiarmed bandit problem (shown in Figure 5.17).

Figure 5.17 Schematic diagram of the multiarmed bandit problem.

In a recommender system, each candidate item is a slot machine, and the system recommending items to users is equivalent to the process of selecting a slot machine. Of course, the recommender system hopes to recommend slot machines with high returns to obtain better overall returns. For example, for a video site, the reward of a slot machine is the user's viewing time. The recommender system recommends a "slot machine" with a higher viewing time expectation to the user to obtain better overall reward and maximize the viewing time of the entire video site.

It is worth noting that in the traditional multiarmed bandit problem, it is assumed that the reward expectation of each slot machine is the same for all users. In other words, this is not a "personalization" problem, but an optimization problem that is separated from the user and only for slot machines. The main algorithms for solving traditional multiarmed bandit problems are ε-Greedy, Thompson Sampling, and UCB.

5.7.1.1 ε-Greedy Algorithm

Here we describe the main process of the ε-Greedy algorithm. Set a number ε in [0,1]. Each time, the probability of randomly choosing from all the slot machines is ε, and the probability of selecting the slot machine with the highest average reward up to now is (1-ε). After pulling the lever, update the reward expectation of the slot machine according to the reward value.

The value of ε here represents the preference for "exploration." Each time, the probability ε is used to "explore," and the probability (1-ε) is used to "exploit," and the reward expectation is updated after the item gets selected. Essentially, "exploration" is actually a process of collecting new information, while "exploitation" is a process of "greedy" utilization of known information. The probability ε is the trade-off between "exploration" and "exploitation."

The ε-Greedy algorithm is a very simple and practical algorithm, but its division of the exploration part and the exploitation part is somewhat rough and blunt. For example, after some iterations of exploration, the benefits of further exploration are not as great as before. At this time, the value of ε should be gradually reduced to increase the proportion of the exploitation part; in addition, exploration with completely "randomized" slot machines is not the most efficient strategy. Some slot machines may have already accumulated enough information, and no further exploration is necessary. At this time, the chance of exploration should be more inclined to the slot machines that have rarely been selected. In order to improve these defects of ε-Greedy algorithm, a heuristic exploration and exploitation algorithm is proposed.

5.7.1.2 Thompson Sampling Algorithm

Thompson Sampling [11] is a classic heuristic exploration vs. exploitation algorithm. The algorithm assumes that the probability of each slot machine winning (assuming the same reward here) is p, and the probability p follows beta (win, lose) distribution. Each slot machine maintains a set of parameters of the beta distribution, namely win, lose. In each trial, choose one slot machine and pull the lever. If it's a win (here, assume the outcome is binary, 0 or 1), then the win parameter of the slot machine is increased by 1, otherwise the lose parameter of the slot machine is increased by 1.

Here is how the slot machine gets selected each time: Use the existing beta distribution of each slot machine to generate a random number b, and do this for each and every machine. Then the slot machine with the largest number will be selected.

In summary, the pseudocode for Thompson Sampling algorithm is shown in Code 5.2.

```
Initialize S_{j,1} = 0, F_{j,1} = 0 for j = 1,...,k
for t = 1,2,..., totalIterations do
    Draw p_{j,t} from Beta(S_{j,t} +1, F_{j,t}+1) for j = 1,...,k
    Play I_t = j for j with maximum p_{j,t}
    Observe reward X_{It,t}
    Update posterior
    Set S_{It,t+1} = S_{It,t}+X_{It,t}
    Set F_{It,t+1} = F_{It,t}+1-X_{It,t}
end for
```

Code 5.2 Pseudocode for Thompson Sampling algorithm

Next, we will further explain why it is assumed that the probability of winning (p) follows beta distribution, and what exactly is beta distribution? The beta distribution is the conjugate prior distribution of Bernoulli distribution. Tossing a coin is a standard Bernoulli process. In this experiment, if a prior distribution is specified for the probability of heads, then this distribution is a beta distribution. Both the CTR scene and the coin tossing can be regarded as a Bernoulli process (the CTR problem can be seen as tossing an eccentric coin, and the click-through rate is the probability of heads). Therefore, Thompson Sampling algorithm is also applicable to use cases such as CTR.

Here is another practical example to explain how Thompson Sampling works. As shown in Figure 5.18, the blue curve for action 1 is beta (600,400) distribution, the green curve for action 2 is beta (400,600) distribution, and the red curve for action 3 is beta (30,70).

Since action 1 and action 2 have each carried out a total of 1000 attempts and accumulated enough data, the uncertainty is already very small. The curves of action 1 and action 2 are very steep, and they peak near their empirical mean of the rewards. But for action 3, however, since only 100 attempts are made, the uncertainty is very large, and the distribution graph is very flat.

When selecting the next action through Thompson Sampling, the expected reward of action 3 is the lowest among the three. If we solely follow the idea of "exploitation," we shall not choose the "slot machine" of action 3; but based on the beta distribution graph of action 3, it is obvious that part of its probability distribution falls on the right side of the distribution of action 1 and 2, and the probability is not small (10–20%). In other words, there is a good chance of selecting the "slot machine" of action 3 through Thompson Sampling. This shows Thompson Sampling's propensity for new items.

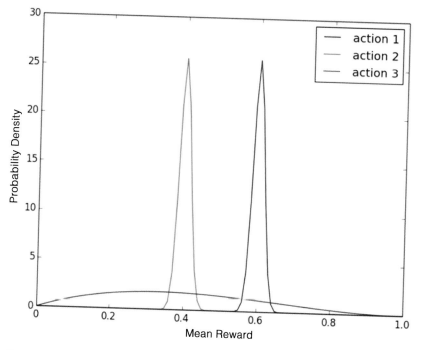

Figure 5.18 Three different beta distributions.

5.7.1.3   UCB Algorithm

UCB is another classic heuristic exploration vs. exploitation algorithm. Similar to the idea of Thompson Sampling, both algorithms use the uncertainty of the distribution as the basis to determine the degree of exploration. But UCB is more convenient for engineering implementation. Here is the algorithm flow of UCB:

(1) Assuming that there are K slot machines, each slot machine is randomly selected m times, and the initial empirical mean $\bar{x}_j$ of machine j's reward is obtained.
(2) Use t to represent the total number of lever-pulls so far, use n_j to represent the number of times the jth machine has been pulled so far, and calculate the UCB value of each machine:

$$\text{UCB}(j) = \bar{x}_j + \sqrt{\frac{2 \log t}{n_j}} \tag{5.12}$$

(3) Select the slot machine i with the largest UCB value, pull the lever, and observe its reward $X_{i,t}$.
(4) Update the expected reward $\bar{x}_i$ of machine i according to $X_{i,t}$.
(5) Repeat steps 2 through 4.

The focus of the UCB algorithm is the calculation of the UCB value. In Equation 5.12, $\bar{x}_j$ represents the expected reward from previous experiments of slot machine j, which can be regarded as the score of "exploitation"; and $\sqrt{\frac{2\log t}{n_j}}$ is the width of the confidence interval, which represents the score of "exploration." The sum of the two is the upper bound of the confidence interval for slot machine j.

Basics: The Origin of the UCB Formula

So where does the UCB formula come from? In fact, the UCB formula is derived based on Hoeffding's inequality.

Suppose there are N independent bounded random variables ranging from 0 to 1, $X_1, X_2, \ldots, X_n$, then the empirical expectation of these n random variables is

$$\overline{X} = \frac{X_1 + \cdots + X_n}{n}$$

Subject to the inequality shown in Equation 5.13:

$$P\left(\overline{X} - E\left[\overline{X}\right] \ge \varepsilon\right) \le e^{-2n\varepsilon^2} \tag{5.13}$$

This is Hoeffding's inequality.

So what is the relationship between Hoeffding's inequality and the upper bound of UCB? Let $\varepsilon = \sqrt{\frac{2\log t}{n_j}}$, and substitute it into Equation 5.13, Hoeffding's inequality can be transformed into Equation 5.14:

$$P\left(\overline{X} - E\left[\overline{X}\right] \ge \sqrt{\frac{2\log t}{n_j}}\right) \le t^{-4} \tag{5.14}$$

From Equation 5.14, we can see that if the upper bound of UCB is $\sqrt{\frac{2\log t}{n_j}}$, then the probability that the difference between the mean value of X and the actual expected value of X is outside the upper bound is very small, less than t^{-4}, which means that using UCB for the upper bound is strict and reasonable.

The rigorous proofs for UCB can be much more theoretical and out of scope of this book. The point here is that the upper bound of UCB is equivalent to the strict confidence interval of the slot machine's expected reward.

Both UCB and Thompson Sampling are common exploration vs. exploitation methods in engineering, but such traditional methods cannot solve the problem of adding personalized features. This severely limits the use of exploration vs. exploitation in personalized recommendation scenarios. Therefore, personalized exploration vs. exploitation methods are proposed.

5.7.2   Personalized Exploration vs. Exploitation Methods

The disadvantage of the traditional exploration vs. exploitation method is that it cannot incorporate the user's context and personalized information, and can only conduct global exploration. In fact, in the user cold start scenario, even a product that has been fully explored is still unfamiliar to the new user, and the user's attitude toward this product is unknown. In addition, the performance of a product in different contexts is also different. For example, a product on the homepage and on the "category" page may have completely different performance due to changes in the context. Therefore, it is very important to incorporate personalized information for traditional exploration vs. exploitation methods. This type of methods is usually called Contextual-Bandit Algorithm. The most representative algorithm is the LinUCB algorithm proposed by Yahoo Labs in 2010 [12].

The name of the LinUCB algorithm reveals its basic principle, where Lin stands for linear, for LinUCB is based on linear recommendation models or CTR prediction models. Its mathematical expression of the linear model is shown in Equation 5.15:

$$E\left[r_{t,a}\,\middle|\,x_{t,a}\right] = x_{t,a}^{\mathrm{T}}\theta_a^*$$

(5.15)

where, $x_{t,a}$ is the feature vector of slot machine a in the tth trial, θ_a^* is the model parameters, and $r_{t,a}$ is the reward obtained by pulling the lever of slot machine a. Therefore, this equation gives the expected return obtained from the slot machine a, under the condition of the feature vector $x_{t,a}$.

In order to obtain the model parameters θ_a^* of each slot machine, Yahoo adopts the classic ridge regression with the linear model, as shown in Equation 5.16.

$$\widehat{\theta_a} = \left(D_a^{\mathrm{T}}D_a + I_d\right)^{-1}D_a^T c_a$$

(5.16)

where I_d is a $d \times d$ unit vector and d refers to the dimension of the feature vector of slot machine a. Matrix D is a $m \times d$ sample matrix. m refers to the m training samples related to slot machine a, and each row of matrix D is the feature matrix of a sample related to slot machine a. Vector c_a is a vector of labels for all samples. It has the same order as the samples in matrix D.

LinUCB follows the basic idea of UCB to calculate the score for exploration, but it needs to extend the traditional UCB method to linear models.

Traditional UCB uses Hoeffding's inequality to obtain the score for exploration, while LinUCB's score for exploration is defined as Equation 5.17:

$$\alpha\sqrt{x_{t,a}^{\mathrm{T}}A_a^{-1}x_{t,a}}$$

(5.17)

where, $x_{t,a}$ is the feature vector of slot machine a, and α is considered to be a hyperparameter that controls the amount of exploration. The definition of matrix A is shown in Equation 5.18:

$$A_a \overset{\text{def}}{=} D_a^{\mathrm{T}}D_a + I_d$$

(5.18)

where, D_a and I_d are defined in Equation 5.16.

This concludes the definitions of the LinUCB algorithm. You may ask – how did the score of the LinUCB exploration part come to be Equation 5.17? The score on the exploration part is essentially an estimate of the uncertainty of the prediction.

The higher the uncertainty, the more likely it is to have a high score. Therefore, the score for exploration in LinUCB is also an estimate of the prediction uncertainty of the linear model.

According to ridge regression, the prediction variance of the model is $x_{t,a}^{\mathrm{T}} A_a^{-1} x_{t,a}$, with $\sqrt{x_{t,a}^{\mathrm{T}} A_a^{-1} x_{t,a}}$ being the standard deviation, which is exactly the score for exploration in LinUCB. Therefore, essentially, whether it is UCB, Thompson Sampling, or LinUCB, it is a measure of prediction uncertainty. For any other predictive model, if you can find a measurement method for prediction uncertainty, you can also construct a corresponding exploration vs. exploitation algorithm.

With the definition of the exploitation part and the exploration part, we can build the algorithm flow of LinUCB, as shown in Code 5.3.

```
for t = 1,2,3,…,T do
    Observe features of all arms a  a ∈ A_t, x_{t,a} ∈ R^d
    for all  a ∈ A_t  do
        if a is new then
```
$$A_a \leftarrow I_d \left(d - dimensional\ identity\ matrix \right)$$
$$b_a \leftarrow 0_{d \times 1} \left(d - dimensional\ zero\ vector \right)$$
```
        end if
```
$$\hat{\theta}_a \leftarrow A_a^{-1} b_a$$
$$p_{t,a} \leftarrow \hat{\theta}_a^{\mathrm{T}} x_{t,a} + \alpha \sqrt{x_{a,a}^{\mathrm{T}} A_a^{-1} x_{t,a}}$$
```
    end for
    Choose arm a_t = arg max_{a∈A_t} p_{t,a} with ties broken arbitrarily,
    and observe a real-valued payoff r_t
```
$$A_{a_t} \leftarrow A_{a_t} + x_{t,a_t} x_{t,a_t}^{\mathrm{T}}$$
$$b_{a_t} \leftarrow b_{a_t} + r_t x_{t,a_t}$$
```
end for
```

Code 5.3 Pseudocode for the LinUCB algorithm

This pseudocode shows that this framework of the algorithm is consistent with that of Thompson Sampling and UCB. The only difference is that it uses LinUCB to calculate the exploration vs. exploitation score when selecting slot machines, and ridge regression is required for updating the model.

Undoubtedly, the proposal of LinUCB has greatly enhanced the accuracy of model prediction and the pertinence of exploration. However, LinUCB also has its limitations. As mentioned, in order to find a suitable exploration score for the linear model, LinUCB needs strict analytical support to obtain the specific form of the predicted standard deviation. As recommendation models enter the era of deep learning, it is difficult to explicitly express the mathematical terms of the deep learning model, and it is almost impossible to obtain the standard deviation of prediction through strict analytical derivation. Under such circumstances, how can we combine the idea of exploration vs. exploitation with deep learning models?

5.7.3 Model-Based Exploration vs. Exploitation Methods

Whether it is the traditional or the personalized exploration vs. exploitation method, there is a significant problem – it cannot be effectively integrated with the deep learning model. For example, for LinUCB, the assumption of the application is that the recommendation model is a linear model. The theoretical framework of LinUCB will no longer work with deep learning models.

So if the CTR prediction model or the recommendation model is a deep learning model, how can we effectively integrate it with the idea of exploration vs. exploitation? Let's review the reinforcement learning model DRN from Section 3.10 one more time.

In DRN, for a trained network Q, a new model parameter $\tilde{W}$ is obtained by adding a small random perturbation ΔW to the parameter W. Here, the network corresponding to $\tilde{W}$ is called the exploration network $\tilde{Q}$. Then the system's real-time feedback is used to decide whether to keep the exploration network $\tilde{Q}$ or to continue using the current network Q.

We can see that DRN is nonheuristic for the exploration process of deep learning models, but being independent of model structure also makes this method applicable to any deep learning model. It effectively combines the idea of exploration vs. exploitation with deep learning models, and explores to optimize the model by randomly perturbing the model parameters.

At the same time, the random perturbation of model parameters also brings changes and updates to the recommendation results, which naturally realizes the exploration of different content, which is direct embodiment of the idea of "exploration vs. exploitation" in the DRN model.

5.7.4 Application of the "Exploration vs. Exploitation" Mechanism in Recommender Systems

There are various applications of exploration vs. exploitation in recommender systems, which mainly includes the following three aspects:

(1) Item cold start. For newly added items or tail items that have no interaction for a long time, the exploration vs. exploitation algorithm has a natural tendency to select, so it can help such items quickly collect user feedback and get through the cold start period. It can effectively find promising items and enrich the item candidate set without undermining the overall revenue of the system.

(2) Discover new interests of users. As mentioned at the beginning of this section, if the recommender system always uses existing data to recommend items for users, it will eventually deplete the user's discovered interests. The user may be satisfied with the current recommendation results for a while, but will very likely get tired quickly and leave. In order to discover new interests of users, it is necessary for the recommender system to carry out a certain degree of exploration to keep the

user's long-term interests. In addition, user interest itself is constantly changing and evolving, and it is necessary to stay on top of the changing trend of user interest through exploration.

(3) Increase the diversity of results. Exploration vs. exploitation algorithms are also means to increase the diversity of recommendation results. There are two main benefits of increasing the results diversity for recommender systems. On the one hand, it allows users to clearly feel the richness of the content; On the other hand, it reduces the boredom of seeing a large amount of homogeneous content appearing together.

In general, the idea of exploration vs. exploitation is an indispensable complement to all recommender systems. Compared with the optimization goal – using existing data to maximize the benefits under current conditions, exploration vs. exploitation is actually focusing on the future. It focuses on the long-term interests of users and the long-term benefits of the company. Not only do engineers need to fully understand this, but also the decision-makers who formulate goals need to have a deeper understanding and make decisions that are more conducive to the long-term development of the company.

References

[1] Xiao Lin. Dual averaging methods for regularized stochastic learning and online optimization. *Journal of Machine Learning Research*, 11, 2010: 2543–2596.

[2] H. Brendan Mcmahan, et al. Ad click prediction: A view from the trenches. Proceedings of the 19th ACM SIGKDD International Conference on Knowledge Discovery and Data Mining, Chicago, IL, USA, August 11–14, 2013.

[3] Paul Covington, Jay Adams, Emre Sargin. Deep neural networks for YouTube recommenders. Proceedings of the 10th ACM Conference on Recommender Systems, Boston, MA, USA, September 15–19, 2016.

[4] Xiao Ma, et al. Entire space multi-task model: An effective approach for estimating post-click conversion rate. The 41st International ACM SIGIR Conference on Research & Development in Information Retrieval, Ann Arbor, MI, USA, July 8–12, 2018.

[5] Robert A. Jacobs, Michael I. Jordan, Steven J. Nowlan, Geoffrey E. Hinton. Adaptive mixtures of local experts. *Neural Computations*, 3, 1991: 79–87.

[6] Jiaqi Ma, Zhe Zhao, Xinyang Yi, Jilin Chen, Lichan Hong, Ed H. Chi. Modeling task relationships in multi-task learning with multi-gate mixture-of-experts. Proceedings of the 24th ACM SIGKDD International Conference on Knowledge Discovery & Data Mining, London, UK, August 19–23, 2018.

[7] Hongyan Tang, Junning Liu, Ming Zhao, Xudong Gong. Progressive layered extraction (PLE): A novel multi-task learning (MTL) model for personalized recommendations. Proceedings of the 14th ACM Conference on Recommender Systems, Brazil [virtual event], September 22–26, 2020.

[8] Fernando Amat, et al. Artwork personalization at Netflix. Proceedings of the 12th ACM Conference on Recommender Systems, Vancouver, BC, Canada, October 2–7, 2018.

[9] Mehdi Elahi, Francesco Ricci, Neil Rubens. A survey of active learning in collaborative filtering recommender systems. *Computer Science Review*, 20, 2016: 29–50.

[10] Peter Auer, Nicolo Cesa-Bianchi, Paul Fischer. Finite-time analysis of the multiarmed bandit problem. *Machine Learning*, 47(2–3), 2002: 235–256.

[11] Olivier Chapelle, Lihong Li. An empirical evaluation of Thompson sampling. *Advances in Neural Information Processing Systems*, 24, 2011: 1872.

[12] Lihong Li, et al. A contextual-bandit approach to personalized news article recommender. Proceedings of the 19th International Conference on World Wide Web, Raleigh, NC, USA, April 26–30, 2010.

6 Engineering Implementations in Deep Learning Recommender Systems

In previous chapters, we introduced the key technical points of deep learning recommender systems from multiple perspectives, mainly from the theoretical and algorithm aspects. However, algorithms and models are only "good wine"; after all, they must be served in a suitable "container" to present the best taste. The "container" here refers to the engineering platform that implements the recommender systems.

From an engineering perspective, recommender systems can be divided into two parts – data and model. The data part mainly covers the related engineering implementations of the data pipeline needed by recommender systems, while the model part refers to the development of the recommendation model. Furthermore, the model development can be further divided into offline training and online serving based on the different stages of model application. Following the overall engineering architecture of recommender systems, this chapter is presented in three parts:

(1) Data pipeline of recommender systems. We will introduce the main framework of the big data platform associated with data pipeline in a recommender system and the mainstream technologies for implementing the big data platform.
(2) Offline training of deep learning recommendation models. It mainly introduces the popular platforms for training deep learning recommendation models, such as Spark MLlib, Parameter Server (parameter server), TensorFlow, and PyTorch.
(3) Online deployment of deep learning recommendation models. We will cover the technical approaches to deploying deep learning recommendation models and the process of model online serving.

In addition to the engineering frameworks, we will also discuss the trade-off between engineering implementation and theory. Then we will share some of our thoughts on how algorithm engineers should make trade-offs balance between practice and theory.

6.1 Data Pipeline in Recommender Systems

In this section, we will walk through the data processing pipeline for training and serving recommendation models. Since 2003, when Google successively published three foundational papers in the field of Big Table [1], Google File System [2], and Map Reduce [3], the recommendation system has also entered the big data era. With

TB or even PB size of training data, the data pipeline of recommender systems must be closely integrated with the big data processing and storage infrastructure to complete efficient training and online inferencing.

The development of big data platforms has gone through various stages from batch processing to stream computing, and then to full integration. The continuous development of architectural patterns has brought a substantial improvement in the freshness and flexibility of data processing. Following the order of development, the big data platform mainly includes four architectural modes: batch processing, stream computing, Lambda, and Kappa.

6.1.1   Batch Processing

Before the birth of the big data platform, it was difficult for traditional databases to deal with the storage and processing of massive data. In response to this problem, a distributed storage system represented by Google GFS and Apache HDFS was developed, which solved the problem of mass data storage. In order to further solve the problem of data processing, the Map Reduce framework was introduced, where data are distributed and computed across machines in "Map" steps followed by "Reduce" operation to achieve massive data manipulation in parallel. The "distributed storage + Map Reduce" architecture can only process static data that has been placed on the disk in batches but cannot process data during the data collection and transfer. That's also where the name "batch processing" is from.

Compared with the classic data processing process on a traditional database, the batch processing architecture replaces the original data storage and computing method relying on the traditional file system and database with the distributed file system and Map Reduce. The schematic diagram of the batch processing architecture is shown in Figure 6.1.

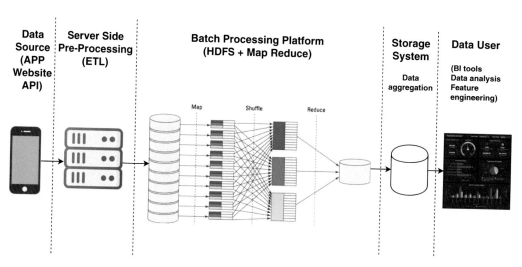

Figure 6.1 Schematic diagram of batch processing.

However, this architecture can only process the data loaded in a distributed file system, so there will be significant data delay, which can cause a significant impact on the real-time performance of some applications. As a result, the stream processing solution came into being.

6.1.2 Big Data Stream Processing

The big data stream processing architecture consumes and processes the data stream during data generation and transfer (as shown in Figure 6.2). The concept of sliding windows in stream processing is very important. Within each "window," data is temporarily cached and then consumed. After completing the data processing of one window, the stream computing platform slides to the next time window for a new round of processing. Therefore, in theory, the delay of data in stream processing is only determined by the size of the sliding window. In practical applications, the size of the sliding window is basically at the minute level, which greatly improves the data delay by several hours compared with the batch processing approach.

There are multiple open-source stream processing frameworks that are popular in the market, including Storm, Spark Streaming, Flink, and others. Flink emerged in recent years. It treats all data as streams and considers batch processing as a special case of stream processing. So Flink can be viewed as a native stream processing framework.

The stream processing framework can not only process a single data stream, but also perform join operations on multiple different data streams to combine the data within the same time window. In addition, the output of a stream process can also become the input of downstream applications, and the entire stream computing architecture is flexible and reconfigurable. Therefore, the advantages of stream computing big data architecture are obvious, that is, small data delay and flexibility in data pipeline configuration. This is very helpful for data monitoring, real-time updates of recommender systems' features, and online training of recommendation models.

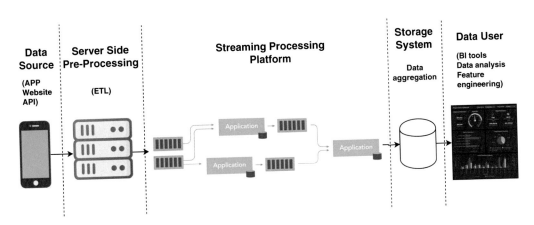

Figure 6.2 Schematic diagram of stream processing.

However, the stream processing architecture has drawbacks in some application use cases, such as data legality check, data playback, and full data analysis. Especially when the sliding window is very small, log disordering and data loss induced by join operations will accumulate data errors. So the data pipeline with solely stream processing is not perfect for all cases. This requires that some new big data architecture can integrate stream processing and batch processing to a certain extent and take advantage of each other's strengths.

6.1.3   Lambda Architecture

Lambda architecture is an important architecture in the field of big data. The data platforms of most first-tier internet companies are basically built based on the Lambda architecture or its subsequent variants.

The data pipeline of the Lambda architecture splits the data collection stage into two branches – stream computing and offline processing. The stream computing branch maintains the stream processing architecture to ensure the freshness of data, while the offline processing part is mainly based on batch processing, which ensures the eventual consistency of data and provides the system with more data processing options. Figure 6.3 shows the schematic diagram of the Lambda architecture.

To maintain the freshness of data, stream computing is mainly based on incremental computing, while the offline processing part performs full operations on the data to ensure its eventual consistency and the diversity of the final recommendation systems features. Before storing the statistical data in the final database, the Lambda architecture often merges the streaming data and the offline data. Then it uses the offline data to check and correct the streaming data, which is an important step in the Lambda architecture.

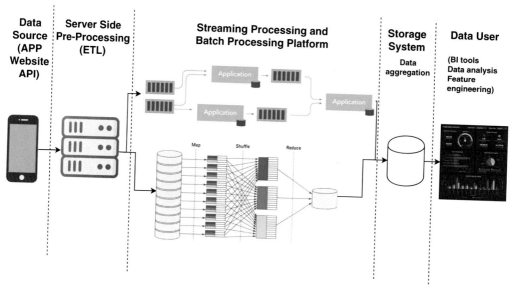

Figure 6.3 Schematic diagram of Lambda architecture.

Lambda architecture can simultaneously possess both real-time processing and batch processing capabilities. It is a popular framework currently adopted by many companies. However, due to the large amount of logical redundancy in the streaming and offline processing parts, there are lots of repetitive codes thus many computing resources are wasted. Is it possible to further integrate the streaming and offline pipelines?

6.1.4 Kappa Architecture

Kappa architecture was created to solve the code redundancy problem in the Lambda architecture. Kappa architecture adheres to the principle of "Everything is streaming." With this principle, all the data processing is treated as stream processing no matter it is actual real-time streaming or offline processing. In this case, offline batch is just a special case of "stream processing." In a sense, the Kappa architecture can also be seen as an "upgraded" version of the stream processing architecture.

So specifically, how does the Kappa architecture handle batch processing through the same stream processing framework? In fact, batch processing also has the concept of a time window. But compared with stream processing, this time window is relatively large. The time window of stream processing may be five minutes, while batch processing may use one day. Considering this, batch processing can fully share the computing logic of stream processing.

Since the time window of batch processing is too long, it is impossible to implement it by stream processing in an online environment. Then, the problem becomes how to use the same stream processing framework to perform data batch processing in an offline environment.

In order to solve this problem, two new components, raw data storage and data replay, need to be added to the stream processing framework. Raw data storage saves the original data or logs in the distributed file system, and data replay components replay these original data in chronological order and process them with the same stream processing framework to achieve batch processing offline. This is the main idea of the Kappa architecture (as shown in Figure 6.4).

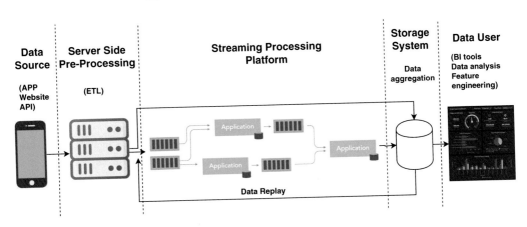

Figure 6.4 Schematic diagram of Kappa architecture.

Kappa architecture fundamentally completes the unification of stream and offline processing from Lambda architecture. It is a very beautiful and concise big data architecture. However, in the process of engineering implementation, there are still some difficulties in the Kappa architecture, such as the efficiency of the data replay and the issue of whether batch processing and stream processing operations can be fully shared. Therefore, Lambda architecture is still dominating the industry. But there have been some trends to gradually migrate to the Kappa architecture.

6.1.5 Integration of Big Data Platforms and Recommender Systems

The relationship between big data platforms and recommender systems is very close. In Section 5.3, we have introduced the importance of freshness in recommender systems in detail. Both the freshness of model features and the model itself heavily depend on the big data processing speed. More specifically, the integration of big data platforms and recommender systems is mainly reflected in two aspects:

(1) Training data processing.
(2) Feature precomputation.

As shown in Figure 6.5, no matter which big data architecture is adopted, the main task of the big data pipeline in the recommender system is to process features and training samples. According to different business use cases, after the feature processing is completed, the training sample and feature data eventually flow in two directions:

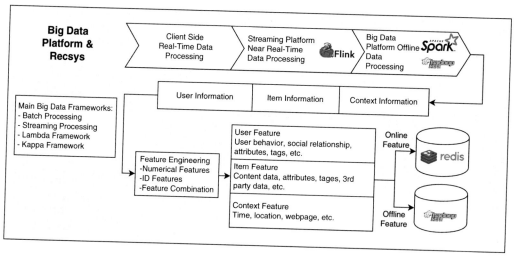

Figure 6.5 Integration of big data platform and recommender systems.
Apache Hadoop, Hadoop, the Apache Hadoop Logo, Apache Flink, Flink, the Apache Flink Logo, Apache Spark, Spark, the Apache Spark Logo and Apache are either registered trademarks or trademarks of the Apache Software Foundation. Redis is a registered trademark of Redis Ltd. Any rights therein are reserved to Redis Ltd. Any use by Cambridge is for referential purposes only and does not indicate any sponsorship, endorsement or affiliation between Redis and Cambridge.

(1) The offline big data storage is represented by HDFS. It is mainly responsible for storing samples for offline training.

(2) The online feature store is represented by Redis. It is mainly responsible for providing real-time features for online inferencing.

The choice of big data architecture is closely related to how the recommendation model is trained. If the recommendation model wants to perform near-real-time or even real-time training updates, the requirements of the big data pipeline's processing capabilities will be very high. It requires a stream processing framework to perform feature engineering calculations in real-time, joining operations on multiple data streams, and integrating the model updates in the data pipeline.

The architecture with the machine learning layer included is also known as unified big data architecture. The machine learning layer is added to the stream processing layer in a Lambda or Kappa architecture, which deeply integrates machine learning training and data processing.

After all, the relationship between recommender systems and big data platforms is inseparable in internet applications which generate massive data. All the cutting-edge recommender systems in the industry need deep integration with big data technologies to complete the entire process of training, updating, and online serving.

6.2   Spark MLlib for Offline Recommendation Model Training

We would like to make an analogy between recommender systems and cooking. Whether a chef can make a good dish depends on three key points:

(1) Qualities of the cooking ingredients, like whether they are sufficient and fresh.
(2) Cooking skills of the chef.
(3) Performance while cooking. Whether the chef can make the best use of the materials and how well the chef can perform while cooking.

Correspondingly, the data collected in recommender systems are the "cooking ingredients," and the richness and freshness of data are equivalent to the "sufficiency" and "freshness" of these ingredients. The offline training model of the recommender system corresponds to the chef's training process. The more the chef is trained, the more types of cooking materials he has tried, the better his cooking skills could be. The online serving of recommendation systems can be analogized to the process of the chef "presenting his cooking skills." A good dish cooked by the chef on-site doesn't not only require all the ingredients to have consistently high quality as usual, but also requires high standards during the cooking process and making suitable adjustments based on the customer's taste.

Next, we will introduce how the recommender system trains its "cooking skills" in an offline environment, and how to keep "high performance" on-site, so that the online service can provide real-time recommendations that best suit the user's "taste."

In internet applications such as recommendation, advertising, and search, the massive data volume in the size of terabyte or even petabyte-level makes it almost impossible to complete the model training in a single-machine environment. Distributed machine learning training provides a solution. With respect to the offline model training, we will introduce three mainstream solutions for distributed machine learning training, respectively – Spark MLlib, Parameter Server, and TensorFlow. They are not the only frameworks to choose from, but also represent three main approaches in distributed training. In this section, we will start with Spark MLlib and describe how it handles the problem of parallel training as the most popular big data framework.

Although challenged by rising stars such as Flink, Spark is still the most popular computing framework in the industry. Many companies choose Spark's native machine learning framework, MLlib, for model training to maintain consistency with the technology stack adopted in the data and model pipeline. Spark MLlib became the first choice for distributed training in machine learning, not only because Spark is widely adopted, but also because Spark MLlib's parallel training approach represents a naive and intuitive solution.

6.2.1   Distributed Computing Mechanism in Spark

Before introducing the distributed machine learning method in Spark MLlib, let's first review Spark's distributed computing mechanisms.

Spark is a distributed computing platform. Here, distributed computing means that computing nodes do not share memory and need to exchange data through network communication. It should be noted that the most typical application mode of Spark is to build on a large number of cheap computing nodes, which can be cheap hosts or virtual Docker Containers. This method is different from CPU+GPU architecture, as well as the high-performance server architecture with shared massive memory and multiprocessors. Knowing this is important for understanding the following computing mechanisms of Spark.

As illustrated in the Spark architecture diagram (Figure 6.6), the Spark program is scheduled and organized by the cluster manager (a cluster management node). Specific computing tasks are conducted on worker nodes, and results are returned to the driver program. Data may also be divided into different partitions on a physical worker node. It can be said that a partition is the basic processing unit of Spark.

When executing a specific program, Spark will disassemble it into a task DAG (directed acyclic graph), and then determine the execution method of each step of the program according to the DAG. Figure 6.7 shows the DAG of a sample Spark job. The job reads files from textFile and hadoopFile, respectively, joins after a series of operations, and finally obtains the processing result.

When executing the DAG shown in Figure 6.7 on the Spark platform, the most critical process is to find which components can be processed in parallel and which components must be shuffled and reduced.

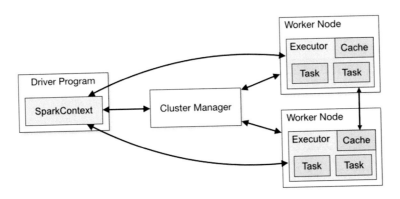

Figure 6.6 Spark architecture diagram.

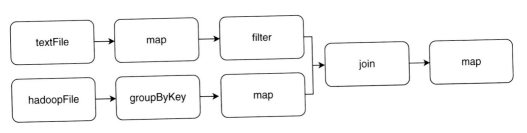

Figure 6.7 A DAG example of one Spark job.

The shuffle here means that the data needs to be redistributed to all partitions before proceeding to the next step. The most typical operations where shuffle can occur are the groupByKey operation and the join operation. Taking the join operation as an example, the textFile data and hadoopFile data must be matched globally to obtain the result data frame (a data structure in Spark) after joining. The group-ByKey operation needs to merge all the same keys in the data, thus also needs a global shuffle to complete.

In contrast, operations such as map and filter only need to process data one by one, and do not need to perform operations between data entries. This is so each partition can process its own data share, and data partitions can be processed in parallel.

In addition, before the program renders the final output, it needs to perform a reduced operation to summarize the results from each partition. As the number of partitions gradually decreases, the parallelism of the reduced operation gradually decreases until the final results are aggregated to the master node.

It can be said that the occurrence of shuffle and reduce operations determines the boundaries of purely parallel processing stages. As shown in Figure 6.8, Spark's DAG is divided into different parallel processing stages.

It should be emphasized that the shuffle operation requires data transfer between different worker nodes, which consumes a lot of computing, communication, and storage resources. Therefore, the shuffle operation should be avoided as much as

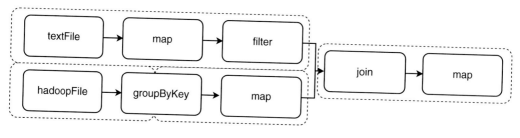

Figure 6.8 DAG split by shuffle operations.

possible in any Spark jobs. In summary, the components inside each stage can be computed parallelly and efficiently, and the shuffle operation or the reduce operation that consumes the most resources usually defines the stage boundary.

6.2.2   Parallel Training Mechanism in Spark MLlib

With the foundation of Spark's distributed computing process, you can more clearly understand the model parallel training mechanism in Spark MLlib.

The model structure can determine the degree of parallelism it has in the training process. For example, a Random Forest model can fully perform data-parallel model training, while the structural characteristics of GBDT determine that it can only be trained sequentially. In this section, we will focus on the implementation of gradient descent method, because the parallelism of gradient descent directly determines the training speed of deep learning models.

In order to more accurately understand the specific implementation of the Spark parallel gradient descent method, we will dive deep into the source code of Spark MLlib, and directly post the source code of Spark for minibatch gradient descent (the code is taken from the runMiniBatchSGD function of the Spark 2.4.3 GradientDescent class):

```
while (!converged && i <= numIterations) {
  val bcWeights = data.context.broadcast(weights)
  // Sample a subset (fraction miniBatchFraction) of the
    total data
  // compute and sum up the subgradients on this subset (this is
    one map-reduce)
  val (gradientSum, lossSum, miniBatchSize) = data.sample
    (false, miniBatchFraction, 42 + i)
    .treeAggregate((BDV.zeros[Double](n), 0.0, 0L))(
      seqOp = (c, v) => {
        // c: (grad, loss, count), v: (label, features)
        val l = gradient.compute(v._2, v._1, bcWeights.value,
          Vectors.fromBreeze(c._1))
        (c._1, c._2 + l, c._3 + 1)
      },
```

```
    combOp = (c1, c2) => {
// c: (grad, loss, count)
       (c1._1 += c2._1, c1._2 + c2._2, c1._3 + c2._3)
    })
 bcWeights.destroy(blocking = false)

 if (miniBatchSize > 0) {
   /**
     * lossSum is computed using the weights from the previous
       iteration
     * and regVal is the regularization value computed in the
       previous iteration as well.
     */
   stochasticLossHistory += lossSum / miniBatchSize + regVal
   val update = updater.compute(
     weights, Vectors.fromBreeze(gradientSum / miniBatchSize.
       toDouble),
     stepSize, i, regParam)
   weights = update._1
   regVal = update._2

   previousWeights = currentWeights
   currentWeights = Some(weights)
   if (previousWeights != None && currentWeights != None) {
     converged = isConverged(previousWeights.get,
       currentWeights.get, convergenceTol)
   }
 } else {
   logWarning(s"Iteration ($i/$numIterations). The size of
     sampled batch is zero")
 }
 i += 1
 }
```

This code looks complicated at first glance. But after we extract the key operations as shown next, the main process of Spark gradient descent calculation turns easy to understand.

```
while (i <= numIterations) {      //limit the maximum iterations
    val bcWeights = data.context.broadcast(weights)//broadcasting
      all the weights
    val (gradientSum, lossSum, miniBatchSize) = data.sample
      (false, miniBatchFraction, 42 + i)
    .treeAggregate()      //compute the gradient in each sample,
      then get gradientSum using treeAggregate function
    val weights = updater.compute(weights, gradientSum /
      miniBatchSize)//update the weights based on gradients
    i += 1                          //iteration + 1
 }
```

This simplified code is quite easy to understand. Basically, Spark's minibatch process has three steps:

(1) Broadcast the current model parameters to each data partition (which can be used as a virtual computing node).
(2) Each computing node performs data sampling to obtain minibatch data, calculates the gradients separately, and then aggregates the gradients through the treeAggregate operation to obtain the final gradientSum.
(3) Use gradientSum to update model weights.

In this way, the boundaries of stages in each iteration are very clear. The parallel part inside each stage is the process of sampling and calculating the gradient of each node separately, and the boundary of stage is the process of summarizing and summing the gradient of each node. Here we will highlight the operation treeAggregate, which aggregates the gradients from all the nodes. This operation is a layer-by-layer aggregation based on a tree-like structure. The whole process is a reduce operation and does not include a shuffle operation. In addition, a hierarchical tree operation is used. Tree node operations are performed in parallel, so the whole process is very efficient.

After the number of iterations reaches the upper limit or the model has sufficiently converged, the model stops training. This is the whole process of minibatch gradient descent calculation in Spark MLlib, and it is also the most representative implementation of distributed model training in Spark MLlib.

In summary, Spark MLlib's parallel training process is actually through data parallelism, which does not involve a complex gradient update strategy, and does not implement parallel training through parameter parallelism. This method is simple, intuitive, and easy to implement, but there are also some limitations.

6.2.3   Limitations of Spark MLlib Parallel Training

Although Spark MLlib is based on distributed computing and uses data parallelism to achieve parallel training of gradient descent, the limitations of Spark MLlib parallel training are also very obvious while training a complex neural network. The issues are mainly slow training speed and memory overflow when there are too many model parameters. Specifically, Spark MLlib's distributed training method has the following drawbacks:

(1) The global broadcast method is adopted to broadcast all model parameters before each iteration. As we all know, Spark's broadcasting process consumes a lot of resources, especially when the parameter scale is very large. The broadcasting process and maintaining a copy of the weight parameters at each node are extremely resource-intensive, which induces poor performance with complex models.
(2) While using the block gradient descent method, each round of gradient descent is determined by the slowest node. From the source code of Spark gradient descent, it can be seen that the minibatch process of Spark MLlib is to

aggregate the gradient layer by layer after all nodes calculate their respective gradients, and finally generate the global gradient. If some problem such as data skew causes a node to take too long to calculate the gradient, it will block all other nodes from performing the next tasks. This synchronized block distributed gradient calculation method is the main reason for the low efficiency of Spark MLlib parallel training.

(3) Spark MLlib does not support complex deep learning network structures and large-scale hyperparameter tuning. Additionally, Spark MLlib only supports standard MLP training in its standard library, and does not support complex network structures such as RNN and LSTM. It cannot conduct large-scale hyperparameter tuning such as different activation functions. All these drawbacks make Spark MLlib less competitive in deep learning applications.

As a result, we need a more robust deep learning framework with higher training efficiency and support for more flexible network structures. Considering these, Parameter Server becomes the mainstream framework for distributed machine learning with its efficient distributed training methods. And deep learning platforms such as TensorFlow and PyTorch have become the top choices in distributed machine learning systems due to their flexibility on network structure adjustments, and comprehensive training and serving support. The next section introduces the main mechanisms of Parameter Server and TensorFlow, respectively.

6.3 Parameter Server for Offline Recommendation Model Training

In Section 6.2, we gave a detailed introduction to the parallel training method in Spark MLlib. Spark adopts a simple and direct data-parallel method to solve the problem of model parallel training. But Spark's parallel gradient descent method is using synchronized blocking approach, and the model parameters need to be transferred to all nodes through global broadcasting. These processes make Spark's parallel gradient descent calculation relatively inefficient.

In order to solve this problem, the Parameter Server [4,5], a distributed and scalable framework, was proposed in 2014. It almost perfectly solves the distributed training problem of machine learning models. Today, Parameter Server is not only directly adopted in the machine learning platforms of some big companies, but also integrated into mainstream deep learning frameworks such as TensorFlow and MXNet, as an important solution for distributed training of machine learning.

6.3.1 Mechanisms of Distributed Training in Parameter Server

First, take a general machine learning problem as an example to explain the mechanism of Parameter Server distributed training.

$$Fw = \sum_{i=1}^{n} \ell\left(x_i, y_i, w\right) + \Omega\left(w\right) \tag{6.1}$$

Equation 6.1 shows a general loss function with a regularization term, where n is the total number of samples, $\ell(x_i, y_i, w)$ is the loss function for calculating a single sample i. x_i is the feature vector, y_i is the sample label, and w represents the model parameters. The training objective of the model is to minimize the loss function $F(w)$. To solve $\arg\min F(w)$, gradient descent is often used. The main function of the Parameter Server is to perform the gradient descent calculation in parallel, and update of the model parameters until the final convergence. It should be noted that the regularization term in the formula requires summarizing all model parameters, which makes it difficult to perform fully parallel training. Therefore, Parameter Server adopts the same data-parallel training approach as Spark MLlib to generate local gradients, and then aggregate all the gradients to update the model weights.

The pseudocode of parallel gradient descent calculation in Parameter Server are shown in Code 6.1:

```
Task Scheduler:
  issue LoadData() to all workers        //Overall parallel training task
                                          //distribute the data to each
                                          //   worker node
  for iteration t = 0,…,T do             // conduct T iterations
    Issue WORKERITERATE(t) to all workers // execute WORKERITERATE function on
                                          //   each worker
  end for

Worker r = 1,…,m:
  function LOADDATA()                     //initialize worker
    load a part of training data {y_{i_k}, x_{i_k}}_{k=1}^{n_r}   //load training data into each
                                          //   worker node
    pull the working set w_r^{(0)} from servers  //each worker node pull the related
                                          //   initial model
                                          //weights from the server
  end function
  function WORKERITERATE(t)               //iterative function for worker
                                          //   node
    gradient g_r^{(t)} ← Σ_{k=1}^{n_r} ∂l(x_{i_k}, y_{i_k}, w_r^{(t)})  //calculate the gradient using the
                                          //   local training data
    push g_r^{(t)} to servers             //push the gradient to server
    pull w_r^{(t+1)} from servers         //pull the new model weights
  end function

Servers:
  function SERVERITERATE(t)               //iterative function on server node
    aggregate g^{(t)} ← Σ_{r=1}^{m} g_r^{(t)}  //aggregate the gradients after
                                          //   receiving from m
                                          //worker nodes
    w^{(t+1)} ← w^{(t)} - η(g^{(t)} + ∂Ω(w^{(t)}))  //combine the aggregated gradient and
                                          //   regulation
                                          //term gradient to get the update
                                          //   total gradient
end function
```

Code 6.1 Parallel gradient descent process in Parameter Server

It can be seen that the Parameter Server consists of server nodes and worker nodes, and their main functions are as follows:

- The main function of the server node is to save the model weights, receive the local gradient calculated by the worker node, aggregate and calculate the global gradient, and update the model parameters.
- The main function of the worker node is to load some training data, pull the latest model parameters from the server node, calculate the local gradient based on the training data, and upload it to the server node.

From the perspective of the framework architecture, the manager–worker structure of Parameter Server and Spark are basically the same, as shown in Figure 6.9.

As illustrated in Figure 6.9, Parameter Server consists of two major components – server group and multiple worker groups. The resource manager is responsible for overall resource allocation and scheduling.

The server node group contains multiple server nodes, each of which is responsible for maintaining some parameters. The server manager in the server node group is responsible for maintaining and allocating server resources.

Each work node group corresponds to an application (that is, a model training task). There is no communication between the work node groups or the task nodes within the same work node group. The task nodes only communicate with the server.

Based on the architecture of Parameter Server, the process of parallel training process is depicted in Figure 6.10.

Two important operations in the parallel gradient descent process of Parameter Server are push and pull:

- **Push Operation:** The worker node uses the local training data to calculate the local gradient and upload it to the server node.
- **Pull Operation:** The worker node pulls the latest model parameters from the server node to the local to perform the next round of gradient calculation.

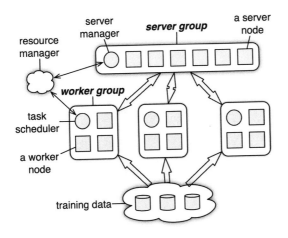

Figure 6.9 Architecture of Parameter Server.

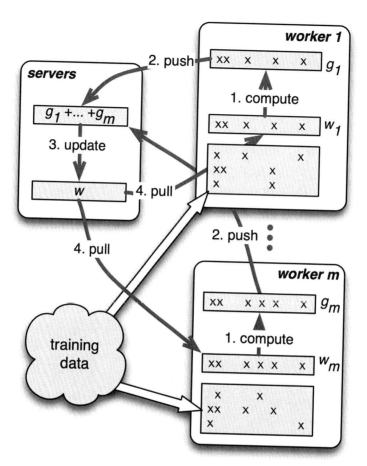

Figure 6.10 Schematic diagram of the parallel training process in Parameter Server.

Following the illustration in Figure 6.10, the whole parallel training process in Parameter Server can be summarized as follows:

(a) Each worker node loads a portion of the training data.
(b) Each worker node pulls the latest model parameters from the server node.
(c) Each worker node calculates the gradient based on local training data.
(d) Worker nodes push the gradients to the server node.
(e) The server node collects all the gradients and aggregates to update the model.
(f) Repeat from step (b) until the total iterations reach the upper limit or the model has converged.

6.3.2 Trade-Off between Consistency and Parallel Efficiency

When summarizing Spark's parallel gradient descent mechanism, we mentioned that the reason of low efficiency in Spark was caused by the "synchronized blocking" in the calculation.

This parallel gradient descent process requires that (1) the gradients of all nodes are calculated, (2) the master node aggregates the gradients, and (3) the new model parameters are updated before the next round of gradient calculation can begin. This means that the "slowest" node blocks the gradient update process of all other nodes.

On the other hand, the "synchronized blocking" parallel gradient descent is the most "consistent" gradient descent method, because its calculation results are strictly consistent with those of sequential gradient descent on a single machine.

So is there any way to improve the parallel efficiency of gradient descent with some balance of consistency?

Parameter Server replaces the original "synchronized blocking" method with "asynchronized non-blocking" gradient descent. Figure 6.11 shows the process of calculating the gradients in multiple iterations of a worker node. It can be seen that when the node is conducting the 11th iteration (iter 11) calculation, the push and pull process of the 10th iteration has not ended. That is to say, the latest model parameters after iter 10 have not been pulled to the local in iter 11. In iter 11, the node calculates the gradient still using the same model parameters as those used in iter 10. This is the so-called asynchronized non-blocking gradient descent method, and the progress of other nodes in calculating the gradient will not affect the gradient calculation of current node. All nodes are always working in parallel and will not be blocked by other nodes.

Of course, any technical solution is based on certain trade-offs. Although the asynchronized gradient update method greatly speeds up the training speed, it sacrifices the model consistency. That is to say, the results of parallel training are inconsistent with the results of the original single-thread sequential training, and such inconsistency will have a certain impact on the speed of model convergence. So the final choice of synchronized update or asynchronized update depends on the sensitivity of different models to consistency. This is similar to a model hyperparameter selection problem, which requires specific validations case by case.

In addition, between synchronized and asynchronized, you can also control the degree of asynchronized calculation by setting parameters such as max delay. For example, we can configure that the model parameters must be updated at once within three iterations. If a worker node has calculated three gradients and has not completed the process of pulling the latest model parameters from the server node, the worker node must stop and wait for the completion of the pull operation. This is a compromise between synchronized and asynchronized calculation.

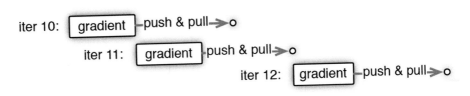

Figure 6.11 The process of calculating the gradient in multiple iterations.

This section describes the difference between synchronized and asynchronized updates in the parallel gradient descent method. In terms of efficiency, users need to monitor the following two indicators:

(1) How much waiting time can be saved by "asynchronized" updates?
(2) "Asynchronized" updates will reduce the consistency of gradient updates. Will it take the model longer to converge?

In response to these two questions, the original Parameter Server paper provided a comparison of the efficiency of asynchronized and synchronized updates (based on Sparse logistic regression model training). In Figure 6.12, it compares the computing time and waiting time between synchronized gradient update strategy and asynchronized gradient update strategy adopted by Parameter Server.

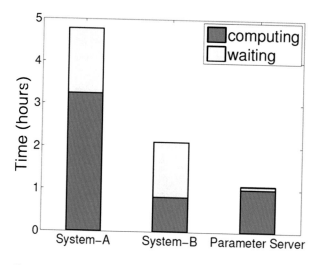

Figure 6.12 Comparison of computing time and waiting time between synchronized and asynchronized strategies.

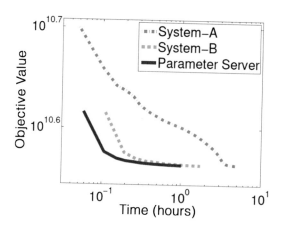

Figure 6.13 Convergence speed of different strategies.

In Figure 6.12, System-A and System-B are two systems that both update gradients synchronously, and Parameter Server is using an asynchronous update strategy. It indicates that the computing time of Parameter Server is much higher than that of the systems with synchronous update strategy, which proves the efficiency has been significantly improved in Parameter Server.

Also, the convergence speed of two strategies is compared in Figure 6.13.

As shown in Figure 6.13, the convergence speed of asynchronized update strategy in Parameter Server is faster than that of System-A and System-B with synchronized update strategy adopted. This proves that the impact of the inconsistency caused by the asynchronous update is not as great as expected.

6.3.3 Coordination and Efficiency in Multiserver Mode

Another cause for the inefficiency of parallel training in Spark MLlib is that each iteration requires the master node to broadcast the model weight parameters to the worker nodes. This leads to two problems:

(1) The master node becomes the bottleneck with the constraints on resources. As a result, the efficiency of the overall model parameters transfer is not high.
(2) All model parameters are broadcast synchronously, which makes the overall network load of the system very heavy.

So how does Parameter Server solve the problem of inefficient single master mode? As can be seen from the architecture diagram shown in Figure 6.9, the Parameter Server adopts the architecture of multiserver in the server node group, and each server is just responsible for partial model parameters. The model parameters are in the form of key-value pairs, so each server is responsible for parameter updates within a parameter key range.

Then another question comes, how does each server decide which part of the parameter range it is responsible for? If a new server node is added, how can a new node be added while ensuring that the existing parameter range does not change significantly? The answers to these two questions involve the principles of consistent hashing. Figure 6.14 shows the consistent hashing ring composed of server nodes.

In the server node group of Parameter Server, the process of applying consistent hashing to manage parameters is roughly as follows:

(1) Map the keys of model parameters to a hash ring space. For example, if there is a hash function that can map any key to the hash space of $0 \sim 2^{32} -1$, just connect the bucket $2^{32} -1$ with bucket 0, then this space becomes a hashing ring space.
(2) According to the number of server nodes n, the hashing ring space is divided into nm ranges, and each server is allocated with m hash ranges alternatively. The purpose of this is to ensure load balance and avoid uneven server load caused by some hotspot hashing ranges.
(3) When a new server node is added to the group, the new server node will find the insertion point on the hash ring. Afterwards, the new server will be responsible

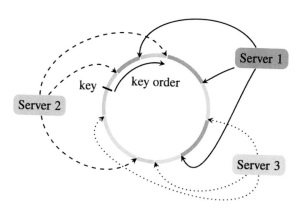

Figure 6.14 Consistent hashing ring composed of server nodes.

for the hashing range between the insertion point and the next range boundary. The hashing segment is divided into two parts, where the new server node is responsible for the second half, and the original node is responsible for the first half. This will not affect the hash allocation of other hash ranges, thus there is no problem of large data shuffling caused by hashing rearrangement.

(4) When a server node is deleted, the insertion point associated with it is removed, and the adjacent node is responsible for the hash range of the removed node.

Applying the consistent hashing to the server node group of Parameter Server can effectively reduce the bottleneck problem caused by the original single-sever mode. With usage of multiserver mode, when a worker node wants to pull new model parameters, the node will send separate range pull requests to different server nodes, after which each server node can send the model parameters that it is responsible for to the worker node in parallel.

In addition, since the server nodes can also coordinate efficiently while processing the gradient, and after a worker node calculates its own gradient, it only needs to use the range push operation to send the gradient to the related server nodes. Of course, this process is also related to the model structure and needs to be combined with the implementation of the model itself. In general, Parameter Server provides the ability to pull and push parameter ranges based on consistent hashing, making the implementation of model parallel training more flexible.

6.3.4   Summary of Technical Key Points in Parameter Server

The key points of Parameter Server in distributed machine learning model training are as follows:

- Replace the synchronized blocking gradient descent strategy with an asynchronized non-blocking distributed gradient descent strategy.
- Implement a multiserver node architecture to avoid bandwidth bottlenecks and memory bottlenecks caused by a single-server node.

- Utilize engineering methods such as consistent hashing, parameter range pulling, and parameter range pushing to achieve minimal data transfer. This design avoids global network congestion and bandwidth waste caused by broadcast operations.

Parameter Server is only a framework to manage the parallel training and does not involve specific model implementation. Therefore, Parameter Server is often used as a component of MXNet and TensorFlow. To implement a machine learning model specifically, it is necessary to rely on general and comprehensive machine learning frameworks. Section 6.4 introduces the mechanism of modern machine learning frameworks represented by TensorFlow.

6.4   TensorFlow for Offline Training of Recommendation Models

The application of deep learning is increasingly deepening in various fields, and the development of major deep learning platforms is also advancing by leaps and bounds. Google's TensorFlow [6,7], Amazon's MXNet, Facebook's PyTorch, Microsoft's CNTK, and others are all deep learning frameworks launched by major technology giants. Unlike Parameter Server, which mainly focuses on model parallel training, the aforementioned deep learning frameworks include almost all steps related to deep learning models, such as model building, parallel training, and online serving. This section takes TensorFlow as an example and introduces model training mechanisms in the deep learning framework, especially the technical details of parallel training.

6.4.1   Fundamentals of TensorFlow

The name "TensorFlow" very accurately expresses the fundamental idea of this framework – constructing a DAG based on the deep learning model architecture, and allowing data to flow in it in the form of tensors.

A tensor is a high-dimensional extension of a matrix, and a matrix is a special form of tensor in a two-dimensional space. In deep learning models, most of the data is represented in matrices or even higher-dimensional tensors. It is very appropriate that Google named its deep learning platform "TensorFlow."

In order to make tensors flow, a task relationship graph consisting of vertices and edges is built for each deep learning model following its structure, where each vertex represents a certain operation, such as pooling operation, activation function, and so on. Each vertex can receive 0 or more input tensors and output 0 or more output tensors. These tensors flow along the directed edges between the points until the final output layer.

Figure 6.15 shows a simple TensorFlow task relationship graph, where vector b, matrix W, and vector x are the inputs of the model. The purple vertices MatMul, Add, and ReLU are operation vertices, representing operations such as matrix multiplication,

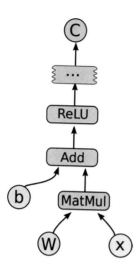

Figure 6.15 A simple TensorFlow-directed graph.

vector addition, and ReLU activation functions, respectively. The model input tensors W, b, and x flow among vertices after being processed by the operation vertices.

In fact, any complex model can be transformed into the form of a task relationship graph of operations. It is not only conducive to the modularization of operations and the flexibility to define and implement model structures, but also clarifies the dependencies between operations. Additionally, this graph representation also determines which operations can be executed in parallel and which can only be executed in serial, which lays the foundation for maximizing training efficiency in the parallel training platform.

6.4.2   Parallel Training Process in TensorFlow Based on Task Graph

After constructing a task relationship graph composed of "operations," TensorFlow can perform flexible task scheduling based on the task relationship graph to maximize the usage of parallel computing resources like multiple GPUs or distributed computing nodes. The general principle of scheduling is that the task nodes or subgraphs with dependencies need to be executed serially, and the task nodes or subgraphs without dependencies can be executed in parallel. Specifically, TensorFlow uses a task queue to solve the dependency scheduling problem. Here, we take an official task relationship graph of TensorFlow as an example (as shown in Figure 6.16) to illustrate the specific process.

As shown in Figure 6.16, the original operation node relationship graph is further processed into a relationship graph composed of operation nodes and task subgraphs. Among them, the subgraph is composed of a set of serial operation nodes. Due to the pure sequential relationship, it can be treated as an indivisible task node in parallel task scheduling.

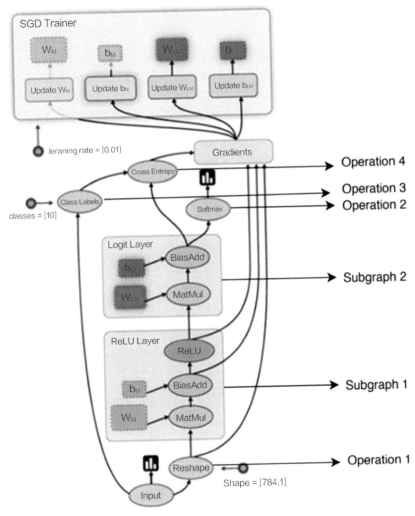

Figure 6.16 An example of a task relationship graph given by TensorFlow.

In the specific parallel task scheduling process, TensorFlow maintains a task queue. When all the pre-order tasks of a task are executed, the current task can be pushed to the end of the task queue. When there is an idle computing node, the computing node pulls a task at the head of the queue from the task queue for execution.

Taking Figure 6.16 as an example, after the input node, Operation 1 and Operation 3 will be pushed to the task queue at the same time. At this moment, if there are two idle GPU computing nodes, Operation 1 and Operation 3 will be popped out, and executed in parallel. After the execution of Operation 1, Subgraph 1 and Subgraph 2 will be pushed to the task queue for subsequent execution. After Subgraph 2 is executed, the pre-order dependencies of Operation 2 are removed, and Operation 2 is pushed to the task queue. The pre-order dependencies of Operation 4 are Subgraph 2 and Operation 3. Operation 4 will be pushed to the task queue only when these two pre-order dependencies are all completed. When the tasks on all computing nodes have been executed and there are no pending tasks in the task queue, the entire training process ends.

The task relationship graph of TensorFlow and the DAG task relationship graph of Spark have similarities in principle. The difference is that the role of Spark DAG is to clarify the sequence of tasks, and the granularity of tasks remains at the transformation operation level such as join, reduce, and so on. Spark's parallel mechanism is more of parallel execution within tasks. However, TensorFlow's task relationship graph decomposes tasks into very fine-grained operation levels, and accelerates the training process by executing independent subtasks in parallel.

6.4.3   Single-Machine Training vs. Distributed Training in TensorFlow

TensorFlow's computing platform has two main modes: one is single-machine training, and the other is multimachine distributed training. For single-machine training, although the parallel computing process of CPU and GPU is also included in the execution process, it is generally in a shared memory environment, so there is no need to consider communication problems too much. The training method in a cluster environment is composed of independent computing nodes. The computing nodes need to rely on network communication to transfer the data, so it can be considered as a computing environment similar to the Parameter Server introduced in Section 6.3.

As shown in Figure 6.17, the single-machine training of TensorFlow is performed on a worker node, and the single worker node performs parallel computing among different GPU+CPU nodes according to the task relationship graph. In a distributed environment, there are multiple worker nodes. If TensorFlow's Parameter Server strategy (tf.distribute.experimental.ParameterServerStrategy) is used, each worker node will be trained in a data-parallel manner. That is to say, each worker node is trained in the same task relationship graph, but the training data is different, and the generated gradients are aggregated and updated in the form of Parameter Server.

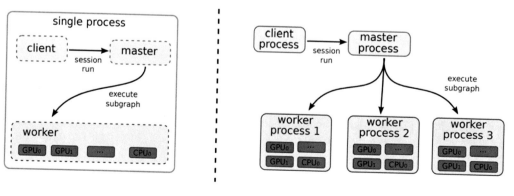

Figure 6.17 Single-machine and distributed training environments for TensorFlow.

Here, we will introduce specific task allocation of the CPU and GPU within each worker node. The GPU has the advantage of multicore, so it has a huge advantage over the CPU when dealing with tensor operations such as matrix addition and vector multiplication. When processing a task node or task subgraph, the CPU is mainly responsible for data and task scheduling, while the GPU is responsible for computationally intensive tensor operations.

For example, when processing the element multiplication operation of two vectors, the CPU will act as the central scheduler, send the elements of the corresponding ranges of the two vectors to the GPU for processing, then collect the processed results, and finally generate the result vector. From this perspective, the combination of CPU+GPU is also like a "simplified" Parameter Server.

6.4.4 Summary of TensorFlow Technical Key Points

This section presents the operation of the deep learning platform represented by TensorFlow from the perspective of the training mechanism. The technical key points can be summarized as follows:

(1) The principle of TensorFlow is to convert the model training process into a task relationship graph. The training data flows in the task relationship graph in the form of tensors to complete the entire training.
(2) TensorFlow performs task scheduling and parallel computing based on the task relationship graph.
(3) For distributed training in TensorFlow, its training process can be divided into two layers. One layer is the data-parallel training process based on the Parameter Server architecture, and the other layer is the parallel computing process at the CPU+GPU task level inside each worker node.

Learning TensorFlow and its tuning will involve a lot of basic knowledge. The models, operations, and training methods supported by TensorFlow are also very comprehensive. We don't intend to give a very in-depth introduction. Interested readers can use the contents of this chapter as a starting point, and use the official documents and tutorials provided by TensorFlow as a guide for more systematic learning.

6.5 Online Serving of Deep Learning Recommendation Model

The previous sections introduced the offline training platform for deep learning recommendation models. Whether it is TensorFlow, PyTorch, or the traditional Spark MLlib, they all provide a relatively mature offline parallel training environment. The recommended model must be used in the online environment after all. How to deploy the offline trained model to the online production environment for online real-time inference has always been a difficult task in the industry. This section will introduce the mainstream methods for deploying recommendation models.

6.5.1   Pre-Stored Recommendation Results or Embeddings

For online serving of the recommendation model, the simplest and most straightforward method is to generate the recommendation results of each user in an offline environment, and then pre-store the results in an online database such as Redis. You can directly extract the pre-stored data in the online environment and recommend it to the user online. The pros and cons of this method are obvious. The pros are as follows:

(1) There is no need to implement the process of model online inference. The offline training platform is completely decoupled from the online service platform, and any offline machine learning tool can be flexibly selected for model training.
(2) There is no complicated calculation in the online service process, so the online latency of the recommender system is extremely low.

The cons of this method are as follows:

(1) It needs to store the recommendation results for the combinations of users, items and application scenarios. When the number of users and items is very large, it can easily encounter combination explosion, and the online database cannot support the storage of such large-scale results.
(2) The online contextual features cannot be introduced, so the performance of the recommender system is limited.

Considering these pros and cons, the method of directly storing recommendation results is usually adopted only for small user scales, or some special application scenarios such as cold start and popular lists.

Pre-computing and storing the embeddings for user and item is another way to replace online inferencing with stored data. Compared with directly storing the recommendation results, the method of storing embeddings greatly reduces the amount of storage. It only needs to conduct the inner product or cosine similarity operation to obtain the final recommendation result online, which is a method that is often used in the industry to deploy the model.

This method cannot support the introduction of online contextual features, and cannot perform online inference by complex model. As a result, the expressivity of the recommendations is limited. Therefore, complex models still require a recommender system capable of online inferencing.

6.5.2   Self-Developed Model Online Serving Platform

Whether in the era when deep learning was just emerging a few years ago, or today when TensorFlow and PyTorch have become popular, self-developed machine learning training and online serving platforms are still a popular option for many large and medium-sized companies. Why do these companies not use the flexible and mature frameworks such as TensorFlow, but still develop their own model training and serving platform from scratch?

An important reason is that general-purpose platforms such as TensorFlow need to support a large number of redundant functions for flexibility and versatility, which makes the platform too heavy and difficult to modify and customize. The advantage of the self-developed platform is that it can be customized according to the company's business and actual needs, as well as taking into account the efficiency of model serving.

The author has participated in the implementation of Follow the Regularized Leader (FTRL), neural network models, and the development of customized online serving platforms. Since it does not depend on any third-party tools, the online serving process can be designed based on the actual production environment. For example, if a Java server is used for online service, the process of online FTRL is to obtain model parameters from the parameter server or in-memory database, and then use customized Java code to implement the model inferencing logic.

Another reason is that most deep learning frameworks cannot support cases when the model has special needs, such as some retrieval models in recommender systems, "exploration and utilization" models, and cold start algorithms that are very tightly coupled with the specific business use case. The online serving code of such models usually needs to be self-developed.

The disadvantages of self-developed platforms are obvious. It is feasible to develop one or two models with customized code. But it is difficult to implement, compare, and tune dozens of models due to the high cost of implementing models. Nowadays, the iteration cycle of self-developed models is too long considering the emergence of new models. Therefore, self-developed platforms and models are often only used by large companies, when the model structure is already determined. In this case, the model inferencing code also needs to be manually implemented.

6.5.3   Pre-Trained Embedding and Lightweight Online Model

Fully adopting a self-developed platform has clear drawbacks, like heavy engineering efforts and poor flexibility. Today, with the rapid evolution of various complex models, the disadvantages of the self-developed model are clearer. Is there any way to combine the flexibility of the general platform, the diversity of functions, and online inferencing efficiency from the self-developed platform? The answer is yes.

Many companies in the industry have adopted a new recommender system design pattern with offline training of complex networks, generating embeddings, and storing them in in-memory databases. A lightweight model such as logistic regression or shallow neural networks is used for online recommendation. The "two-tower" model introduced in Section 4.3 is a typical example (as shown in Figure 4.5).

The two-tower model uses complex networks to embed the user features and item features, respectively. Before the final cross layer, there is no interaction between the user features and the item features, which forms two independent "towers."

After completing the training of the two-tower model, the final user embeddings and item embeddings can be stored in the in-memory database. When performing online inference, there is no need to reproduce the complex network, and only the logic of the final output layer needs to be implemented. The output layer here is mostly logistic regression or softmax or a shallow neural network. But they are all relatively simple to implement. After the user embedding and the item embedding are fetched from the in-memory database, the final prediction can be obtained through the online calculation of the output layer.

With such architecture, some other contextual features can also be used together with user and item embeddings in the final output layer. This enables us to introduce more real-time features and enrich the feature sources of the model.

Nowadays, when Graph Embedding technology has become very powerful. The offline training method of embeddings can integrate a large amount of user and item information, and the output layer does not need to be very complicated. Therefore, the method of embedding pre-training plus a lightweight online model is a flexible and simple approach for recommender systems without much impact on the model performance.

6.5.4   Model Transformation and Deployment with PMML

The embedding + lightweight model approach is practical and efficient, but it breaks the model into pieces without end-to-end training or deployment. Is there a way to deploy the model directly after training offline? This section introduces a platform-agnostic model deployment method – Predictive Model Markup Language (PMML).

PMML is a general markup language that expresses different model structure parameters in the form of XML. In the process of online model deployment, PMML often acts as an intermediary between the offline training platform and the online inference platform.

Here, Spark MLlib is used as an example to explain the role of PMML in the entire machine learning model training and online deployment process, as illustrated in Figure 6.18.

The example in Figure 6.18 uses JPMML as the library for serializing and parsing PMML files. The JPMML library is being used in two parts of this design: the Spark platform and the Java server. Inside the Spark platform, it completes the serialization of the Spark MLlib model, generates PMML files, and saves them to the database or file system that can be reached by the online server. On the Java inference server, the JPMML library parsed the PMML model file, and generates the model object to integrate with the other business logic code.

JPMML only performs inference on the Java server, and does not need to consider the model training and distributed deployment. Therefore, the library is relatively light and can efficiently complete the inference process. Another similar open-source project is MLeap, which also uses PMML as a medium for model transformation and online serving.

In fact, JPMML and MLeap also have the ability to convert and launch simple models in Scikit-learn and TensorFlow. However, for complex models in TensorFlow, the expressivity of PMML language is not enough. So launching a complex TensorFlow would need a more native solution – TensorFlow Serving.

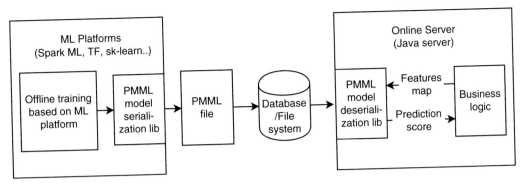

Figure 6.18 Utilizing PMML for model deployment in the Spark MLlib framework.

6.5.5   TensorFlow Serving

TensorFlow Serving is a native model server developed by TensorFlow. Essentially, the workflow of TensorFlow Serving is the same as that of PMML-like tools. The difference is that TensorFlow defines its own model serialization standard. Using the model serialization function that comes with TensorFlow, the trained model parameters and structures can be saved to a designated file.

The most common and convenient way to use TensorFlow Serving is to use Docker to build a model serving API. After the Docker environment is prepared, the installation and preparation of the TensorFlow Serving environment only needs to be done by pulling the image (pull image) using the following command:

```
docker pull tensorflow/serving
```

After starting the docker container, we can also start the model service API with only one line of command:

```
tensorflow_model_server --port=8500 --rest_api_port=8501 \
--model_name=${MODEL_NAME}
--model_base_path=${MODEL_BASE_PATH}/${MODEL_NAME}
```

Here, we just need to change the model file path.

Of course, it is not easy to build a complete set of TensorFlow Serving services, because it involves a series of engineering issues such as model update, maintenance, and on-demand expansion of the entire docker container cluster. The performance of TensorFlow Serving is still criticized by the industry because of its limitations, but its ease of use and support for complex models make it the first choice for launching TensorFlow models.

6.5.6   Flexible Choice of Model Serving Method

The issue in the deep learning recommendation model online serving is essentially an engineering problem, because it is closely tied to the company's online server environment, hardware environment, offline training environment, database/storage system, and so on. Because of this, the approach taken by each company is different. Even if this section has listed five main online methods, it cannot cover all recommended model online methods in the industry. Even within a company, for different business scenarios, the online methods of models are not always the same.

Therefore, as a machine learning engineer, in addition to understanding the mainstream model service methods, one should also comprehensively weigh the company's engineering environment to give the most suitable solution.

6.6   Trade-Off between Engineering and Theory

Engineering and theory can be sometimes conflicting as well as interdependent in the process of solving technical problems. Theory needs to depend on engineering implementation to be productionized. Otherwise, theory will be just a pie in the sky and cannot be applied in the practical applications. However, engineering capabilities can restrict the development of theory. In this section, we will discuss how to make trade-offs between engineering and theory in the field of recommender systems.

6.6.1   Nature of the Engineer's Responsibilities

The trade-off balance between engineering and theory is something that every engineer needs to consider. Every engineer should have an engineering mindset instead of the "research thinking" that scholars have. Recommender systems is a field with a strong emphasis on engineering implementations and aiming at putting theory into production as its primary goal. The importance of an engineering mindset is self-evident. Next, we will explain how to make trade-offs between engineering and theory from the perspective of an engineer.

Whether you are a machine learning engineer, a software engineer, or even an engineer designing an electric vehicle or rockets, your responsibilities are the same. You need to find and utilize the optimal solution to deliver the product given some constraints.

In the recommender systems context, the constraints here can be restrictions from the R&D schedule, limitations of the hardware and software environment, requirements of actual business logic and application scenarios, or from the business objectives defined by the product manager, and so on. Because of these constraints, it is impossible for an engineer to arbitrarily try new technologies and do as many exploratory innovations as researchers in academia. Thus making a balance between cutting-edge theory and engineering implementations is a basic quality an engineer should have. In the following sections, we will use three practical cases to help readers understand how to make technical trade-offs in actual projects.

6.6.2   Trade-Off between Redis Capacity and Online Model Deployment

For online recommender systems, both model parameters and online features are necessary for online model inferencing. In order to ensure real-time performance with low data query latency, many companies use the in-memory database method to host the data. Among the data storage solutions, Redis has become the mainstream choice. However, Redis needs to take a lot of memory resources, and memory resources are relatively scarce and expensive compared with others. Therefore, whether you use AWS (Amazon Web Services, Amazon Web Services Platform), Alibaba Cloud, or a self-built data center, the cost of using Redis is relatively high, and the capacity of Redis has become a key factor restricting the ways how the recommendation model goes online.

Due to such constraints, engineers must consider the problem from two aspects:

(1) The model's parameter scale should be as small as possible. Especially for the deep learning recommendation models, the parameter quantity of the model has been increased by several orders of magnitude compared with the traditional model.

(2) The number of features used for online estimation cannot be increased indefinitely, and a certain degree of trade-off should be made based on the feature's importance.

To launch a recommender system under such constraints, it is necessary to drop some unimportant factors and focus on the key points. An experienced engineer's thinking would be like this:

(1) If the feature dimensions are tens of millions or even higher, theoretically the order of magnitude of parameters is also in the order of tens of millions. It is difficult for online services to support this level of data volume, which requires engineering improvement on the sparsity of the model. It is important to focus on the key features and discard secondary features. Even if it may impact some certain model prediction accuracy, it will help reduce online inferencing latency and reduce the consumption of engineering resources.

(2) What are the key technical points to enhance the model's sparsity? We can add L1 regularization term or adopt a training method with strong sparsity such as FTRL.

(3) There are many technical approaches to achieving the goal. When it is impossible to determine which technology is better, it is a good choice to implement all of them, and use offline and online indicators for comparison.

(4) Determine the final technical approach based on the data and improve the engineering implementation.

This is the simplification method on the model side. Of course, the same idea can be adopted in the online feature reduction. Firstly, the method of principal component analysis can be used for feature screening. Then, the online features can be reduced without significantly impacting the model performance. For the features that are not easy to choose, conduct offline evaluation and online A/B testing to finally reach the level that the engineering system can support.

6.6.3   Research Development Schedule Constraints and Trade-Offs in Technology Selection

In the actual engineering environment, the constraints of the research and development schedule are also a factor that cannot be ignored. This involves the engineer's ability to control the overall project and to estimate the development timeline. No one wants to be the slowest link to drag down other teams in the IT industry, where product iterations are increasingly rapid.

In the process of upgrading the technology stacks, it is necessary to fully weigh the new requirements of the product and the progress of the overall migration. For example, the company hopes to migrate the machine learning platform from Spark to TensorFlow. This is a technical decision to follow the latest technological trends. However, due to the characteristics of the Spark platform, the programming language and model training methods are quite different from TensorFlow. The entire migration must be through a long development cycle. During the migration process, if there are new product requirements, engineers need to make trade-offs and take into account the daily development progress in the process of technology upgrade.

There are two possible technical paths:

(1) Let the entire team focus on completing the migration from Spark to TensorFlow, and then conduct research and development of new models and new functions on the new platform.
(2) Some team members use the mature and stable Spark platform to continue the development and quickly meet product requirements, leaving sufficient time for TensorFlow migration. At the same time, another group of members fully work on TensorFlow to ensure the maturity of the new platform before mass migration.

From a purely technical point of view, since it has been decided to migrate to the TensorFlow platform, theoretically there is no need to spend time developing new models using the Spark platform. However, we need to clarify two key considerations here:

(1) No matter how mature the platform is, it always takes a long time for the entire team to break in and conduct the tuning. It is impossible to let it support important business logic right after the migration.
(2) The technology platform migration is usually a technical decision and requires transparency with the other stakeholders. However, it should not be a direct reason for deprioritizing the business support.

Therefore, from the perspective of project progress and risk, the second technical path should be a more realistic choice for project development.

6.6.4   Trade-Offs between Hardware Platform and Model Structure

Almost all machine learning engineers have had a similar complaint – the company's hardware resources are too limited, and it takes nearly a day to train a model.

Big companies may have relatively more resources, and small companies are more likely to be restricted by hardware constraints due to the limitation of research and development budget. But no matter what size of company, hardware resources are always limited, so we must learn to optimize all engineering implementations related to the model under the condition of limited hardware resources.

The optimization here actually includes two aspects:

(1) One is the optimization of the program itself. We can always hear the complaints that Spark runs too slowly. Sometimes, it is due to the lack of deep understanding of Spark's shuffle mechanism. Such problematic programs usually involve lots of unnecessary data shuffling due to the data skew problem. This kind of issue does not need the technical trade-offs, but requires the engineer to consolidate its technical foundation and understanding of the mechanisms.

(2) In the other scenarios, optimization means some technical trade-offs. Is it possible to greatly improve the speed of model training, reduce the consumption of model training, and improve the online performance of the recommended model by optimizing or simplifying the model structure? Typical cases are mentioned in Section 5.3. In the deep learning model, the overall training convergence speed of the model has a strong correlation with the number of parameters of the model, and the embedding layer usually takes a major portion of the model parameters. Therefore, in order to speed up the training of the model, the embedding components can be pre-trained separately, which can achieve rapid convergence of the other model components. Of course, this approach abandons the consistency of end-to-end training. But under the constraints of hardware conditions, the benefits of enhancing the online performance of the model may be much greater than the benefits of model consistency brought by end-to-end training. Another example is the model structure simplification. If the gains brought by increasing the complexity of the model have become very small, there is no need to waste too many hardware resources to make marginal improvements. Instead, the optimization should be re-directed to improving the online system performance, mining other useful information, and introducing a more effective network structure for the model.

6.6.5   Balance between Whole Picture and Details

These cases cannot cover all the engineering trade-offs people make in practice. We only hope that readers can build a good engineering intuition through these cases, jump out of very specific technical details, and balance between the whole picture and details.

This chapter is only a small part of engineering implementation in deep learning recommender systems. However, if readers can start from this, establish an overall understanding of recommender systems engineering architecture, and understand the principles, advantages, and disadvantages of various technical approaches, it is the beginning of becoming an excellent recommendation engineer.

References

[1] Fay Chang, et al. Bigtable: A distributed storage system for structured data. *ACM transactions on Computer Systems (TOCS)*, 26.2 (2008): 4.

[2] Sanjay Ghemawat, Howard Gobioff, Shun-Tak Leung. The Google file system. 2003.

[3] Jeffrey Dean, Sanjay Ghemawat. MapReduce: Simplified data processing on large clusters. *Communications of the ACM*, 51.1, 2008: 107–113.

[4] Mu Li, et al. Scaling distributed machine learning with the parameter server. 11th USENIX Symposium on Operating Systems Design and Implementation (OSDI 14), Broomfield, CO, USA, October 6–8, 2014.

[5] Mu Li, et al. Parameter server for distributed machine learning. *Big Learning NIPS Workshop*, 6(2), 2013.

[6] Martín Abadi, et al. TensorFlow: Large-scale machine learning on heterogeneous distributed systems: arXiv preprint arXiv: 1603.04467 (2016).

[7] Martín Abadi, et al. TensorFlow: A system for large-scale machine learning. 12th USENIX Symposium on Operating Systems Design and Implementation (OSDI 16), Savannah, GA, USA, November 2–4, 2016.

7 Evaluation in Recommender Systems

The proportion of knowledge related to the evaluation of the recommender system is not large in the entire recommender systems knowledge framework, but its importance is as significant as building a recommender system. The evaluation mainly includes the following three points:

(1) The metrics used in the evaluation of the recommender systems directly determine whether the optimization of the recommendation system is objective and reasonable.
(2) The evaluation is a collaborative effort, which requires the machine learning team to communicate and cooperate with other teams.
(3) The selected metrics directly determine whether the recommender system meets the company's business goals and development vision.

These three points are the keys to the success of a recommender system.

This chapter focuses on the evaluation of recommender systems, from offline evaluation to online experiment. It discusses the methods and metrics of recommendation system evaluation from multiple levels, including the following:

(1) Offline evaluation methods and metrics.
(2) Offline simulation evaluation – replay.
(3) Online A/B testing and online metrics.
(4) Fast online evaluation method – interleaving.

These evaluation methods are not independent. At the end of this chapter, we will discuss how to combine different levels of evaluation methods to form a scientific and efficient multilayer recommender system evaluation architecture.

7.1 Offline Evaluation Methods and Basic Metrics

In the evaluation process of the recommender system, offline evaluation is often treated as the most common and basic evaluation method. As the name suggests, offline evaluation refers to the evaluation performed in an offline environment before deploying the model online. Since there is no need to deploy to the production environment, offline evaluation does not have the engineering risk of online deployment, and there is no need to waste valuable online traffic resources. Additionally, it has many other advantages, such as short test time, multiple parallel tests at the same time, the ability to use abundant offline computing resources, and so on.

Therefore, before the model is launched online, conducting a large number of offline evaluations is the most efficient way to verify the model performance. In order to fully grasp the technical points of offline evaluation, it is necessary to master two aspects of knowledge – the methods and the metrics used in offline evaluation.

7.1.1   Methods of Offline Evaluations

The basic principle of offline evaluation is to divide the dataset into a training set and a testing set in an offline environment. The training set is used to train the model, and the testing set is for model evaluation. According to different dataset partition methods, offline evaluation can be divided into the following three types:

7.1.1.1   Holdout Test

The holdout test is a basic offline evaluation method, which randomly divides the original sample set into two parts – the training set and the testing set. For example, for a recommendation model, the samples can be randomly divided into two parts according to the ratio of 70%:30%, where 70% of the samples are used for model training and 30% of the samples are used for model evaluation.

The disadvantage of the holdout test is obvious. The evaluation metric calculated on the testing set is directly related to the division of the training set and the testing set. If only a small amount of holdout test is performed, the conclusions obtained will be relatively random. In order to eliminate this randomness, the idea of cross-validation is proposed.

7.1.1.2   Cross-Validation

- K-fold cross-validation. In this method, the samples are firstly divided into k partitions. Then, the training and evaluation process will traverse these k subsets in turn. In each turn, we use the current subset as a testing set and use all other subsets as a training set to perform model training. Finally, the average of all the evaluation metrics for k runs is used as the final evaluation result. In practical experiments, k is usually equal to 10.
- Leave-one-out validation. One sample is left as a testing set each time, and all other samples are used as the training set. Assuming the total number of samples is n, all n samples are traversed in turn. Then, n times of evaluation are performed, and the evaluation metrics are averaged to obtain the final performance result. In the case of a large number of samples, the time overhead of the leave-one-out validation method is extremely high. In fact, leave-one-out validation is a special case of leave-p validation. Leave-p validation means leaving p samples as the testing set each time, and there are C_n^p possibilities to select p elements from n elements, so its time complexity is much higher than that of leaving one verification. As a result, it is rarely used in practice.

7.1.1.3 Bootstrap

Both the holdout test and the cross-validation are based on the method of dividing whole datasets into training and testing sets. However, when the sample size is relatively small, sample set division will further reduce the training sample amount, which may affect the training effect of the model. Is there an evaluation method that can maintain the sample size of the training set? The bootstrap approach can solve this problem to a certain extent.

Bootstrap is a test method based on the resampling technique. For a sample set with size of n, random sampling with replacement is performed n times to obtain a training set with size of n. In the n-time sampling process, some samples will be re-sampled, and some samples will not be drawn. The bootstrap method uses these undrawn samples as a testing set for model evaluation.

7.1.2 Offline Evaluation Metrics

After knowing the correct offline evaluation method, to measure the performance of a recommendation model, it is necessary to evaluate the recommender system from multiple perspectives through different metrics and then draw comprehensive conclusions. The following are metrics that are commonly used in offline evaluation.

7.1.2.1 Accuracy

Classification accuracy refers to the ratio of correctly classified samples against the total number of samples, that is,

$$\text{Accuracy} = \frac{n_{\text{correct}}}{n_{\text{total}}} \tag{7.1}$$

where n_{correct} is the number of correctly classified samples and n_{total} is the total sample count.

Accuracy is a relatively intuitive evaluation metric in classification tasks. Although it has strong interpretability, it also has drawbacks. When the proportion of samples in different categories is very imbalanced, the category with a large proportion often becomes a factor that affects the accuracy rate. For example, if negative samples account for 99%, then the classifier can predict all samples as negative samples to obtain 99% accuracy.

For a click-through rate prediction classification problem, the recommendation model can be evaluated with the accuracy rate under the premise of selecting a threshold to determine positive and negative samples. In the actual recommendation scenario, the more common use case is to generate a recommendation list. So the combination of precision and recall are more commonly used to measure the performance of recommendations.

7.1.2.2 Precision and Recall

Precision is the ratio of the number of correctly classified positive samples against the number of predicted positive samples, while recall is the ratio of the number of correctly classified positive samples to the number of true positive samples.

In the ranking model, there is usually no definite threshold to directly judge the prediction result as a positive sample or a negative sample. The precision rate (Precision@N) and recall rate (Recall@N) of the Top N-ranked results are usually used to evaluate the ranking model's performance. In this case, the Top N items are considered the positive samples predicted by the model in the precision rate and recall rate calculation.

Precision rate and recall rate are contradictory indicators. In order to improve the precision rate, the model needs to predict the sample as a positive sample when it has high confidence, but it often misses many true positive samples when the model is not so confident, which results in a lower recall rate.

In order to comprehensively reflect the results of precision and recall, the F1-score is often adopted. F1-score is the harmonic mean of precision and recall, which is defined as follows:

$$F1 = \frac{2 \cdot \text{Precision} \cdot \text{Recall}}{\text{Precision} + \text{Recall}} \tag{7.2}$$

7.1.2.3   Root Mean Square Error

Root mean square error (RMSE) is often used to measure the quality of the regression model. When using the click-through rate prediction model to build a recommender system, the recommender system actually predicts the probability of a positive sample. It can be evaluated by RMSE, which is defined as follows,

$$\text{RMSE} = \sqrt{\frac{\sum_{i=1}^{n} (y_i - \hat{y}_i)^2}{n}} \tag{7.3}$$

where y_i is the ground truth label of i-th sample, $\hat{y}_i$ is the predicted value of the i-th sample, and n is the number of samples.

In general, RMSE can well reflect the degree of deviation between the predicted value of the regression model and the true value. However, in practical applications, if there are individual outliers with a very large degree of deviation, the RMSE can become quite large even if the number of outliers is small. To solve this problem, mean absolute percent error (MAPE) is often adopted to improve the robustness against outliers. The definition of MAPE is as follows,

$$\text{MAPE} = \sum_{i=1}^{n} \left| \frac{y_i - \hat{y}_i}{y_i} \right| \times \frac{100}{n} \tag{7.4}$$

Compared with RMSE, MAPE is equivalent to normalizing the error of each sample, which reduces the impact of absolute error brought by individual outliers.

7.1.2.4   Logarithmic Loss Function

Logarithmic loss function (LogLoss) is another metric that is often used in offline evaluation. In a binary classification problem, LogLoss can be defined as follows,

$$\text{LogLoss} = -\frac{1}{N} \sum_{i=1}^{N} \left(y_i \log P_i + (1 - y_i) \log (1 - P_i) \right) \tag{7.5}$$

Among them, y_i is the ground truth label of the sample x_i, P_i is the probability of predicting that the input sample x_i is a positive sample, and N is the total number of samples.

Readers could find that LogLoss is the loss function of logistic regression. A large number of deep learning models use logistic regression (that is, Sigmoid) or Softmax as the output layer. Therefore, using LogLoss as an evaluation metric can very intuitively reflect the change of the model's loss function. From the perspective of the model, LogLoss is a very suitable evaluation metric for the model's convergence.

7.2   Offline Metrics for Ranking Models

Section 7.1 introduces the main offline evaluation methods and common evaluation metrics of the recommender system, but they are more commonly used as the evaluation of a prediction model such as click-through rate (CTR) prediction, rather than a ranking model. Usually, we hope the outputs of the prediction should have a physical meaning. In the CTR prediction case, the model output should be close to the empirical click-through rate. However, the final output of the recommender system is usually a ranked list. Taking the matrix decomposition method as an example, the similarity between users and items is only a criterion used for sorting, and does not have a physical meaning like CTR. Therefore, it is more appropriate to evaluate recommendation models using metrics that can directly measure the ranking quality. In this section, we will introduce several offline metrics for directly measuring the ranking model performance. These metrics are Precision-Recall (P–R) curve, Receiver Operating Characteristic (ROC) curve, and mean average precision (mAP).

7.2.1   Precision–Recall Curve

Section 7.1 introduces two important metrics for evaluating sorted sequences, Precision@N and Recall@N. In order to comprehensively evaluate the quality of a ranking model, we should not only check the Precision@N and Recall@N of the model under different Top N, but also to draw the Precision-Recall curve (P–R curve) of the model. In this section, we will briefly introduce the method of generating P–R curve.

The horizontal axis of the P–R curve is the recall rate, and the vertical axis is the precision rate. For a ranking model, a point on its P–R curve represents the precision and recall for a given threshold. The threshold is used to determine if prediction output is positive or negative. In other words, if the model prediction output is greater than the threshold, then it is predicted as positive sample, otherwise it is considered as negative sample.

The entire P–R curve is generated by changing the threshold from high to low. As shown in Figure 7.1, the solid line represents the P–R curve of model A, and the dotted line represents the P–R curve of model B. The areas near horizontal axis origin represents the precision and recall of the model when the threshold is maximum.

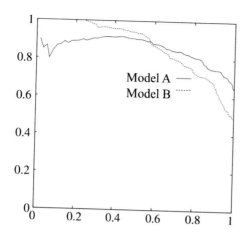

Figure 7.1 Examples of P–R curves.

It can be seen from Figure 7.1 that when the recall rate is close to 0, the precision rate of model A is 0.9, and the precision rate of model B is 1. This implies that the samples with the top scores in model B are all true positive samples, while model A has some prediction errors even when the predicted score is quite high. As the recall rate increases, the precision rate decreases overall. In particular, when the recall rate is 1, the precision rate of model A exceeds that of model B. This demonstrates that the performance of the model cannot be fully measured by using the precision and recall of a single point. The overall model performance should be evaluated using a comprehensive metric such as the P–R curve.

After the P–R curve is generated, we can use the area under the curve (AUC) to quantify the P–R curve. As the name implies, AUC refers to the area under the P–R curve, so calculating the AUC value needs to be integrated along the horizontal axis of the P–R curve. The larger the AUC, the better the ranking model's performance.

7.2.2   Receiver Operating Characteristic Curve

The ROC curve was first introduced in the military field. Then, it was widely used in the medical field, and that's also where the ROC concept in the machine learning domain originated.

The horizontal axis of a ROC curve is the False Positive Rate (FPR) and the vertical axis is the True Positive Rate (TPR). FPR and TPR are defined as follows,

$$\text{FPR} = \frac{\text{FP}}{N}, \text{TPR} = \frac{\text{TP}}{P} \tag{7.6}$$

where P is the number of positive samples, N is the number of negative samples, TP denotes the number of positive samples that the model correctly predicts the positive class, and FP refers to the number of negative samples that are wrongly predicted as positive by the model.

Table 7.1 An example of ranking model prediction outputs

Sample #	Ground Truth Label	Model Predictions	Sample #	Ground Truth Label	Model Predictions
1	P	0.9	11	P	0.4
2	P	0.8	12	N	0.39
3	N	0.7	13	P	0.38
4	P	0.6	14	N	0.37
5	P	0.55	15	N	0.36
6	P	0.54	16	N	0.35
7	N	0.53	17	P	0.34
8	N	0.52	18	N	0.33
9	P	0.51	19	P	0.30
10	N	0.505	20	N	0.1

The definition of the ROC curve seems complicated, but the process of generating the ROC curve is not difficult. Next, we will show how to draw a ROC curve with an example and let readers understand how an ROC curve is used to evaluate the ranking model performance.

Like the P–R curve, the ROC curve is generated by continuously changing the model's positive sample prediction threshold. Here is an example to explain the process.

Assuming that there are 20 samples in the test set, the output of the model prediction is shown in Table 7.1. The first column in the table is the sample index, the second column is the ground truth label of the sample, and the third column is the probability that the model predicts as positive. Samples are sorted from highest to lowest predicted probability. Before deciding the final positive and negative examples, a threshold needs to be specified: samples with a predicted probability greater than the threshold will be considered as positive examples, and samples smaller than the threshold will be considered as negative examples. If the threshold is 0.9, then only the first sample will be predicted as a positive example, and all others will be negative examples. The threshold here is also known as the cut-off point.

Then the threshold is changed to different values, starting from the highest score (actually starting from positive infinity, corresponding to the zero point of the ROC curve), gradually to the lowest score. At each threshold, it generates to a pair of FPR and TPR values. The value pairs are then plotted correspondingly on the ROC graph. Finally, the ROC curve is obtained by connecting all the data points sequentially on the graph.

For this example, when the threshold value is positive infinity, the model predicts all samples as negative examples. Both FPR and TPR are also 0. So the first point of the curve is (0,0). When the threshold is changed to 0.9, the model predicts that sample #1 is a positive sample, and the sample is a real positive example. Therefore, TP=1. In 20 samples, the number of all positive cases is P=10, so TPR=TP/P=1/10. In this example, there is no positive sample that is wrongly predicted, that is, FP=0, and

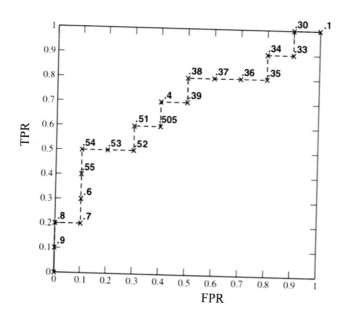

Figure 7.2 ROC curve.

the total number of negative samples is N=10, so FPR=FP/N=0/10=0. It corresponds to the point (0,0.1) on the ROC diagram. Continue changing the threshold value in turn until all the key points are drawn, and then connect the points to get the final ROC curve, as shown in Figure 7.2.

In fact, there is a more intuitive way to draw the ROC curve. First, count the number of positive and negative samples according to the sample label, assuming that the number of positive samples is P and the number of negative samples is N. Next, set the interval of the horizontal axis to 1/N, and the interval of the vertical axis to 1/P Then, sort the samples according to the predicted probability output by the model (from high to low). Traverse the samples in turn and draw the ROC curve starting from 0 point. Draw a unit interval curve along the vertical axis every time a positive sample is encountered, and a unit interval curve along the horizontal axis for each negative sample. Finally, connect the last point with (1,1), and the entire ROC curve is drawn.

Similar to the P–R curve, the AUC can be calculated after ROC curve is generated. The AUC can be used to evaluate the ranking model's performance in the recommender system.

7.2.3   Mean Average Precision

Mean average precision (mAP) is another commonly used evaluation metric in recommender systems and information retrieval. This metric is actually an average of

Average Precision (AP). Before calculating mAP, readers need to understand what average precision is.

Assume that the ranking results of a user test set by the recommender system are shown in Table 7.2, where 1 represents the positive sample, and 0 represents the negative sample.

In the previous section, we introduced how to calculate precision@N. Then what is the precision@N at each position of this ranking list? The results are shown in Table 7.3.

The calculation of AP only takes the precision for different topN for average calculation, that is, $AP = (1/1 + 2/4 + 3/5 + 4/6)/4 = 0.6917$. How about mAP?

If the recommender system sorts the samples of each user in the test set, then we can get an AP value for each user. The average AP value of all users is then the mAP value.

It is worth noting that the calculation method of mAP is completely different from the calculation methods of the P–R curve and the ROC curve, because mAP needs to sort the samples for each user, while both P–R curve and ROC curve can be calculated with the sorted full test set. This difference needs special attention in the actual calculations.

7.2.4 Selecting Reasonable Evaluation Metrics

In addition to three commonly used metrics like P–R curve, ROC curve, and mAP, there are many other metrics used in the recommender system evaluation, such as Normalized Discounted Cumulative Gain (NDCG), coverage, and diversity, and so on. In the actual offline experiment, although it is necessary to evaluate the model from different angles, there is no need to pursue perfection to find the "best" metric. Choosing too many metrics to evaluate the model could sometimes result in a waste of time. The purpose of offline evaluation is to quickly detect the issues, eliminate unreliable candidates, and find promising candidates for online evaluation. Therefore, selecting two to four representative offline metrics based on the business scenarios and conducting efficient offline experiments is the correct path for offline evaluation.

Table 7.2 Example of ranking results

Ranking List	$N = 1$	$N = 2$	$N = 3$	$N = 4$	$N = 5$	$N = 6$
Ground Truth Label	1	0	0	1	1	1

Table 7.3 Examples of precision@N calculation

Ranking List	$N = 1$	$N = 2$	$N = 3$	$N = 4$	$N = 5$	$N = 6$
Ground Truth Label	1	0	0	1	1	1
Precision@N	1/1	1/2	1/3	2/4	3/5	4/6

7.3 Replay: An Offline Evaluation Method Aligned with the Online Environment

The first two sections introduce the offline evaluation methods and commonly used evaluation metrics in the recommender system. Traditional offline evaluation methods have been widely used in various model experiments in academia. However, during the model development in industry, can these methods (such as holdout test and cross-validation) really objectively measure the model's impact on the company's business goal?

7.3.1 Logical Loop for Model Evaluation

To answer this question, it is necessary to revisit the core of model evaluation – how to evaluate a model and determine whether it is a "good" model? Figure 7.3 shows the logical relationship of each component in the model evaluation.

The key point of offline evaluation is to make the results of offline evaluation as close as possible to online ones. To achieve this goal, the offline evaluation process should simulate the online environment as much as possible. The online environment includes not only the online data environment, but also production settings such as model update frequency.

7.3.2 Dynamic Offline Evaluation Method

The disadvantage of the traditional offline evaluation method is that the evaluation process is static. In other words, the model is not updated with the evaluation, which does not reflect the actual condition in production. Assuming that a recommendation model is evaluated with one month's test data, if the evaluation process is static, it means that when the model predicts the data close to the end of the month, the model has stopped updating for nearly 30 days. This is not practical in most industrial applications. It will lead to the drifting in the model evaluation. In order to solve this

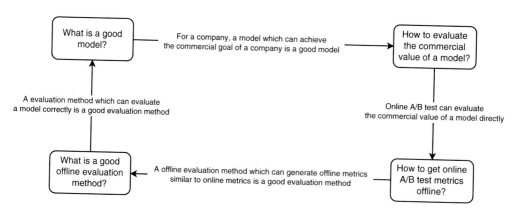

Figure 7.3 Logical relationship of each component in the model evaluation.

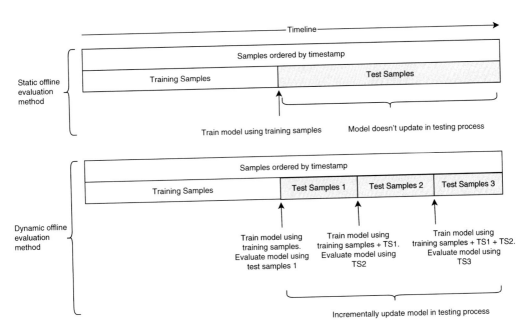

Figure 7.4 Comparison of traditional offline evaluation method and dynamic offline evaluation method.

problem, the entire evaluation process needs to be dynamic to make it closer to an online environment.

The dynamic offline evaluation method first sorts the test samples into chronological order, and then uses the model to predict the test samples in the subsequent time interval. At the time point when the model is updated, the model needs to incrementally learn from the samples before the time point of the model update, and perform its subsequent evaluation after the update. The comparison between the traditional offline evaluation method and the dynamic offline evaluation method is shown in Figure 7.4.

It is easy to see that the dynamic evaluation process is closer to the real online environment, and the evaluation results are closer to the objective situation. If the frequency of model updates continues to increase, the entire dynamic evaluation process becomes an online simulation process of sample playback one by one. This is the classic simulation offline evaluation method – replay.

In fact, replay is the only offline evaluation method for reinforcement learning models [1]. Taking the DRN model introduced in Section 3.10 as an example, since the model needs to continuously receive online feedback and update it online, the replay method must be used offline to simulate the model's online feedback loop and update process.

7.3.3 Replay Evaluation Method Adopted in Netflix

The replay method performs offline testing by replaying online data streams. The principle of the evaluation method is not difficult to understand, but it will encounter some difficulties in actual engineering. The most critical point is that the samples used in a replay cannot contain any "future information" in the simulation data stream. This is to avoid the phenomenon called "data leakage."

For example, the replay method uses the sample data from August 1st to August 31st for replay, and the prediction model has historical CTR as one feature. The calculation of this feature can only be generated through historical data. More specifically, the sample on August 20th can only use the data from August 1st to August 19th to generate historical CTR features and cannot use the data after August 20th. In the evaluation process, if all sample data from August 1st to August 31st were used to generate features for engineering simplification, and then the replay method was used for evaluation, the evaluation result would not be useful since the model uses future knowledge to predict backward samples.

In engineering implementation, Netflix built a complete set of data pipeline architecture (as shown in Figure 7.5) to support the replay evaluation method and gave it a very beautiful name – Time Machine.

It can be seen from the figure that the Time Machine runs once a day. The main function of its primary task, Snapshot Jobs, is to integrate various logs, features, and data of the day to form sample data for model training and evaluation of the day. The date is used in the directory name, and the sample data is stored in the distributed file

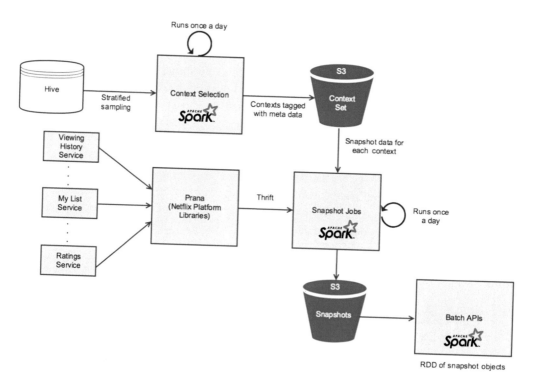

Figure 7.5 Netflix's offline evaluation data pipeline – Time Machine.
Apache Spark, Spark, the Apache Spark Logo and Apache are either registered trademarks or trademarks of the Apache Software Foundation.

system S3. A unified API is provided to external consumers, and these data snapshots can be fetched based on the requested time frame.

From the input of Snapshot Jobs, the information integrated by the Time Machine includes two parts:

(1) Context: it includes relatively static information stored in Hive, such as user profile, device information, item information, and so on.
(2) System log stream: it refers to the logs generated by the system in real time, including the user's viewing history, recommendation impression and user ratings. These logs are generated from different services, and are ingested through Netflix's unified data API – Prana.

Snapshot Jobs retrieve the context information from the context S3 bucket and logs through Prana, then saves the one day's data snapshot to S3 after data processing and feature generation.

After generating the daily data snapshot, it is no longer difficult to use the replay method for offline evaluation. This is because there is no need to perform heavy feature generation during the replay process, and the data snapshot information of the day can be directly used.

On the other hand, it loses flexibility to some extent. Since different models use different features, it is impossible for Snapshot Jobs to generate the required features for all models at once. If some special features are required for a particular model, the Time Machine needs to generate another snapshot for this model based on the common data snapshot.

Based on the framework of the Time Machine, using samples of a certain period of time to perform a replay evaluation is equivalent to having a time travel to this period of time. We hope readers can find their ideal model in this "wonderful" time travel.

7.4 A/B Test and Online Evaluation Metrics

No matter how closely the offline evaluation simulates the online environment, it is impossible to completely reproduce all the online conditions. For almost all internet companies, online A/B testing is the main testing method to validate the effectiveness of new components, new features, and new products.

7.4.1 What Is A/B Test?

A/B test, also known as split test or bucket test, is a random experiment. It usually divided the test group into control (A) and treatment (B). By varying a single variable, it compares the performance of the control and treatment groups correspondingly, and then draws the experiment conclusions based on the collected performance metrics. Specific to the models used in the internet applications, users can be randomly divided into control and treatment groups. Then, the new model is applied to the users in the treatment group, and the old model is applied to the users in the control group.

With some data collection and analysis, the experimenter can get comparisons on the selected online metrics.

Compared with offline evaluation, there are three main reasons why online A/B testing cannot be skipped:

- Offline evaluation cannot completely eliminate the impact of data bias.
- Offline evaluation cannot fully reproduce the online condition. Generally speaking, offline evaluation often does not consider the data latency, data loss, label missing, and so on. Therefore, the offline evaluation results often have some deviation from the reality.
- Some business metrics of the online system cannot be calculated in the offline evaluation. Offline evaluation generally evaluates the model itself, and cannot directly obtain other metrics related to the business target. Taking the new recommendation model as an example, offline evaluation often focuses on improving the ROC curve and PR curve, while online evaluation can fully understand the changes in user click rate, retention time, PV visits, and so on. These metrics can be only obtained through online A/B testing.

7.4.2   Bucketing Mechanism in A/B Testing

In the process of A/B test bucketing, it is necessary to consider the independence of the samples and the unbiasedness of the sampling method. The same user can only be allocated into the same bucket during the entire test, and the user bucketing should be purely random to ensure that the samples in the bucket are not biased.

In the actual industrial online experiment scenario, the website or application often needs to conduct multiple sets of different A/B tests at the same time, such as performing A/B tests on different App UIs at the front end, different middleware efficiencies at the business layer and different algorithms in the recommender system. To avoid the interference of A/B tests at different levels, an effective testing principle must be formulated. Otherwise, the evaluation results can be polluted and misleading caused by improper experiment traffic division. Google's paper [2] introduced in detail the mechanism of experimental traffic layering and partitioning to ensure the high availability of valuable online test traffic.

The mechanism of A/B testing layering and partitioning can be briefly described by two principles:

(1) Orthogonal traffic between layers
(2) Mutually exclusive within the same layer

The orthogonal traffic means that the traffic of each experiment group in the experiment will be randomly partitioned again in the different experiment layers, and evenly distributed in each experiment group in the next layer.

Taking Figure 7.6 as an example, the traffic flow is randomly and equally divided into two parts, X_1 (blue) and X_2 (white) in the Layer X experiment. In the Layer Y experiment, the traffic of X_1 and X_2 should be randomly and evenly distributed to

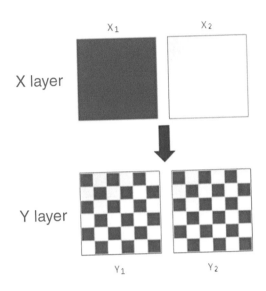

Figure 7.6 Example of orthogonal traffic between layers.

the two buckets Y_1 and Y_2. If the traffic re-distribution of Y_1 and Y_2 is imbalanced in Layer X, then the samples of Layer Y will be biased. As a result, the experimental results of Layer Y will be affected by Layer X. Therefore, the traffic passing through Layer X should be re-randomized and evenly distributed in Y_1 and Y_2.

The meaning of mutually exclusive traffic in the same layer is as follows:

(1) If multiple sets of A/B tests are performed in the same layer, the traffic between different tests should not overlap.
(2) In a group of A/B tests, the traffic of the treatment group and the control group do not overlap.

In user-based A/B testing, "mutual exclusion" means any particular user should only exist in a single treatment group per experiment. Especially for the recommender system, the consistency of user experience is very important, since it usually takes the user some time to adapt to the new recommendation experience. Therefore, it is necessary to ensure that the same user is always assigned to the same group in A/B testing.

The orthogonal and mutually exclusive principles of A/B testing together ensure the objectivity of A/B testing evaluation. Then, how should we choose the evaluation metrics for online A/B testing?

7.4.3 Metrics for Online A/B Testing

Generally speaking, the A/B testing is the last test before the model goes online. The model that passes the A/B test will directly serve the online users to meet the company's business goals. Therefore, the metrics of A/B testing should be consistent with the business key performance indicator (KPI).

Table 7.4 Main evaluation metrics for online A/B testing in various recommender systems

Recommender System Category	Online A/B Metrics
E-commerce	Click-through rate, conversion rate and unit customer spending
News	Retention rate (number of users who are still active after x days/number of total users before x days), average session duration, average number of clicks
Video	Play completion rate (play time/video time), average play time, total play time

Table 7.4 lists the main evaluation metrics for online A/B testing of e-commerce, news and video recommendation models.

Readers should have noticed that the metrics of online A/B testing are quite different from those of offline evaluation (such as AUC, F1-score, and so on). Offline evaluation does not have the conditions to directly calculate the business KPIs, so the next best thing is to choose model-related metrics just for technical evaluation purposes. However, at the company level, there is more interest in the business KPIs that can drive business growth. Therefore, when an online testing environment is available, it is necessary to use A/B testing to verify the effect of the model on improving business KPI. In this case, the role of online A/B testing can never be replaced by offline evaluation.

7.5   Fast Online Evaluation Method: Interleaving

For web applications backed by many recommendation models, in order to continuously iterate and optimize the recommender system, a large number of A/B tests are required to verify the effect of the new algorithm. However, online A/B testing will inevitably take up lots of valuable online traffic resources, and can potentially cause negative impacts to user experience. This generates conflicts between increasing demand for A/B tests and limited resources for online A/B tests.

In response to these problems, a fast online evaluation method – Interleaving – was formally proposed by Microsoft [3] in 2013, and has been successfully applied in production by some companies such as Netflix [4]. Specifically, the Interleaving method is used as the pre-selection stage of the online A/B test, as shown in Figure 7.7, to quickly narrow down the candidate algorithms, and select a small number of "promising" recommendation algorithms from a large number of initial ideas. Then, the traditional A/B testing is performed on the narrowed set of models to measure their long-term impact on user behavior.

In Figure 7.7, light bulbs represent candidate algorithms, with the optimal winning algorithm shown by a red bulb. The Interleaving method can quickly narrow down the initial set of candidate algorithms, determining the best one faster than traditional A/B testing. We'll use Netflix's application scenario as an example to illustrate the principles and characteristics of the Interleaving method.

Traditional A/B Testing

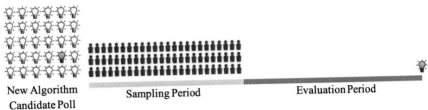

New Algorithm
Candidate Poll
Sampling Period
Evaluation Period

Two Stage Experimental Process

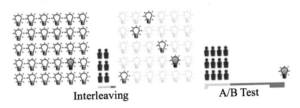

Interleaving
A/B Test

Figure 7.7 Using Interleaving for rapid online testing.

7.5.1 Statistical Issues with Traditional A/B Testing

In addition to efficiency limitations, traditional A/B testing also encounters certain issues with statistical significance. Let's illustrate this with a classic A/B testing example.

Imagine designing an A/B test to assess whether there's a taste preference for Coca-Cola over Pepsi among users. In a traditional setup, participants would be randomly divided into two groups for a blind taste test (where brand labels are hidden). Group A would be given only Coca-Cola, while Group B would only get Pepsi. Consumption over a set period would then indicate a preference for one brand over the other.

While generally effective, this test has potential flaws:

In the test population, consumption habits vary widely, from those who rarely drink soda to heavy daily consumers. Heavy soda drinkers make up a small portion of the sample but may contribute disproportionately to overall consumption. This imbalance could skew results if either group has slightly more heavy consumers, leading to a distorted conclusion.

This issue also arises in online applications like Netflix. A small number of highly active users account for a significant portion of total watch time. So, if more of these active users end up in Group A than in Group B (or vice versa), it can impact the A/B test outcome and obscure the true model performance.

How to address this issue? One solution is to avoid dividing the test population into separate groups. Instead, allow all participants to choose freely between Coca-Cola and Pepsi (while still ensuring the brands remain unlabeled but distinct). At the end of the test, we can calculate each participant's consumption ratio between Coca-Cola and Pepsi, then average these ratios to get an overall preference.

Advantages of this approach include:

(1) It eliminates imbalances in user characteristics between groups.
(2) By assigning equal weight to each participant, it minimizes the impact of heavy consumers on the results.

This approach, where all test options are presented simultaneously to participants and preferences are used to derive evaluation results, is known as the Interleaving method.

7.5.2   Implementing the Interleaving Method

Figure 7.8 illustrates the differences between traditional A/B testing and the interleaving method.

In a traditional A/B test, Netflix will select two groups of subscribers – one group applied with algorithm A, and the other group with algorithm B.

In contrast, in the Interleaving method, there is only one set of subscribers who receive alternate rankings generated by mixing algorithm A and algorithm B.

This allows users to see the recommendation results of both algorithms A and B at the same time in one line (users cannot distinguish whether an item is recommended by algorithm A or B), and then measure the performance of two models using online metrics such as watching time.

While using the Interleaving method for testing, the position bias needs to be considered. The Interleaving method should prevent a particular algorithm from always being ranked first. Therefore, it is necessary to let algorithm A and algorithm B take the lead alternatively with equal probability. This is similar to the process in which the two captains decide who should choose first by tossing a coin and then alternately

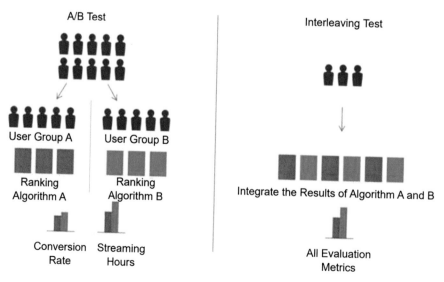

Figure 7.8 Comparison of traditional A/B testing and interleaving method [4].

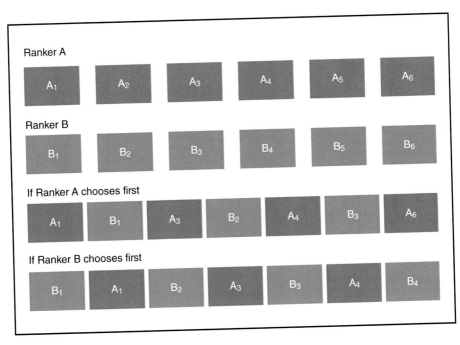

Figure 7.9 Interleaving method on a video ranking page [4].

choose players in a casual sports game. The alternative drafting approach is depicted in Figure 7.9.

After clarifying the specific evaluation process of the Interleaving method, it is necessary to verify whether this method can replace the traditional A/B test and whether it will produce wrong results. Netflix has verified the Interleaving method from two aspects – sensitivity and correctness.

7.5.3 Sensitivity Comparison of Interleaving and Traditional A/B Testing

Netflix's sensitivity experiments measured the sample population size required with the Interleaving method to achieve the same power as traditional A/B testing. Since the resources of online testing are often limited, experimenters always hope to use fewer online resources (for example, sample size, experiment period, and so on) for fast model evaluation.

Figure 7.10 shows the experimental results of the sensitivity comparison. The horizontal axis is the number of samples involved in the experiment, and the vertical axis is the p-value. It can be seen that the Interleaving method uses 10^3 samples to determine whether algorithm A is better than B, while the traditional A/B test requires 10^5 samples to reduce the p-value to below 5%. It shows the Interleaving method only needs 1% of the user sample to determine which algorithm is better. This means that 100 sets of Interleaving experiments can be done with the same level of resources needed by a single traditional A/B test, which undoubtedly greatly enhances the capacity of online testing.

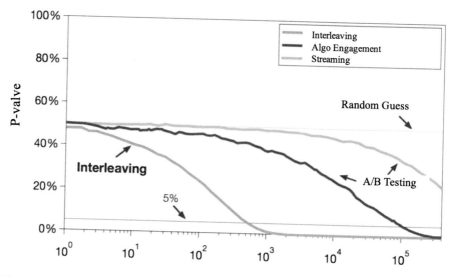

Figure 7.10 Sensitivity test for Interleaving and traditional A/B Testing [4].

7.5.4 Correlation of Metrics in Interleaving and A/B Testing

In addition to sensitivity, the result consistency between Interleaving method and A/B testing is the other key to determine the feasibility of Interleaving.

Figure 7.11 shows the correlation between the metrics from the Interleaving method and the A/B testing. Each data point represents a recommendation model. There is a very strong correlation between the Interleaving metric and the A/B test evaluation metric, which demonstrates that the algorithm that wins in the Interleaving experiment is also very likely to win in the subsequent A/B test.

It should be noted that although the correlation between the two test metrics is extremely strong – the pages displayed in the experiment of the Interleaving method are not actual production pages generated by algorithm A or algorithm B alone. So Interleaving can't totally replace A/B testing in order to measure the actual impact of the new algorithm. A/B testing is still the most authoritative testing method to get a comprehensive evaluation of model performance.

7.5.5 Advantages and Disadvantages of the Interleaving Method

The advantages of the Interleaving method are that it requires fewer samples, the test speed is fast, and the results are not significantly different from traditional A/B tests. However, readers should be clear that the Interleaving method also has certain limitations. The limitations are mainly in the following two aspects:

(1) The engineering framework is more complex than traditional A/B testing. The experimental logic and business logic of the Interleaving method are convoluted, so the business logic may be affected. In order to implement the Interleaving

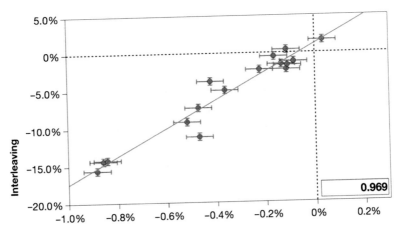

Figure 7.11 The correlation of Interleaving measurement with the A/B testing metric [4].

method, it is necessary to add a large number of auxiliary data identifiers to the entire data flow, which is a difficulty in engineering implementation.

(2) The Interleaving method is only a relative measurement of the user's response to the recommendation results, and cannot obtain the true performance of an algorithm. If you want to know how much one algorithm can improve the business KPIs, it is impossible to draw conclusions using the Interleaving method. To this end, Netflix designed a two-stage experimental structure of Interleaving + A/B testing to improve the entire online testing framework.

7.6   Recommender Systems Evaluation Architecture

This chapter introduces the main evaluation methods and metrics of recommender systems. These model evaluation methods are not independent. A mature evaluation architecture should comprehensively consider the evaluation efficiency and correctness. It needs to use fewer resources to quickly screen out models with better performance. This section systematically discusses how to build a mature recommender system testing and evaluation architecture using the introduced evaluation methods.

As Section 7.3 discusses, for a company, the most fair and reasonable evaluation method is to conduct online A/B testing to evaluate whether the model can better achieve the business goals of the company or the team.

In this case, why can't any model improvement be tested? The reason is given in Section 7.5 while introducing the Interleaving method. This is because online A/B testing takes up lots of online traffic resources and may also negatively impact user experience. However, the limited online testing bandwidths are far from satisfying the needs of model iteration and development. In addition, online testing often needs to last for several days or even weeks, which will greatly slow down the model iteration cycle.

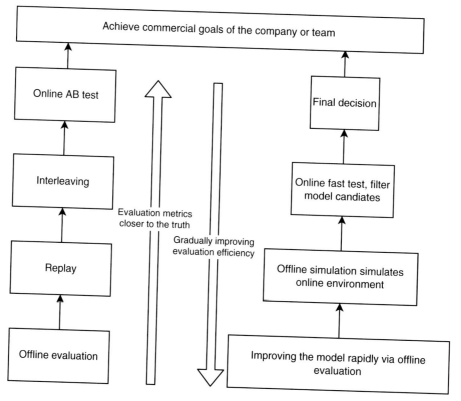

Figure 7.12 Recommender system evaluation architecture.

Because of the limitations of online testing, offline testing has become the next best choice for model evaluation. Offline testing can use nearly unlimited offline computing resources to quickly obtain evaluation results, thereby quickly achieving iterative optimization of the model.

Between online A/B testing and traditional offline testing, there are evaluation methods such as Replay and Interleaving. The Replay method can simulate the online test process in the offline environment to the greatest extent, and the Interleaving method can establish a fast online test environment. This multilevel evaluation and testing method together constitute a complete recommender system evaluation architecture as shown in Figure 7.12, achieving a balance between evaluation efficiency and correctness.

In the schematic diagram of the evaluation architecture shown in Figure 7.12, the left side shows different evaluation methods, and the right side is the pyramid-shaped model screening process. It can be seen that the lower the level, the more models need to be screened, and the more improvement ideas need to be verified. Due to the huge number of possibilities, evaluation efficiency has become a more critical consideration, and the requirements for evaluation correctness are not so strict. At this time, a more efficient offline evaluation method should be used.

As candidate models are screened out layer by layer, the closer it is to the stage of final launch, the stricter the evaluation method's requirements for evaluating correctness should be. Before the model is officially launched, the final model evaluation should be done with the A/B test that is closest to the real production experience. After the most convincing online measurements are produced, the final model can be launched, and the iterative process of model improvement can be completed.

References

[1] Lihong Li, et al. Unbiased offline evaluation of contextual-bandit-based news article Recommender algorithms. Proceedings of the 4th ACM International Conference on Web Search and Data Mining, Hong Kong, China, February 9–12, 2011.

[2] Diane Tang, et al. Overlapping experiment infrastructure: More, better, faster experimentation. Proceedings of the 16th ACM SIGKDD International Conference on Knowledge Discovery and Data Mining, Washington, DC, USA, July 25–28, 2010.

[3] Filip Radlinski, Nick Craswell. Optimized interleaving for online retrieval evaluation. Proceedings of the 6th ACM International Conference on Web Search and Data Mining, Rome, Italy, February 4–8, 2013.

[4] Joshua Parks, et al. Innovating Faster on Personalization Algorithms at Netflix Using Interleaving. Netflix Technology Blog. 2017. https://netflixtechblog.com/interleaving-in-online-experiments-at-netflix-a04ee392ec55

8 Frontier Practice of Deep Learning Recommender Systems

Recommender system is one of the application fields where deep learning is extensively implemented and generates the greatest business value. Some of the most cutting-edge research results come from the practice of industry giants. From the GBDT+LR combination model proposed by Facebook in 2014, which led the direction of feature engineering modeling, to the Deep Crossing model proposed by Microsoft in 2016, the Wide&Deep model architecture released by Google, and YouTube's deep learning recommender system, the industry ushered in the wave of deep learning recommender systems. Today, whether it is the continuous innovation of the Alibaba team in the field of e-commerce recommender systems, or Airbnb's cutting-edge application of deep learning in search and recommendation, deep learning has become a well-deserved mainstream in the field of recommender systems.

For practitioners or readers who aspire to become a recommender systems engineer, it is undoubtedly fortunate to be in this era of open-source code and knowledge sharing. We can almost zero-distance access the cutting-edge recommender systems applications through industry pioneers' papers, blogs, and technical speeches. This chapter's content starts with the basics and gradually delves into the framework and details, explaining several deep learning recommender systems introduced by Meta (previously Facebook), Airbnb, YouTube, and Alibaba. We hope readers can focus on the technical details and engineering implementations of these cutting-edge recommender system applications in the industry, integrate the knowledge, and apply it to their practice based on the knowledge foundation from the previous chapters.

8.1 Deep Learning Recommender Systems by Facebook

In 2014, Facebook (currently Meta, the following uses Facebook as the company name, since the paper was published in 2014) published a paper on their advertising recommender system, *Practical Lessons from Predicting Clicks on Ads at Facebook* [1], which proposed the classic GBDT+LR CTR model structure. Strictly speaking, the GBDT+LR model structure does not belong to the category of deep learning. However, at that time, this work opened up a new stage of feature engineering modeling and automation using the GBDT model for automatic feature combination and selection. Since then, deep learning techniques such as Deep Crossing and Embedding have been applied to feature engineering and gradually transitioned to full deep learning networks. In a sense, Facebook's advertising recommender system based on GBDT+LR became a bridge connecting the era of traditional machine learning recommender systems and the era of deep learning recommender systems. In addition, its online learning, online data integration, downsampling on negative samples, and other technologies adopted as early as 2014 still have strong engineering significance today.

In 2019, Facebook released their latest deep learning model, DLRM (Deep Learning Recommender Model) [2], which uses a classic deep learning model architecture and is trained on a CPU+GPU platform. It is an innovative attempt at a deep learning recommender system in the industry.

This section will first introduce Facebook's implementation of the recommender system based on the GBDT+LR combination model and then delve into the model details and implementation of DLRM.

8.1.1   Application Scenarios

The application scenario of Facebook's advertising recommender system is a standard CTR (click-through rate) prediction use case. The system takes in relevant features of users, ads, and context, predicts the CTR, and then uses the CTR for ad ranking and recommendation. It is important to note that other modules of Facebook's advertising system use the CTR to calculate ad bidding, return on investment (ROI), and other estimated values. Therefore, the predicted value of the CTR model needs to be an accurate value with actual physical meaning, rather than just the higher or lower relevance of ads (which is a crucial difference between advertising and recommender systems). Facebook also specifically introduces a CTR calibration method to correct the deviation between the output value of the CTR prediction model and the actual value.

8.1.2   CTR Prediction Model Based on GBDT+LR

Section 2.6 introduces the model structure of GBDT+LR in detail, which we will briefly review.

In summary, Facebook's CTR prediction model uses the GBDT+LR model structure, which automatically performs feature selection and combination through GBDT, generates a new discrete feature vector, and then uses it as the input of the LR model to predict CTR.

The GBDT model for feature engineering and the LR model for CTR prediction are trained independently with the same optimization objective. Therefore, there is no complicated training problem of how to backpropagate the gradient of LR to GBDT.

Compared with individual LR and GBDT models, the GBDT+LR model significantly improves performance. As shown in Table 8.1, the hybrid model reduces loss by about 3% compared to single LR or GBDT models.

In the practical application of models, hyperparameter tuning is an important step that affects the model performance. In the GBDT+LR model, in order to determine the optimal GBDT subtree size, Facebook has provided a relationship curve between the subtree size and the model loss (as shown in Figure 8.1).

Table 8.1 Performance comparison of the GBDT+LR model against other models

Model	Normalized cross-entry relative to the GBDT model (%)
GBDT+LR	96.58
LR	99.43
GBDT	100 (as the baseline)

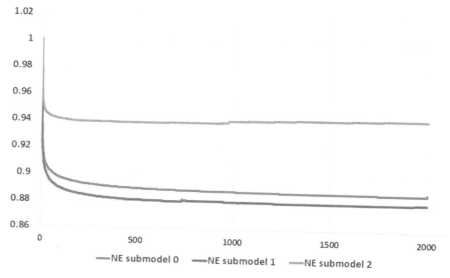

Figure 8.1 The relationship between GBDT subtree size and model loss.

After the subtree size exceeds 500, increasing the size of the subtree has little contribution to model loss reduction. Especially, the last 1000 subtrees only contributed to a 0.1% reduction in loss. It concludes that the gains of increasing the complexity of the model are almost negligible. Finally, Facebook chose 600 as the subtree size in the production.

Section 5.3.3 introduced the GBDT+LR model update method. Due to the fact of massive data collected at Facebook and the difficulty of parallelizing GBDT training, Facebook's engineers adopted a model update strategy – updating the GBDT part every few days and the LR part near real-time in the production system. This strategy balances the model freshness and model training complexity.

8.1.3   Real-Time Streaming Architecture

In order to achieve near real-time training of the model and the features (as detailed in Section 5.3 on knowledge related to the real-time nature of recommendation models and features), Facebook has built a real-time data streaming architecture based on Scribe (a log collection system developed and open-sourced by Facebook). This data

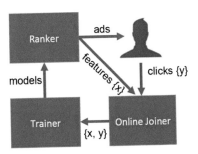

Figure 8.2 Structures of online joiner module and other components in Facebook recommender systems.

streaming architecture is called the online data joiner. The relationship between this module and other modules in the recommender systems is shown in Figure 8.2.

The most important function of this module is to integrate data from different data streams in near real-time to generate training samples, and finally join with click data to get the final labeled data. Throughout the process, the most important things to note are the following three aspects:

8.1.3.1 Waiting Window

The waiting window refers to how long to wait after an impression occurs before it can be determined whether an impression leads to a positive click. If the waiting window is too large, the real-time performance of the data will be affected; if the waiting window is too small, some click data will be missed. Both can result in a discrepancy in the labeled CTR of training samples. This is a problem of engineering tuning, and it is necessary to find a waiting window that matches the actual business pattern. In addition, missing data is sometimes inevitable during data streaming. So it requires the data platform to reprocess all the data in stages to avoid the accumulation of errors generated by the stream processing platform.

8.1.3.2 Unified Action ID in Distributed Systems

In order to achieve the combination of impression data and click records in a distributed system, in addition to generating a globally unified request ID for each behavior, Facebook also established a HashQueue to cache the impression records. The impression in the HashQueue will be considered as a negative sample if no matching click data is found within the waiting window. Facebook uses the Scribe framework to implement this process. Some other companies use Kafka to cache the big data, and use stream computing frameworks such as Flink and Spark Streaming to complete subsequent real-time computing.

8.1.3.3 Data Stream Protection Mechanism

Facebook specifically mentioned the protection mechanism of the online data joiner. Once the data joiner fails due to some abnormality (for example, the click data stream cannot be correctly joined with the impression data stream due to a bug in the action

ID generation), all samples will become negative samples. Since the model is trained and served in real-time, the accuracy of the model will be immediately affected by the wrong sample data, which will directly affect advertising and company profits. The consequences are very serious. To this end, Facebook has specially set up an anomaly detection mechanism. Once the data distribution of the real-time sample stream changes, it will immediately cut off the online learning process to prevent the prediction model from being affected.

8.1.4   Downsampling and Model Calibration

In order to control the data size and reduce training overhead, Facebook has implemented two downsampling methods – uniform subsampling and negative sampling. Uniform sampling is an indiscriminate random sampling of all samples. In order to select the optimal sampling frequency, Facebook experimented with four sampling rates of 1%, 10%, 50%, and 100%. Figure 8.3 compares the model loss with different sampling rates.

It can be seen that when the sampling rate is 10%, compared with the model trained on the full amount of data (100% histogram on the far right), the model loss only increases by 1%. When the sampling rate is reduced to 1%, the model loss has a significant increase of 9%. Therefore, the 10% sampling rate is a more appropriate choice for balancing engineering consumption and model performance.

Another method, negative sampling, retains all positive samples and only downsamples the negative samples. In addition to improving training efficiency, negative sampling also directly solves the problem of imbalance between positive and negative samples. Facebook empirically selected a negative sampling rate from 0.0001 to 0.1, and the experimental results are shown in Figure 8.4.

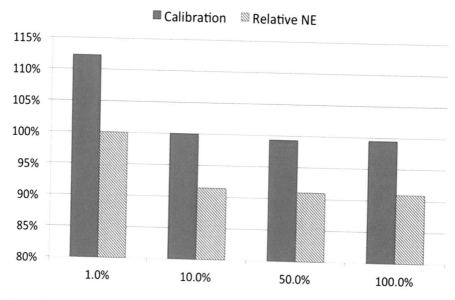

Figure 8.3 Model loss under different sampling rate.

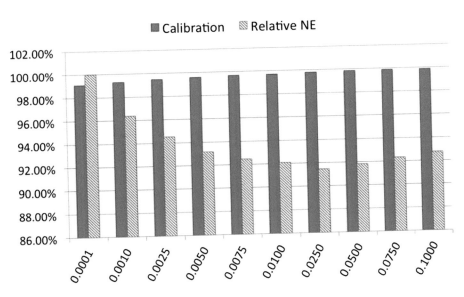

Figure 8.4 Model loss under different negative sampling rates.

It can be seen that when the negative sampling rate is 0.0250, the model loss reaches the lowest compared to those with other sampling rates. Although Facebook did not make a further explanation in the paper, the most likely reason is the data imbalance issue is mostly resolved under this sample rate. In practice, Facebook uses a negative sampling rate of 0.0250.

The problem caused by negative sampling is the drift of the estimated CTR value. Assuming that the real CTR is 0.1%, after negative sampling of 0.01, the predicted CTR will increase to about 10%. In order to support accurate bidding and ROI estimation, the CTR prediction model must provide accurate and physically meaningful CTR values. Therefore, after negative sampling, it is necessary to correct the CTR to make the expected value of the CTR model return 0.1%. The correction formula is shown in Equation 8.1:

$$q = \frac{p}{p + (1-p)/w} \tag{8.1}$$

where q is the corrected CTR, p is the CTR prediction from the model, and w is the negative sampling rate. The process of correcting CTR through negative sampling is not complicated, and interested readers can manually derive this formula following the negative sampling process.

8.1.5 Facebook's Engineering Practice of GBDT+LR Combination Model

Although Facebook's advertising recommender system based on the GBDT+LR combination model was developed in 2014, we can still learn a lot from it in terms of model transformation and engineering implementation. The three most valuable lessons are summarized next:

8.1.5.1   Modelization of Feature Engineering

In 2014, while many practitioners were still experimenting with various feature combinations through experience and parameter tuning, Facebook's innovative approach of using models for automatic feature combination and selection was a groundbreaking idea. It was also around that time that various deep learning and embedding ideas began to emerge, promoting the concept of modelization of feature engineering.

8.1.5.2   Balancing Model Complexity and Effectiveness

The use of different update frequencies for GBDT and LR is a highly engineering-oriented and valuable practical experience, and it is also the solution that maximizes the advantages of each part of the combination model.

8.1.5.3   Use Data to Verify Ideas

In our work, we often have many intuitive conclusions, such as the impact of data and model real-time performance, how many subtrees GBDT should set, and whether to use negative sampling or random sampling. In response to these questions, Facebook reminds us to let data speak. No matter how small a choice is, it should be supported by data, which is the rigorous work attitude that every engineer should have.

8.1.6   Facebook's Deep Learning Model DLRM

After five years, Facebook released its recommender system deep learning model, the DLRM in 2019. Compared with GBDT+LR, DLRM is a thorough attempt to apply deep learning models. The model structure, training method, and performance evaluation of DLRM will be introduced next.

The model structure of DLRM is shown in Figure 8.5, and the functions of each layer of the model are as follows:

Feature Engineering: All features are divided into two categories – sparse features generated by one-hot encoding (such as category and ID-type features), and the continuous numerical features.

Embedding Layer: After each categorical feature is converted into a one-hot vector, the embedding layer is used to convert it into an n-dimensional embedding vector. In other words, the sparse features are transformed into dense embedding vectors. Continuous features such as age and income are concatenated into a feature vector and input into the yellow MLP module in Figure 8.5, which is also transformed into an n-dimensional vector. At this point, both the sparse features composed of categorical features and the feature vectors composed of continuous features have been transformed into n-dimensional embedding vectors after passing through the embedding layer.

Neural Network Layers: Above the embedding layer are the neural network layers represented by triangles. That is to say, after obtaining n-dimensional embedding vectors, each type of embedding may be further transformed through the neural network layer. However, this process is optional and based on tuning and performance evaluation to determine whether to introduce the neural network layer for further feature processing.

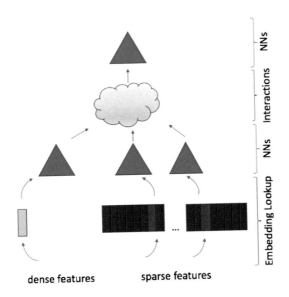

Figure 8.5 Model structure of DLRM.

Interaction Layers: This layer calculates the inner product of each pair of the embeddings and connects them with the corresponding embeddings of the continuous features, and then inputs them into the following MLP. So this step is actually the same as the PNN model introduced in Section 3.5, which aims to enable sufficient cross-interactions between features. After the combination, the inputs enter the upper MLP to make the final target fitting.

Objective Fitting Layers: The blue triangle on the top of the structural diagram represents another fully connected multilayer neural network. The final CTR prediction is generated using the sigmoid function in the last layer. This is also a very standard setting for the output layer of deep learning models.

From the DLRM model structure, it can be seen that the model structure is not complex, and there are no attention mechanisms, sequence models, or reinforcement learning model ideas. It is a very standard deep learning recommendation model in the industry. This is attributed to Facebook's practical technical culture, and also shows that simple model structures can play a good role in the background of massive data.

8.1.7 Parallel Training Method in the DLRM Model

As a paper from the industry, the actual training methods of the DLRM model can often benefit peers in the industry. Due to the huge amount of data at Facebook, the single-node model training cannot support the model training task in time. Therefore, model parallel training is a necessary solution.

In short, the DLRM model uses a combination of model parallelism and data parallelism, adopting model parallelism for the embedding part and data parallelism for the MLP part. The purpose of using model parallelism for the embedding part is to alleviate the memory bottleneck problem caused by a large number of embedding layer parameters. Data parallelism is used for the MLP and interaction layers to parallelize forward and backward propagation.

Model parallel training of the embedding layer means that only a portion of the embedding layer parameters are saved on one device or computing node, and each device only updates the embedding layer parameters on its own node during parallel mini-batch gradient updates.

Data parallel training of the MLP and interaction layers means that each device already has all the model parameters, and each device calculates gradients using part of the data, and then uses the AllReduce method to summarize all the gradients for parameter updates.

8.1.8   DLRM Model Performance

DLRM was trained on Facebook's proprietary AI platform, the Big Basin platform. The platform's specific configuration is Dual Socket Intel Xeon 6138 CPU @ 2.00GHz + 8 Nvidia Tesla V100 16GB GPUs.

Obviously, the Big Basin platform is a high-performance CPU+GPU combination platform, which does not adopt a distributed hardware architecture like the Parameter Server introduced in Section 6.3. This saves a lot of network communication costs, but lacks scalability compared with the Parameter Server.

In terms of performance comparison, DLRM chose Google's DCN proposed in 2017 as the performance benchmarking baseline. By comparing DLRM with DCN introduced in Section 3.6, it can be found that the main difference between DLRM and DCN lies in the different feature cross methods. DLRM adopts the cross-product method of two different feature fields, while DCN adopts a more complex cross-layer feature cross method. Tested on the Criteo Ad Kaggle data, the performance comparison between the two is shown in Figure 8.6.

As can be seen, DLRM slightly outperforms DCN in terms of accuracy. Of course, the model's performance is closely related to the choice of the dataset and the tuning of the

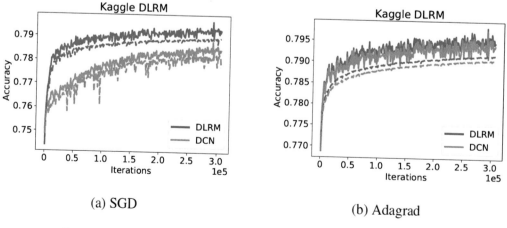

(a) SGD   (b) Adagrad

Figure 8.6 Performance comparison of DLRM and DCN models.

parameters. Moreover, the advantage of DLRM under the Adagrad training method has been negligible. The performance evaluation shown here is only for a reference purpose.

8.1.9 Summary of Facebook's Deep Learning Recommender System

Whether it is the GBDT+LR combination model or the latest DLRM model, Facebook's technical choices always give people a very practical feeling, which are simple and direct with problem-solving as their centric goal. Although, from an academic perspective, both models are not very innovative, practitioners in the industry can still learn a lot of engineering practices from them. The DLRM model is a very standard and practical deep learning recommendation model. If a company is just starting to transition from traditional machine learning models to deep learning models, it can completely adopt DLRM as the standard implementation. The feature engineering modelization and model combination ideas conveyed by the GBDT+LR combination model have a profound impact on the development of recommender system technology.

8.2 Airbnb's Real-Time Search Recommender System Based on Embedding

In 2018, Airbnb published a paper titled "Real-time Personalization using Embeddings for Search Ranking at Airbnb" [3] at KDD, which was awarded the best paper at the conference. The first author of the paper, Mihajlo, Airbnb's senior machine learning scientist, has also shared Airbnb's search recommender system at multiple technical conferences.

As one of the "core operations" of deep learning, embedding technology can not only convert a large number of sparse features into dense features as the inputs of deep learning networks, but also encode the semantic representations of items through embedding, and directly search for similar items through similarity calculation. Airbnb fully exploited these two advantages of embedding and built its real-time search recommender system based on it.

8.2.1 Application Scenarios

As the world's largest short-term rental website, Airbnb provides an intermediary platform connecting hosts and short-term rental guests/users. The user interaction with Airbnb is a typical search recommendation application scenario. After the user provides location, price, keywords, and other information, Airbnb will provide a search recommendation list of housing resources.

After showing the list of recommended housing resources, the interactions between tenants and landlords are of several types (as shown in Figure 8.7):

- The tenant clicks on a housing listing.
- The tenant immediately books a housing listing.
- The tenant makes a booking request, and the landlord may reject, accept, or not respond to the tenant's booking request.

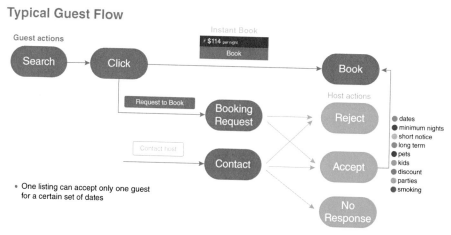

Figure 8.7 Different interaction types in Airbnb.

Airbnb's search application is based on such a business scenario, using historical data generated by several interaction methods to build a real-time search ranking model. In order to capture the user's "short-term" and "long-term" interests, Airbnb did not directly input the clicked listing IDs or booked listing IDs in the user's historical data into the ranking model. Instead, it first generates embedding representations of the tenants and housing resources, and then uses the results of embedding to build many features as the inputs of the ranking model.

In terms of embedding methods, Airbnb generated two different embeddings to encode the user's "short-term" and "long-term" interests, respectively. The purpose of generating embeddings for short-term interests is to recommend similar housing resources and provide real-time personalized recommendations for users within a session. The purpose of generating long-term interest embeddings is to take care of the user's previous booking preferences in the final recommendation results and provide personalized search experiences.

8.2.2   Housing Embedding Method Based on Short-Term Interests

Airbnb uses the in-session click data to embed the listings, capturing the user's short-term interests during a single search. The session click data refers to a sequence of listings that a user clicks during a single search, which must meet two conditions: (1) the user must stay on the listing detail page for more than 30 seconds to be counted as a data point in the sequence; (2) if the user has no action for more than 30 minutes, the sequence will be interrupted and is no longer considered a session. This is done for two purposes, which are to filter out noise and negative feedback signals, and to avoid the generation of nonrelevant sequences.

With the sequence of clicked listings, it is possible to embed them like a sentence sample, just like the Item2vec method described in Section 4.3. Airbnb chose the skip-gram model from Word2vec, which was introduced in Section 4.2, as the framework for the embedding method, modifying the objective function of Word2vec to approximate Airbnb's business objectives.

The method of Word2vec was introduced in detail in Section 4.1 of this book. Here, we list the objective function of the skip-gram model of Word2vec:

$$\arg\max_{\theta} \sum_{(w,c)\in D} \log p(c|w) = \sum_{(w,c)\in D} \left(\log e^{v_c \cdot v_w} - \log \sum_{c'} e^{v_{c'} \cdot v_w} \right) \tag{8.2}$$

After adopting the training method of negative sampling, the objective function is transformed into the following form,

$$\arg\max_{\theta} \sum_{(w,c)\in D} \log \sigma(v_c \cdot v_w) + \sum_{(w,c)\in D'} \log \sigma(-v_c \cdot v_w) \tag{8.3}$$

where σ is the sigmoid function, D is the positive sample set, and D' is the negative sample set. The first half of Equation 8.3 represents the objective function of the positive samples, while the second half represents the function of negative samples (with an added negative sign).

Returning to the Airbnb listing embedding problem, the positive samples in the embedding process are naturally taken from the listing within the sliding window of the click sequence in the session, while the negative samples are randomly selected from the corpus (that is, all the available listings) after determining the central listing.

Therefore, Airbnb's initial objective function is almost identical to that of Word2vec,

$$\arg\max_{\theta} \sum_{(l,c)\in \mathcal{D}_p} \log \frac{1}{1+e^{-V_c'V_l}} + \sum_{(l,c)\in \mathcal{D}_n} \log \frac{1}{1+e^{V_c'V_l}} \tag{8.4}$$

On the top of original Word2vec embedding, Airbnb's engineers wanted to introduce historical booking information into the embedding process. This can make Airbnb's search results and similar listings more likely to recommend the items based on previous bookings. From this motivation, Airbnb divided session click sequences into two categories: booking sessions and exploratory sessions.

In each booking session, only the last item is the listing that is finally booked. In order to introduce this booking behavior into the objective function, whether the booked listing is in the Word2vec sliding window or not, it is assumed that the booked listing is related to the central listing in the sliding window. This introduces a global context into the objective function. Therefore, the objective function becomes as follows,

$$\arg\max_{\theta} \sum_{(l,c)\in \mathcal{D}_p} \log \frac{1}{1+e^{-V_c'V_l}} + \sum_{(l,c)\in \mathcal{D}_n} \log \frac{1}{1+e^{V_c'V_l}} + \log \frac{1}{1+e^{-V_{l_b}'V_l}} \tag{8.5}$$

In the last term, l_b represents the booked listing, and because booking is a positive sample behavior, this term also has a negative sign in front of it. It should be noted that there is no Σ symbol in front of the last term like the preceding terms. It is because the central listing in the sliding window is related to all other listings in the sliding window.

To better discover the differences between listings within the same marketplace, Airbnb added another set of negative samples. These are randomly sampled from the set of listings in the same marketplace as the central listing. Similarly, they can be added to the objective function as follows,

$$\underset{\theta}{\arg\max} \sum_{(l,c)\in \mathcal{D}_p} \log\frac{1}{1+e^{-V_c'V_l}} + \sum_{(l,c)\in \mathcal{D}_n} \log\frac{1}{1+e^{V_c'V_l}} + \log\frac{1}{1+e^{-V_{l_b}'V_l}}$$
$$+ \sum_{(l,m_n)\in \mathcal{D}_{m_n}} \log\frac{1}{1+e^{V_{m_n}'V_l}} \tag{8.6}$$

Among them, $\mathcal{D}_{mn}$ refers to the collection of negative samples in the same region in the new dataset.

Thus, the objective function for the listing embeddings is defined, and the training process for the embeddings is the standard process of using negative sampling as in Word2vec, which will not be further elaborated here.

In addition, the paper also introduces a method to solve the cold start problem. In short, if there is a new housing missing an embedding vector, the average of the embedding vectors of three nearby housing units of the same type and similar price will be taken, which is a good practical engineering experience.

8.2.3 User Embeddings and Housing Embeddings Based on Long-Term Interests

Short-term interest embeddings use user click data to construct housing embeddings, which can effectively find similar housing units, but are deficient in that they do not include users' long-term interest information. For example, if a user booked a housing unit six months ago, it includes the user's long-term preferences for attributes such as housing prices and types. However, because the previous embeddings only used session-level click data, they lost the user's long-term interest information.

To capture users' long-term preferences, Airbnb uses booking session sequences. For example, if user j has booked five housing units in the past year, then their booking session would be $s_j = (l_{j1}, l_{j2}, l_{j3}, l_{j4}, l_{j5})$. Since there is a set of booking sessions, can we apply Word2vec's method to embeddings as we did with click sessions? The answer is no, because we would encounter a very tricky problem of data sparsity.

Specifically, the data sparsity problem of booking sessions manifests itself in the following three ways:

(1) The total number of booking behaviors is much smaller than the number of click behaviors, so the size of the booking session set is much smaller than that of the click session set.

(2) The number of booking behaviors for a single user is very small. Many users only booked one housing unit in the past year, which means that many booking session sequences have a length of only one.

(3) Most housing units are booked very few times. To train meaningful and stable embeddings using Word2vec, an item needs to appear at least 5–10 times, but many housing units are booked less than five times, which makes it impossible to obtain effective embeddings.

How to solve such a serious data sparsity problem and train meaningful user and housing embeddings? Airbnb's solution is to aggregate similar users and similar housing units based on certain attribute rules. For example, housing unit attributes are shown in Table 8.2.

You can use attribute names and bucket IDs (referring to the index number of attribute values) to form an attribute identifier. For example, if a listing is located in the US, has a listing type of "Ent" (bucket 1), and a nightly price range of $56–59 (bucket 3), you can use "US_lt1_pn3" to represent the attribute identifier of this listing.

The definition of user attributes follows the same logic. As shown in Table 8.3, user attributes include device type, whether the user has filled in a profile, whether they have a profile picture, and their history of bookings. These user attributes are fundamental and can be used to generate a user attribute identifier (or user type) using the same method as for listing attribute identifiers.

Table 8.2 Housing attributes

Bucket ID	1	2	3	4	5	6	7	8
Country	US	CA	GB	FR	MX	AU	ES	...
Listing Type	Ent	Priv	Share					
Price per Night	<40	40–55	56–69	70–83	84–100	101–129	130–189	190+
Num of Beds	1	2	3	4+				
5-star rating%	0–40	41–60	61–90	90+				

Table 8.3 User attributes

Bucket ID	1	2	3	4	5	6	7
Market	SF	NYC	LA	PHL	AUS	LV	...
Language	En	Es	Fr	Jp	Ru	Ko	De
Device Type	Mac	Msft	Andr	iPad	Tablet	iPhone	...
Full Profile	Yes	No					
Profile Photo	Yes	No					
Num of Historical Booking	0	1	2–7	8+			
Price Per Night	<40	40–55	56–69	70–83	84–100	101–129	130–189

With user and listing attributes, a new booking session sequence can be re-generated through the aggregation of data. User attributes can directly replace the original user ID, generating a booking sequence consisting of all historical bookings for that particular user. This method solves the problem of sparse user booking data.

After obtaining the booking sequence for a certain user attribute, how can the embeddings for user and listing attributes be obtained? To ensure user attribute ID and listing attribute ID embeddings generated in the same vector space, Airbnb uses a somewhat counterintuitive method.

For a booking session $(l_1, l_2, \ldots, l_m)$ sorted by time for a given user ID, the original listing item is replaced by a tuple (user_type, listing_type), resulting in the sequence $((u_{\text{type1}}, l_{\text{type1}}), (u_{\text{type2}}, l_{\text{type2}}), \cdots, (u_{\text{typeM}}, l_{\text{typeM}}))$. Here, l_{type1} refers to the listing attribute corresponding to listing l_1, and u_{type1} refers to the user attribute at the time of booking listing l_1. Since a user's attributes can change over time, $u_{\text{type1}}, u_{\text{type2}}$ may not be the same even they are from the same user.

Once the sequence is defined, the next question is how to train embeddings so that user and listing attribute embeddings can be in the same vector space. The training objective function used is completely in line with the form of the objective function defined in Section 8.2.2. However, since the (user type, listing type) tuple is used to replace the original listing, determining the "central item" becomes a critical issue. In fact, Airbnb did not disclose the technical details in the related paper, but based on its general description, this section presents a training method that is closest to the original paper.

Airbnb provides the objective functions for training user type embeddings and listing type embeddings when the "central item" in the sliding window is user type (u_t) and listing type (l_t), respectively,

$$\underset{\theta}{\arg\max} \sum_{(u_t, c) \in \mathcal{D}_{\text{book}}} \log \frac{1}{1 + e^{-V_c' V_{u_t}}} + \sum_{(u_t, c) \in \mathcal{D}_{\text{neg}}} \log \frac{1}{1 + e^{V_c' V_{u_t}}} \tag{8.7}$$

$$\underset{\theta}{\arg\max} \sum_{(l_t, c) \in \mathcal{D}_{\text{book}}} \log \frac{1}{1 + e^{-V_c' V_{l_t}}} + \sum_{(l_t, c) \in \mathcal{D}_{\text{neg}}} \log \frac{1}{1 + e^{V_c' V_{l_t}}} \tag{8.8}$$

where $\mathcal{D}_{\text{book}}$ is the set of user and listing attributes near the central item. Therefore, during the training process, user and listing attributes are treated equally, and these two target functions are exactly the same.

It can be said that Airbnb flattened all the tuples in the training process, treating user and listing attributes equivalently when training embeddings, ensuring that they naturally generate in the same vector space. Although this process wastes some information from two types of attributes, it is a good engineering solution.

Once the objective function for embedding is defined, and both user and listing embeddings are mapped to the same vector space, training can be conducted using Word2vec negative sampling. The cosine similarity between user and listing embeddings represents the user's long-term interest preference for a certain listing.

8.2.4   Embedding for Airbnb Search Queries

In addition to computing embeddings for users and listings, Airbnb also applied embeddings for search queries in its search recommender system. Similar to the method for user embeddings, the search queries and listings are embedded in the same vector space, and then sorted based on their cosine similarity. The search ranking generated using the embedding method differs from the traditional text similarity approach.

Before the introduction of embeddings, the search results could only be based on the input keywords. However, with the introduction of embeddings, the search results can even capture the semantic information of the search query. For example, when inputting "France Skiing," although none of the location names in the results contain the keyword "Skiing," the associated results are all ski resorts in France. This undoubtedly provides results that are closer to the user's intention.

8.2.5   Airbnb's Real-Time Search Ranking Model and Its Feature Engineering

Earlier, we introduced Airbnb's method of computing embeddings for users' short-term and long-term interests in listings. It is important to note that Airbnb does not directly rank search results based on embedding similarity, but instead generates different user-listing pair features based on embeddings, which are then input into the search ranking model to obtain the final ranking results.

So what features does Airbnb generate based on embeddings? And how do these features drive online personalized search results? Table 8.4 lists all the embedding-based features.

It is clear that the last feature, UserTypeListingTypeSim, refers to the similarity between the user type and listing type. This feature similarity is calculated using the long-term interest embeddings of user types and listing types. In addition, all other features apply to short-term interest embeddings. For example, EmbClickSim refers to the similarity between a candidate listing and the listing that the user most recently clicked on.

A careful reader may have a question – where does the "real-time" aspect of Airbnb's system come into play? In fact, the answer to this question can be found in the feature design. Among these embedding-related features, Airbnb has added

Table 8.4 List of embedding-based user and listing features

Feature Names	Feature Descriptions
EmbClickSim	Similarity between candidate listings and user's clicked listings
EmbSkipSim	Similarity between candidate listings and user's skipped listings
EmbLongClickSim	Similarity between candidate listings and user's long clicked listings
EmbWishlistSim	Similarity between candidate listings and user's saved listings
EmbInqSim	Similarity between candidate listings and user's inquired listings
EmbBookSim	Similarity between candidate listings and user's booked listings
EmbLastLongClickSim	Similarity between candidate listings and user's last long clicked listings
UserTypeListingTypeSim	Similarity between candidate listing type and user type

Table 8.5 Airbnb evaluation of different feature importance

Feature Name	Coverage (%)	Feature Importance Ranking
EmbClickSim	76.16	5/104
EmbSkipSim	78.64	8/104
EmbLongClickSim	51.05	20/104
EmbWishlistSim	36.50	47/104
EmbInqSim	20.61	12/104
EmbBookSim	8.06	46/104
EmbLastLongClickSim	48.28	11/104
UserTypeListingTypeSim	86.11	22/104

features such as similarity to the most recently clicked listing (EmbClickSim) and similarity to the last long clicked listing (EmbLastLongClickSim). Due to the presence of these features, users can receive real-time feedback during the browsing process, and search results can change in real-time based on user click behavior.

After obtaining these embedding features, they are input into the search ranking model for training together with other features. Here, Airbnb uses a GBDT model that supports pairwise Lambda Rank [4] as the search ranking model, which has been open-sourced by Airbnb engineers. Finally, Table 8.5 shows the evaluation results of Airbnb's feature importance for reference.

8.2.6   Summary of Airbnb's Real-Time Search Recommender System

This section introduces the content related to Airbnb's real-time search recommender system. Overall, there are several aspects of the system that are worth emphasizing.

8.2.6.1   Excellent Integration of Engineering and Theory
In this work, the Airbnb team modified the classic Word2vec method and completed the embedding of users and listings. Also, they addressed the data sparsity issue by aggregating user and listing attributes through bucketizing. These highly practical methods are a valuable approach for machine learning engineers to learn.

8.2.6.2   Excellent Integration of Business and Knowledge
During the modification of the embedding objective function, there were multiple instances where the objective terms were closely aligned with business goals, thereby linking the algorithm development to the company's business and commercial models. This is an ability that many academically oriented machine learning engineers should develop.

8.3   YouTube's Deep Learning Video Recommender System

This section introduces YouTube's deep learning video recommender system. In 2016, YouTube published a paper titled "Deep Neural Networks for YouTube

Recommenders" [5]. Even though the novelty is not very significant nowadays, the proposed approach in this paper has become one of the most classic deep learning architectures in the recommender systems industry. Readers can gain insights not only from the classic architecture of deep learning recommender systems but also from the technical details and engineering practices, which are invaluable.

8.3.1   Application Scenarios

As the world's largest video-sharing website, almost all videos on the YouTube platform are from user-generated content (UGC). This content has two common characteristics:

(1) Unlike Netflix or some other major video streaming services, which mainly purchase or produce top content, YouTube's content is very diverse. This makes its business mode quite different from the other streaming services. The main effect of YouTube's content is not as obvious as those of streaming providers.

(2) Due to the vast number of videos on YouTube, it is difficult for users to discover content they like.

These characteristics of YouTube's content make the recommender system more critical than other streaming services. In addition, YouTube's main source of profit comes from video advertising, and the exposure opportunities of advertisements are directly proportional to the user's viewing time. Therefore, the YouTube recommender system is the foundation of its business model.

Based on YouTube's business model and content characteristics, its recommendation team built two deep learning networks that consider recall and precision requirements, respectively. They also constructed a ranking model with user watch time as the optimization goal to maximize user watch time and generate more advertising exposure opportunities. The following describes in detail the model structure and technical specifics of the YouTube recommender system.

8.3.2   YouTube Recommender Systems Architecture

As mentioned earlier, the vast number of videos on YouTube requires its recommender system to perform personalized recommendation on a scale of millions of videos. Considering the latency issue of online systems, it is not suitable to directly use a complex network to sort all massive candidate sets. Therefore, YouTube uses a two-level deep learning model to complete the entire recommendation process as shown in Figure 8.8.

The first stage uses a candidate generation model to quickly screen candidate videos. In this step, the candidate video set is reduced from millions to hundreds. This is equivalent to the recall layer in the classic recommender system architecture.

The second stage uses a ranking model to perform precise ranking on hundreds of candidate videos. This is equivalent to the ranking layer in the classic recommender system architecture.

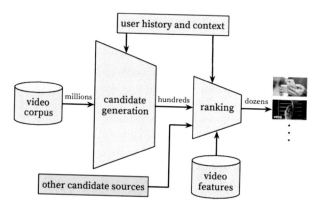

Figure 8.8 Overall architecture of YouTube recommender system.

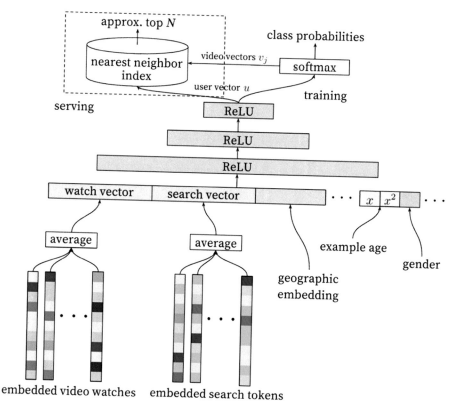

Figure 8.9 Architecture of the YouTube candidate generation model.

8.3.3   Candidate Generation Model

First, we introduce the architecture of the candidate generation model (as shown in Figure 8.9). Looking at this network from the bottom up, the input of the bottom layer is the user's historical video embedding vector and search query embedding vector.

To generate video embedding and search query embedding, YouTube uses a method similar to the Airbnb embedding method introduced in Section 8.2. It uses the Word2vec method to embed videos and search queries based on the user's viewing and search sequences, and then uses them as inputs to the candidate generation model. The specific method can refer to the process of Airbnb embedding for house listings in Section 8.2. In addition to pre-embedding, an embedding layer can also be directly added to the deep learning network for end-to-end training with the upper MLP layers. The pros and cons of these two methods have been discussed in Section 4.5.

Apart from the video and search term embedding vectors, the feature vectors also include the user's geographic feature embedding, age, gender, and so on. All the features are then concatenated and input into a ReLU neural network for training.

After three layers of neural networks, the softmax function is used as the output layer. YouTube sees the problem of selecting a candidate video set as a next-watch recommendation problem for users. The final output of the model is a probability distribution over all candidate videos. Clearly, this is a multiclassification problem, which is why softmax is used as the final output layer.

Overall, the candidate generation model of the YouTube recommender system is a standard deep neural network model that uses pre-trained embedding features.

8.3.4 Unique Online Serving Method for Candidate Generation Models

Readers may have noticed that the model serving method in the upper left corner of Figure 8.9 is completely different from the model training method. During the online serving of the candidate generation model, YouTube does not directly use the trained method, but instead uses a nearest neighbor search method, which is a result of balancing engineering and theoretical considerations.

Specifically, during the model online serving, if the inference process of the candidate generation network is run end-to-end for each request, the computational cost of the entire inference process will be very high because the network structure is relatively complex, especially since the number of output layer parameters is enormous. Therefore, after obtaining the user and video embedding through the candidate generation model, the efficiency of the model online serving can be greatly improved by using the nearest neighbor search method based on embedding. This way, it is not even necessary to move the model inference logic to the server. It is sufficient to store the user embedding and video embedding in a memory database such as Redis or server memory. If the nearest neighbor search method (such as LSH, introduced in Section 4.6) is used, the computational complexity of the model service can even be reduced to a constant level. This is a tremendous efficiency improvement for candidate generation processes with millions of candidates.

If we continue to explore, we can get some very interesting information. An arrow is drawn from the softmax to the model service module in the architecture diagram (Figure 8.9), which represents the generation of video embedding vectors. How are these video embeddings generated? Since the last layer is softmax, the parameters of this softmax layer are essentially an $m \times n$ dimensional matrix, where m refers to the dimension of the last layer (ReLU layer), and n refers to the total number of classifications, which is the total number of YouTube videos. Therefore, the video embeddings are the column vectors of this $m \times n$ dimensional matrix. This method of embedding generation is actually the same as the method of generating word vectors in Word2vec.

In addition, the generation of user vectors is straightforward to understand. Since all the input feature vectors are user-related features, when using a user's feature vector as the model input, the output vector of the last ReLU layer can be used as that user's embedding vector. After training the model, inputting all user feature vectors into the model one by one will produce all user embedding vectors, which can then be imported into the online embedding database. When predicting a user's video candidate set, the user's embedding vector is first obtained, and then the top K nearest neighbors of this user embedding vector in the video embedding vector space are searched using local sensitive hash method, and k candidate video sets can be quickly obtained.

8.3.5　Ranking Model

Using the candidate generation model, hundreds of candidate videos are generated, and then the ranking model is used for precise ranking. The ranking model of YouTube's recommender system is shown in Figure 5.8.

At first glance, readers may think that the network structure of the ranking model is not much different from that of the candidate set generation model. Indeed, this is the case in terms of model structure. Here, we need to focus on the input layer and output layer of the model, that is, the feature engineering and optimization objectives of the ranking model.

Compared with the candidate generation model, which needs to screen millions of candidate sets, the ranking model only needs to sort hundreds of candidate videos, so more features can be introduced for precise ranking. Specifically, the features from left to right in the input layer are:

(1) The embedding of the current candidate video (impression video ID embedding).
(2) The average embedding of the last N videos watched by the user (watched video IDs average embedding).
(3) The embedding of the user's language and the embedding of the current candidate video's language (language embedding).
(4) The time interval since the user last watched a video on the same channel (time since last watch).
(5) The number of times the video has been exposed to the user (#previous impressions).

Among these five features, the meanings of the first three are intuitive. Here we will focus on the fourth and fifth features, as these two features effectively capture YouTube's observations of user behavior.

The fourth feature, "time since last watch" represents the interval time between the user watching videos of the same type. From the user's perspective, if a user has just watched a video from the "Classic DOTA Game Review" channel, the user is likely to continue watching videos from this channel. This feature captures this user behavior very well.

The fifth feature "#previous impressions" introduces the "exploration and exploitation" mechanism described in Section 5.7 to avoid continuous ineffective exposure of the same video to the same user and increase the possibility of the user seeing new videos.

It should be noted that the ranking model not only introduces the original feature values for the fourth and fifth features, but also performs square and square root operations. As a new feature input to the model, this operation introduces nonlinearity of the features and improves the model's ability to express the features.

After passing through a three-layer ReLU network, the ranking model uses a different output layer from that of the candidate generation model. The candidate generation model chooses softmax as its output layer, while the ranking model chooses weighted logistic regression as the model output layer. At the same time, the output layer function chosen during the model serving phase is $e^{(Wx+b)}$. Why does YouTube choose different output layer functions for training and serving phases?

Starting from YouTube's business model, increasing user watch time is the main optimization goal of its recommender system. Therefore, when training the ranking model, the expected watch time per impression should be a more reasonable optimization objective. Therefore, in order to directly predict the watch time, YouTube uses the watch time of positive samples as the sample weight and trains with weighted logistic regression, which enables the model to learn the information of actual watch time.

Assuming the probability of an event happening is p, a new concept called "odds" is introduced here, which refers to the ratio of the event happening to not happening. For logistic regression, the probability p of an event happening is obtained from the sigmoid function, as shown,

$$p = \text{sigmoid}\left(\theta^{\mathrm{T}} x\right) = \frac{1}{1 + e^{-(Wx+b)}} \tag{8.9}$$

Here, the variable Odds is defined as shown in Equation 8.10 and by substituting it into Equation 8.9, we get,

$$\text{Odds} = \frac{p}{1-p} = e^{Wx+b} \tag{8.10}$$

It is obvious that YouTube uses the variable Odds as the output of the model in the model serving. Why does YouTube predict the variable Odds? What is the physical meaning of Odds?

Further explanation is needed based on the principle of weighted logistic regression. Since weighted logistic regression introduces the information of positive sample weights, in the YouTube scenario, the viewing time T_i of positive sample i is its sample weight. Therefore, the probability of a positive sample occurrence becomes T_i times the original probability, and the Odds of positive sample i becomes,

$$\text{Odds}(i) = \frac{T_i p}{1 - T_i p} \tag{8.11}$$

In the video recommendation scenario, the probability p of a user opening a video is often a very small value (usually around 1%), so Equation 8.11 can be further simplified:

$$\text{Odds}(i) = \frac{T_i p}{1 - T_i p} \approx T_i p = E(T_i) = \text{Expected watching time}$$

It can be seen that the physical meaning of the variable Odds is the expected viewing time for each impression, which is exactly the optimization target that the ranking model hopes to achieve. Therefore, using weighted logistic regression for model training and $e^{(Wx+b)}$ for model service is the most suitable technical implementation for optimizing this target.

8.3.6   Training and Testing Samples Processing

To improve the model's training efficiency and accuracy, YouTube has implemented various engineering measures to process training samples, including the following three experiences for readers to reference:

(1) The candidate generation model transforms the recommendation problem into a multiclassification problem. In the scenario of predicting the next viewing, each candidate video is a category, so there are millions of categories in total. Using softmax for training is undoubtedly inefficient. How did YouTube solve this problem? YouTube adopted the negative sampling training method commonly used in Word2vec to reduce the number of classifications predicted each time and accelerate the convergence speed of the entire model. The specific method has been introduced in Section 4.1. In addition, YouTube also tried another commonly used training method in Word2vec, hierarchical softmax, but did not achieve good results. Therefore, the more convenient negative sampling method was chosen in practice.

(2) In the preprocessing of the training set, YouTube did not use the raw user logs, but extracted an equal number of training samples for each user. Why did they do this? The purpose of this approach is to reduce the excessive influence of highly active users on the model loss, preventing the model from becoming biased toward the behavioral patterns of active users and ignore the experience of more numerous long-tail users.

(3) Why does YouTube use the user's most recent viewing behavior as the test set instead of using the classic random holdout method for the test set? Using only the last viewing behavior as the test set is mainly to avoid introducing future information in the model training process.

YouTube's training and testing processes are based on the observation and understanding of business data, which is a very good engineering practice to follow.

8.3.7   How to Handle User Preferences for New Videos

For UGC platforms, user preferences for new content are quite clear. For most content, the first few days after it is uploaded is its peak traffic period, which quickly declines

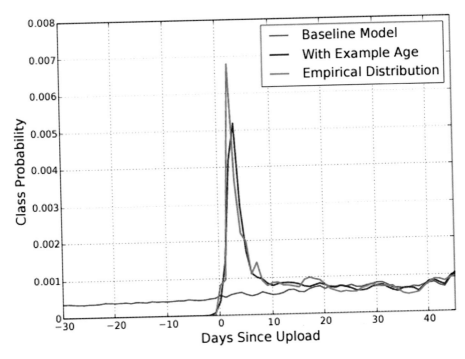

Figure 8.10 The impact of changes in positive sample probability estimates over time for different models.

and then stabilizes (as shown by the green curve in Figure 8.10). So how well user preferences for new videos are handled directly affects the accuracy of predictions.

To fit user preferences for new content, YouTube's recommender system introduced the "Example Age" feature, which is defined as the time between the moment the training sample was produced and the current time. For example, if a training sample was produced 24 hours ago, the Example Age feature value is 24. When serving the model, regardless of what the candidate video is, this feature value can be set to 0 or even a small negative value, as the training sample will be generated shortly in the future when the recommendation result is produced.

The logic behind YouTube's choice of a time feature to reflect the freshness of a training sample is not easy to understand, and readers may have different interpretations of the motivations. The authors' understanding of this feature is that it does not contain any information itself, but when it is crossed with other features in a deep neural network, it serves as a timestamp. By crossing this timestamp with other features, the weights of the other features over time are saved, and the final prediction includes information about time trends.

YouTube has validated the importance of the Example Age feature through experimentation. The blue curve in Figure 8.10 is the model's prediction before introducing the Example Age feature, which is not significantly correlative with time. However, after introducing the Example Age feature, the model's prediction value is very close to the empirical distribution.

Usually, the "freshness" feature is defined as the number of days since the video was uploaded. For example, even though an impression sample was generated 24 hours ago, if the video in the sample was uploaded 90 hours ago, the feature value should be 90. When doing online estimation, the value of this feature is not 0, but the interval between the current time and the upload time of each video. This is undoubtedly a way to save time information. YouTube apparently did not adopt this method, and the author speculates that this method is not effective because it leads to freshness feature distribution being too discrete. The training process will include videos that have just been uploaded, as well as videos that have been uploaded for one or even five years, which will make it difficult for freshness features to describe recent changes. Of course, readers are recommended to implement both methods and evaluate their effectiveness to reach a final conclusion.

8.3.8   Summary of YouTube's Deep Learning Video Recommender System

This section introduces YouTube's deep learning video recommender system, model structure, and technical details. The paper shared by YouTube is the most comprehensive engineering-oriented recommender system paper the authors have seen so far. Every reader can learn from YouTube engineers' open, sharing attitude and practical spirit. Even if readers have read the contents of this section, we strongly recommend that they read the original paper carefully and understand each technical detail.

8.4   Evolution of Alibaba's Deep Learning Recommender System

Since the publication of the LS-PLM model in 2017 [6], Alibaba's advertising recommendation team has been evolving its product recommender system with astonishing speed and execution. This includes not only DIN [7] and its evolved version DIEN [8], introduced in Sections 3.8 and 3.9, but also the recommendation model Multi-channel User Interest Memory Network (MIMN [9]) released in 2019. In this section, we summarize the technological iteration process of Alibaba's deep learning recommender system over a larger time span, and hope to present a full picture of Alibaba's approach to model iteration and technological upgrades.

8.4.1   Recommender Systems Application Scenarios

Alibaba's application scenarios are commonly seen in most e-commerce. Whether it is Tmall or Taobao, the main function of Alibaba's recommender system is to recommend products of interest to users in different recommendation positions on the website or app based on the user's historical behavior, input search terms, and other product and user information.

When solving recommendation problems, it is important to know the details and elements of the application scenario and the different stages of user interaction. For example, when a user wants to buy a "wireless mouse" on Tmall, they generally need

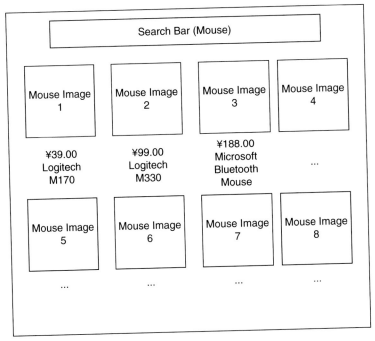

Figure 8.11 Recommendation results when the user searches for "wireless mouse" on Tmall.

to go through the following stages, from logging in to Tmall to successfully making the purchase (Figure 8.11 shows the recommended results when the user searches for "wireless mouse").

(1) Login
(2) Search
(3) Browse
(4) Click
(5) Add to Cart
(6) Payment
(7) Purchase Successful

Each step could possibly cause user's churn, with Browse to Click and Click to "Add to Cart" being the most critical. So should separate CTR and CVR models be established for these two stages or should they be modeled together? Alibaba's technical team addresses this issue in their multiobjective optimization model ESMM [10].

In the recommendation process, various types of product information can be used, including text-based descriptions, numeric information such as prices and purchase quantities, and the important product image information. How can all these modalities of information be better used to drive the recommendation engine? Alibaba's technical team provides a solution in their multimodal CTR model paper (Image Matters: Visually modeling user behaviors using Advanced Model Server [11]).

In addition to this, Alibaba has been rapidly iterating and upgrading its recommendation models from the initial LS-PLM to basic deep learning models, then to DIN with attention mechanisms and subsequent evolution versions such as DIEN and MIMN.

8.4.2   Recommendation Model Systems in Alibaba

From the introduction in Section 8.4.1, readers can see that even for giant IT companies, their technical teams consider problems from a detailed perspective. It is the coordination of multiple objectives, multiple modalities, and the use of various recommendation models that efficiently drives so many recommendation scenarios and solves numerous use cases in recommender systems. Figure 8.12 roughly outlines the system of Alibaba's recommendation models.

Most of the models in the figure have been discussed in earlier chapters, such as LS-PLM in Section 2.7, DIN in Section 3.8, DIEN in Section 3.9, and ESMM in Section 5.4. Next, the author will mainly introduce the main ideas of the models and link the development process of Alibaba's recommendation models together.

8.4.3   Evolution Process of Alibaba's Deep Learning Recommendation Model

Alibaba's deep learning recommendation model has evolved through four stages:

8.4.3.1   Basic Deep Learning Model
Based on the classical Embedding+MLP deep learning model architecture, the embedding of user behavior history is simply added and pooled, then connected with other user features, ad features, and scene features before being input to the upper neural network for training. The model structure is shown in Figure 8.13(a).

8.4.3.2   DIN Model
Replace the Sum Pooling operation of the basic model with an attention mechanism to determine the weight of each historical behavior based on the relationship

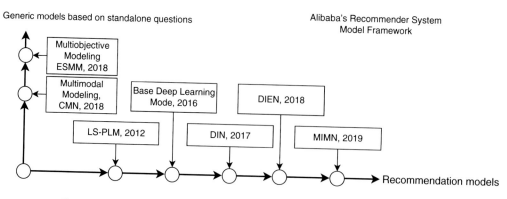

Figure 8.12 Recommender model system in Alibaba.

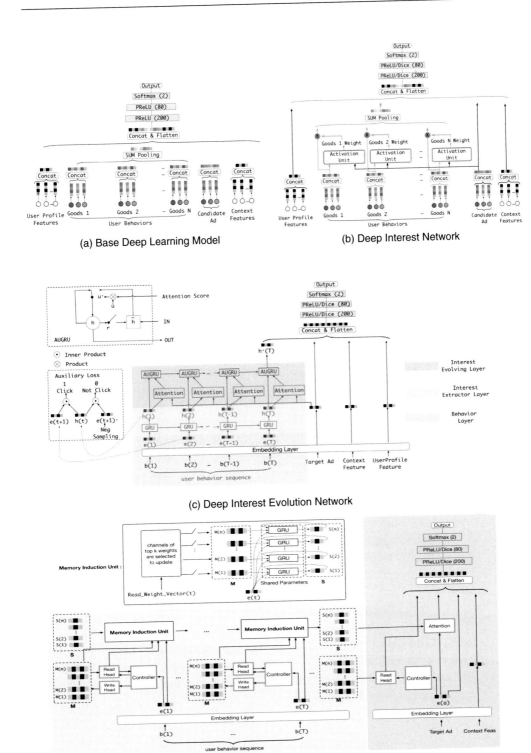

(a) Base Deep Learning Model

(b) Deep Interest Network

(c) Deep Interest Evolution Network

(d) Multi Channel Interest Memory Network

Figure 8.13 Four stages in the evolution of Alibaba's deep learning recommendation models.

between the candidate ad and the user's historical behavior. The model structure is shown in Figure 8.13(b).

8.4.3.3   DIEN Model

On top of DIN, further improve the modeling of user behavior history by using sequence models to extract user interests on top of user behavior history and simulate the evolution of user interests. The model structure is shown in Figure 8.13(c).

8.4.3.4   MIMN Model

Based on DIEN, further divide the user's interests into different interest channels to simulate the evolution of users on different interest channels and generate memory vectors for different interest channels. Then use the attention mechanism on multiple layers of neural networks. The model structure is shown in Figure 8.13(d).

The key to the evolution of Alibaba's recommendation models lies in the utilization of a user's historical behaviors. Users' historical behaviors do play a crucial role in recommendations. Additionally, thanks to Alibaba's high-quality data and its leading position in the e-commerce industry, its data can effectively capture the purchase interests of most users, thus enabling effective modeling. Figure 8.14 shows the purchase history of a female user. This example (each picture represents a product that the user has purchased) explains well the considerations during the development of different models for user behaviors.

Figure 8.14(a) represents the basic deep learning model that treats all user behavior equally without distinction. In Figure 8.14(b), each product has a weight represented by a progress bar, which is learned through an attention mechanism based on the relationship between the purchased product and candidate products. This allows the model to focus on different user behaviors. In Figure 8.14(c), user behavior has a time dimension, and the DIEN model considers the trend of user behavior and interest over time, enabling the model to predict the user's next purchase. In Figure 8.14(d), user behavior is not only arranged in a sequence based on time, but also based on different product categories, allowing the MIMN model to model multiple "interest channels" of users more accurately and avoid interference between different interests.

It can be seen that Alibaba's recommendation models have made several improvements based on the key point of "user interest," and the whole improvement process has made the model's understanding of user interest more accurate, resulting in better performance. Based on the AUC performance of various models on Taobao and Amazon datasets (as shown in Table 8.6), Alibaba's improvement of the model based on user interests has been successful.

8.4.4   Technical Architecture of Online Serving

For complex models, model online serving has always been a challenge in the industry. Using approximate methods to simplify the model will result in the degradation

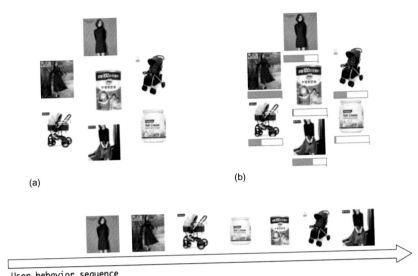

(a)

(b)

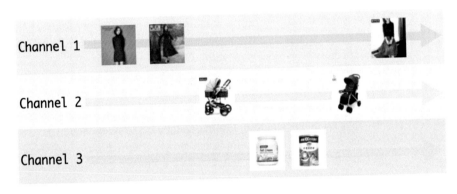

User behavior sequence

(c)

(d)

(e)

Figure 8.14 Different modeling approaches on user behaviors. a) Base deep learning model. (b) Deep interest network. (c) Deep interest evolution network. (d) Multichannel interest memory network. (e) Session based deep interest network.

Table 8.6 AUCs of different models by Alibaba

Model	Taobao Dataset (mean ± std)	Amazon Dataset (mean ± std)
Basic Deep Learning Model	0.8709 ± 0.00184	0.7367 ± 0.00043
DIN	0.8833 ± 0.00220	0.7419 ± 0.00049
DIEN	0.9081 ± 0.00221	0.7481 ± 0.00102
MIMN	0.9179 ± 0.00325	0.7593 ± 0.00150

of the model's performance. Deploying a complex model end-to-end to the online system will result in high latency, which affects user experience. This dilemma also troubles Alibaba engineers. For models with sequence structures, such as DIEN and MIMN, this problem is particularly prominent because the sequence structure in the model implies a serial inference process, and the model cannot be parallelized for acceleration, making model online serving a bottleneck in the entire recommendation process.

So how to solve this problem? The original paper of MIMN released relevant solutions (as shown in Figure 8.15).

Figures 8.15(a) and (b) represent two different online serving architectures, with the horizontal dashed line in the middle representing the separation between online and offline environments. The main difference between the two architectures lies in how user behavior is processed, with two key distinctions:

8.4.4.1   User Interest Representation Module

The "User Behavior Features Online Database" in Architecture A is replaced by the "User Interest Representation Online Database" in Architecture B. This change is very important for the model inference process. Whether it is DIEN or MIMN, the final form of expressing user interests is the interest embedding vector. If the user behavior feature sequence is obtained online, a complex sequence model inference process needs to be run to generate the user interest vector on the real-time prediction server. If the user interest vector is available in an online feature store, the real-time prediction server can skip the sequence model inferencing phase and start the MLP calculation directly. The number of layers in MLP is much smaller than that in the sequence model and is easier to compute in parallel. Therefore, the latency of entire online inferencing can be significantly reduced.

8.4.4.2   User Interest Center Module

Architecture B adds a service module called User Interest Center (UIC). UIC is used to generate user interest vectors based on the user behavior sequence. For DIEN and MIMN, UIC runs the part of the model that generates user interest vectors. At the same time, the way of updating real-time user behavior events also changes. For Architecture A, when a new user behavior event occurs, it is inserted into the user behavior feature database, while for Architecture B, a new user behavior event will trigger the update logic of UIC, and UIC will use the event to update the corresponding user's interest embedding vector.

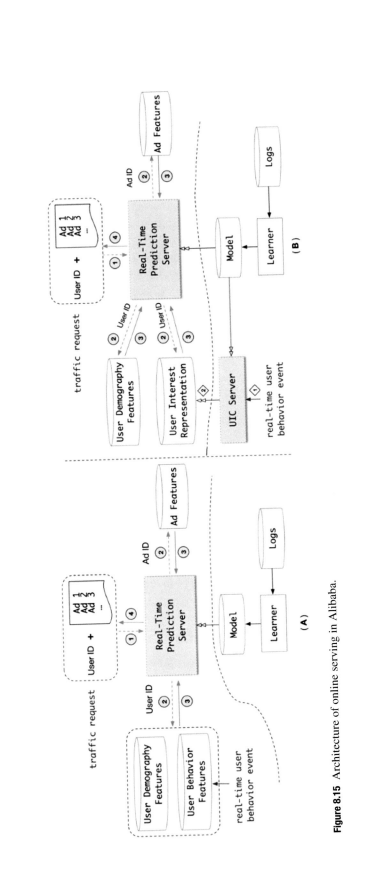

Figure 8.15 Architecture of online serving in Alibaba.

After understanding the user interest representation module and the role of the UIC, the roles of other modules are basically the same in both architectures. The offline and online running logic of these modules are as follows:

- **Offline Component:** The learner module regularly trains and updates the model using system logs. After the model is updated, the new model is directly deployed in the real-time estimation server in Architecture A. Meanwhile in Architecture B, the model is split, and the component that generates the user interest representation (the left part of Figure 8.15(b)) is deployed in the UIC, and the remaining part is deployed in the real-time estimation server.
- **Online Components:** The online request flow is as follows:
  (1) Traffic request is received along with user ID and candidate product ID to be ranked.
  (2) The real-time estimation server obtains user and product features (ad features) based on the user ID and candidate product ID. User features include demographic features and user behavior features (Architecture A) or user interest representation vectors (Architecture B).
  (3) The real-time prediction server uses user and product features to conduct ranking, and returns the final ranking result to the client.

Architecture B decomposes the most time-consuming sequence model and greatly reduces the total latency of the model online inferencing. According to the public data released by Alibaba, the estimated latency of the DIEN model was reduced from 200 milliseconds to 19 milliseconds with 500 QPS. From an engineering perspective, this is undoubtedly the gain from optimizing the model serving process.

This is a good example of online deployment optimizations for deep learning recommendation models introduced in Section 6.5. In fact, Architecture A essentially adopts an end-to-end deployment solution such as TensorFlow Serving, while Architecture B adopts the deployment scheme of pre-trained embedding + lightweight online models. Alibaba's design provides the best examples for these online deployment solutions.

8.4.5   Summary of Alibaba's Recommender Systems Architecture

From 2016 to 2019, a series of papers published by the Alibaba Advertising Recommendation team established a complete set of recommender system architecture. Whether in terms of deep learning theory or engineering implementations, it is highly recommended that readers follow this series of articles and focus on the learnings from the following three aspects:

8.4.5.1   Best Engineering Practices

Papers that focus on best engineering practices have two common characteristics. One is that the application scenario comes from business directly, and the other is that the solution to the problem is easier to implement. This is made possible by Alibaba's profound engineering foundations and leading business model, coupled with the continuous contributions of outstanding engineers, enabling the development of many solutions born from practice.

8.4.5.2 Accurate Observation of User Behavior Patterns

In improving the recommender system, we need to start by observing and understanding users' behavior patterns, and then map these learnings to the techniques in the models. The evolution of Alibaba's difference recommendation model accurately captures user behavior patterns. This work is meticulous and effective.

8.4.5.3 Micro-Innovation of the Model

These papers present a roadmap of micro-innovation at multiple levels – from low-dimensional to high-dimensional, from discrete to continuous, and from standalone development to the fusion of multiple models. Alibaba's models introduce attention mechanisms and sequence models that are popular in the field of natural language processing into the recommendation field, which is another typical and effective innovation method. In addition, each model iteration is not a complete rebuild, but an incremental micro-innovation based on the previous model. This efficient iteration approach also provides the industry with a great example of continuous model development and business improvement.

References

[1] Xinran He, et al. Practical lessons from predicting clicks on ads at Facebook. Proceedings of the Eighth International Workshop on Data Mining for Online Advertising, New York, NY, USA, August 24–27, 2014.

[2] Maxim Naumov, et al. Deep learning recommendation model for personalization and recommendation systems: arXiv preprint arXiv:1906.00091 (2019).

[3] Mihajlo Grbovic, Haibin Cheng. Real-time personalization using embeddings for search ranking at Airbnb. Proceedings of the 24th ACM SIGKDD International Conference on Knowledge Discovery & Data Mining, London, UK, August 19–23, 2018.

[4] Christopher JC Burges. From ranknet to lambdarank to lambdamart: An overview. *Learning* 11(23–581), 2010: 81.

[5] Paul Covington, Jay Adams, Emre Sargin. Deep neural networks for YouTube recommendations. Proceedings of the 10th ACM Conference on Recommender Systems, Boston, MA, USA, September 15–19, 2016.

[6] Kun Gai, et al. Learning piece-wise linear models from large scale data for ad click prediction: arXiv preprint arXiv:1704.05194 (2017).

[7] Guorui Zhou, et al. Deep interest network for click-through rate prediction. Proceedings of the 24th ACM SIGKDD International Conference on Knowledge Discovery & Data Mining, London, UK, August 19–23, 2018.

[8] Guorui Zhou, et al. Deep interest evolution network for click-through rate prediction. Proceedings of the AAAI Conference on Artificial Intelligence, Vol. 33, Honolulu, Hawaii, USA, January 27–February 1, 2019.

[9] Qi Pi, et al. Practice on long sequential user behavior modeling for click-through rate prediction. Proceedings of the 25th ACM SIGKDD International Conference on Knowledge Discovery & Data Mining, Anchorage, AK, USA, August 4–8, 2019.

[10] Xiao Ma, et al. Entire space multi-task model: An effective approach for estimating post-click conversion rate. The 41st International ACM SIGIR Conference on Research & Development in Information Retrieval, Ann Arbor, MI, USA, July 8–12, 2018.

[11] Tiezheng Ge, et al. Image matters: Visually modeling user behaviors using advanced model server. Proceedings of the 27th ACM International Conference on Information and Knowledge Management, Torino, Italy, October 22–26, 2018.

9 Build Your Own Recommender Systems Knowledge Framework

This is the last chapter of this book. After discussing all the technical details of recommender systems, we hope you are ready to return to the overall architecture and understand the general knowledge framework from a higher perspective.

Back in Chapter 1, we initially described the technical architecture diagram of recommender systems; we suggested that you may temporarily ignore the details in the diagram and only keep the framework in mind. Now, as the technical details of each module were gradually revealed in subsequent chapters, you may have already filled in the architecture diagram in your own way.

To understand a certain field, it is most important to build your own knowledge framework. Only by establishing a knowledge framework can you check and make up for gaps based on this framework; only then can you see the details and dive deep without ignoring the whole picture. We hope that this book provides not only a specific method to solve your recommender systems problems, but also a high-level technical overview of the industry.

In this chapter, we will review all the technical content of this book in three ways and establish the logical connection between them.

Section 9.1 will look into further technical details based on the architecture diagram in Chapter 1, so that you can establish the final "comprehensive knowledge architecture diagram of recommender systems."

Section 9.2 will focus on the core recommendation model part of the diagram, and review the model development in a timeline, especially the evolution process of the deep learning model.

Section 9.3 will talk about the core qualities that a qualified recommender systems engineer should possess from a practical perspective.

9.1 The Overall Architecture Diagram of Recommender Systems

Figure 9.1 is a summary framework of the entire book, which echoes Figure 1.4, and supplements most of the technical details involved in this book.

This diagram can be viewed as a technical index of the entire book. Here, each module and each term in the diagram refers to a specific technical detail. There is a maxim of war that goes, "Until you see the whole battlefield, don't make a move." Only by understanding the whole picture can we find the best solution in "one domain" and achieve a true global optimum.

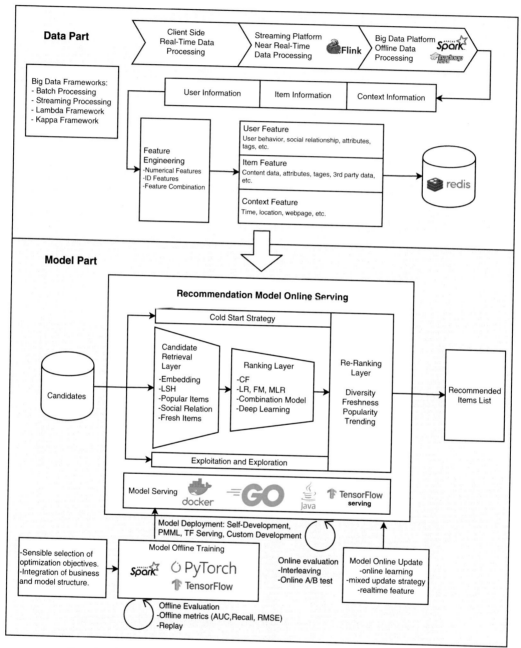

Figure 9.1 The comprehensive knowledge architecture of recommender systems.
Oracle and Java are registered trademarks of Oracle and/or its affiliates. Used with Permission.
Apache Hadoop, Hadoop, the Apache Hadoop Logo, Apache Flink, Flink, the Apache
Flink Logo, Apache Spark, Spark, the Apache Spark Logo and Apache are either registered
trademarks or trademarks of the Apache Software Foundation. Redis is a registered trademark
of Redis Ltd. Any rights therein are reserved to Redis Ltd. Any use by Cambridge is for
referential purposes only and does not indicate any sponsorship, endorsement or affiliation
between Redis and Cambridge.

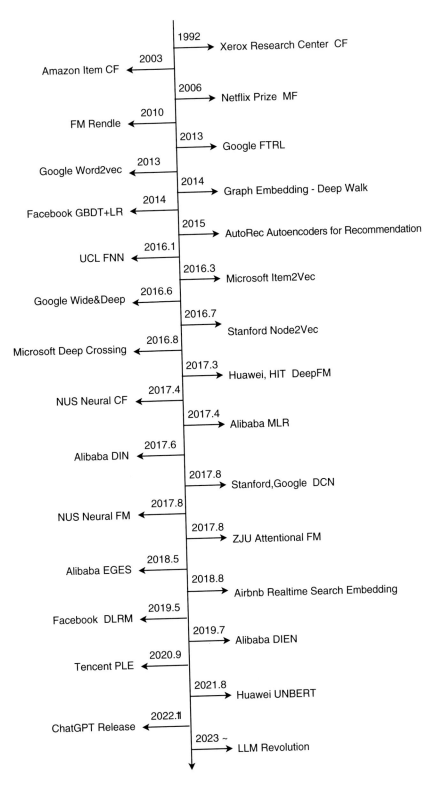

Figure 9.2 Timeline of recommendation model development.

Although we try to summarize deep learning recommender systems in the diagram as much as possible, but "technical solutions are always diverse and cannot be unique." Figure 9.1 is the enterprise-level recommender system architecture adopted by most companies, and it is not the only "correct" answer. We have our own limitations in information and may have missed some excellent approaches as well. In practical applications, machine learning engineers should take their own objective environment as the starting point to build the most "suitable" rather than the most "correct" recommender system.

9.2   Timeline of Recommendation Model Development

Figure 9.2 summarizes the timeline of the development of recommendation models introduced in this book.

Noticeably, the iterative evolution of deep learning recommendation models has accelerated since 2016. In the meantime, more and more excellent Internet companies have participated, bringing many best practices to the industry.

While writing this book, there must still be many new excellent technologies and models being proposed and applied. The content of this book is static, but the development of technology is dynamic, and you will need to keep track of the cutting-edge content and never stop learning.

9.3   How to Become an Excellent Recommender Systems Machine Learning Engineer

In this section, we will be discussing the basic competencies that are required of an excellent machine learning engineer. This role requires not only good knowledge of machine learning, but also outstanding abilities in all aspects related to business practice.

9.3.1   The Four Competencies for Machine Learning Engineers

Regardless of the specific job requirements, let's look at this from a higher perspective. The technical competencies of a machine learning engineer can basically be broken down into the following four aspects: knowledge, tools, analytics, and business.

The radar charts in Figure 9.3 roughly show the skills and capabilities required for several positions related to recommender systems and machine learning. It reveals the nuances of the ability requirements of these positions.

Simply put, any machine learning engineer of recommender systems should meet the minimum requirements of four skills, because before becoming an "excellent" engineer, one should first be a qualified engineer. Not only should you have

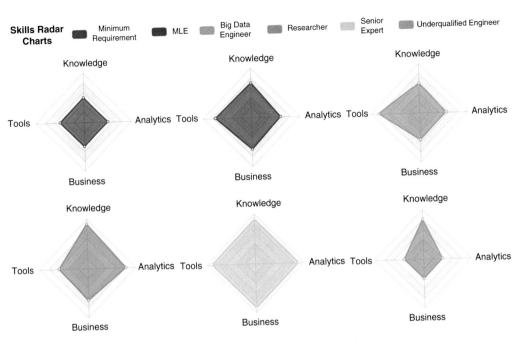

Figure 9.3 Radar charts of job skills related to machine learning.

domain-related knowledge, but you should also have the ability to transform the knowledge into a practical system. One of the authors of this book once interviewed a machine learning engineer candidate who had published some papers and patents related to machine learning. From the perspective of "knowledge" in the field, he was a good candidate, but when asked about his engineering ability, he clearly expressed his unwillingness to write code. Maybe there was something hidden about his reluctance to write code at the time, but for the interviewer, the candidate's ability to use "tools" was not sufficient, and his ability might be seriously "biased." This person was, after all, not a qualified machine learning engineer. Generally speaking, the minimum qualifications required for a machine learning engineer should be the following:

- **Knowledge:** Basic knowledge and understanding of recommender systems.
- **Tools:** Ability to write programs and utilize related engineering tools.
- **Analytics:** Basic knowledge of algorithms; ability for analytical thinking and reasoning.
- **Business:** Ability to understand the business applications of recommender systems.

Based on these minimum qualifications, different positions have different requirements for abilities. With the skills radar charts shown in Figure 9.3, the characteristics of the capabilities of different positions are as follows:

- **Machine learning engineer:** The ability requirements of a machine learning engineer are relatively comprehensive. As implementers and applicators of algorithm models, machine learning engineers are required to have a solid machine learning foundation, the ability to improve and implement algorithms, the ability to use tools, and insight into business.
- **Big data engineer:** Big data engineers need to pay more attention to improving big data tools and platforms, and need to maintain the entire data flow related to the recommender system, so the ability to use tools is the most emphasized.
- **Algorithm researcher:** Algorithm researchers are responsible for proposing new algorithms, new model structures, and other research tasks, so they have the highest requirements for knowledge and analytical abilities.
- **Engineers with "biased" ability:** Some engineers don't pay attention to the accumulation of knowledge in tool use and business understanding. When they are looking for a job, they rush to supplement their knowledge with coding problems. It may be effective in some interview situations, but to become an excellent machine learning engineer, one will also need to make up for their own shortcomings.

Of course, it is somewhat too general to describe the qualifications required for machine learning engineers with only four words: "knowledge," "tools," "analytics," and "business." So let's explain these four skills:

- **Knowledge:** This mainly refers to the knowledge and theories related to recommender systems, such as recommendation models, methods of embedding, and so on.
- **Tools:** This is the ability to use tools to apply knowledge to actual business. The tools related to recommender systems mainly include model training tools such as TensorFlow and PyTorch, big data processing tools such as Spark and Flink, and some tools related to model servicing.
- **Analytics:** This is the ability for analytical inference, problem-solving, divergent thinking, and the mastery of general algorithms.
- **Business:** This is the ability to understand the recommender system's application scenarios and business models, to discover user motivations, formulate corresponding optimization goals, and improve the algorithms.

Please note that skills learning should be targeted to the area that is most needed based on the specific positions and specific projects.

9.3.2   Depth and Breadth of the Capabilities

With a specific job, the ability of an excellent machine learning engineer should be comprehensive – be able to provide solutions with "depth" and "breadth." For example, the company hopes to improve the current recommendation model, so you are proposing a model improvement plan with DIN as the main structure. This requires you to have a comprehensive understanding of the principles and implementation of DIN in both depth and breadth.

In terms of depth, it is necessary to understand a series of problems, from model motivation to implementation details. An example of a learning path from generalization to specificity is as follows:

- What is the motivation behind the DIN model? Is it suitable for the current scenario and data characteristics of your company? (Business understanding)
- What is the model structure of the DIN model? What are the engineering difficulties in its implementation? (Knowledge, tool applications)
- What is the attention mechanism emphasized by the DIN model? How does the attention mechanism improve the recommendation outcome? (Knowledge, business understanding)
- The DIN model generates embeddings for users and products. How is the embedding implemented? (Knowledge, analytical thinking)
- Should you implement the DIN model by improving the existing model, or use a new offline training method to train the DIN model? (Tool application, analytical thinking)
- What are the potential problems and solutions for online deployment and service of DIN models? (Tool application)

From this example, you can see that forming a complete set of model improvement plans requires the machine learning engineer to have an in-depth understanding of the details of the new model. Without thorough research, the improvement plan could encounter directional errors during implementation, which can be costly to correct.

In addition to an in-depth understanding of the technical details of the solutions, the engineer will also need to understand the pros and cons of various possible alternatives, so as to obtain the optimal solution under the current application scenario through comprehensive considerations. Following this example of model improvement, the engineer also needs to consider the following aspects in breadth:

- What are the models similar to DIN, and are they suitable for the current application scenario?
- What are the embedding methods used in the DIN model, and what are the advantages and disadvantages of these methods?
- What are the methods for training and deployment of DIN models? How will they integrate with your company's technology stack?

With an in-depth understanding of a technical solution, the understanding of other alternatives can be generalized. But the key points and characteristics of each solution must also be clear, and if necessary, through A/B testing, peer communication and consultation, prototype testing, and other methods to rule out candidates and determine the most suitable option.

In addition, the ability to balance between engineering and research mentioned in Section 6.6 is also one of the indispensable skills for a machine learning engineer. It is an essential ability for one to make a reasonable compromise between reality and ideal in order to accomplish a functional comprehensive technical solution.

9.3.3   Summary of the Competencies Required for Machine Learning Engineers

To become an excellent machine learning engineer in recommender systems, or even an excellent machine learning engineer in general, you should comprehensively improve your abilities in the four aspects of "knowledge," "tools," "analytics," and "business." Solving a problem will require the engineer to have knowledge and technical capabilities in depth and breadth, make trade-offs and compromises under practical constraints, and finally come up with a feasible and optimal technical solution.

Afterword

From the beginning of writing this book to the final draft, it took a whole year. In this year, the development of deep learning recommender systems has never ceased. Even if the scope of knowledge included in this book has been adjusted several times, trying to keep up with the new technology, it still cannot cover all the latest developments. As the authors often said when introducing the work to others, "A machine learning engineer is a job that is struggling on the verge of being eliminated at any time." That is why we say, when you close the book, it's not the end, but another beginning.

The situation is not so pessimistic. As introduced at the beginning of Chapter 9, once you have established your own recommender system knowledge framework, all that remains is to grow branches and leaves from this big tree. We believe that the process for deep learning to change the recommender system is far from over. The classic models that have been settled before will eventually become important nodes on this tree of knowledge, so that everyone will benefit from them. We also hope that this book can become a phased portrait of this tree. For us, this is definitely not the end. In the near future, we will continue to update the content of this book, so that the knowledge framework of the book is also flourishing.

Until then, keep learning.

Printed in the United States
by Baker & Taylor Publisher Services